CALCIO'S GREATEST FORWARDS

CALCIO'S GREATEST FORWARDS

SERIE A'S FINEST ATTACKERS

GEORGE RINALDI

pitch

First published by Pitch Publishing, 2016

Pitch Publishing
A2 Yeoman Gate
Yeoman Way
Durrington
BN13 3QZ
www.pitchpublishing.co.uk

A CIP catalogue record is available for this book from the British Library.

ISBN 978-1-78531-118-5

Typesetting and origination by Pitch Publishing

Printed by Bell & Bain, Glasgow, Scotland

Contents

ABOUT THE AUTHOR

George Rinaldi is a 21-year-old sports journalist currently covering European football while mainly focusing on Italy's Serie A. He is currently writing for Football Italia and Forza Italian Football, and is also freelancing across multiple publications. These include most recently *FourFourTwo* in the UK, *Howler* magazine in the United States, and *Soccer360* magazine. He is a supporter of English side Wolverhampton Wanderers and Italian club Fiorentina, attending his first match back in 2011 – a rather typical 0-0 draw at the Stadio Artemio Franchi versus Sampdoria.

ACKNOWLEDGEMENTS

THIS was a project that would never have taken shape without the help of some of the finest football journalists and writers around, alongside working with a fantastic publishing firm and some very talented illustrators.

Firstly we come to Giancarlo Rinaldi. Despite sharing a rather fetching surname and the support of Fiorentina, we really are no relation! This man was able to give me a kick-start in working with Italian football and made me rekindle my love for calcio once again. To top it off, he contributed to the book as well. I would also like to thank Gabriele Marcotti, who took the time out of his hectic schedule to write a fantastic foreword. When you have the backing of Gab you know you're doing something right.

Of course, I would like to pay thanks to Paolo Bandini, Andy Brassell, Susy Campanale, Adam Digby, John Foot, Richard Hall, James Horncastle, Antonio Labbate and Dov Schiavone for contributing with player introductions, transforming a good read into a truly superb read. Their insight into a player they feel a connection with gives a great start to certain sections. I'm also indebted to the help of Sophie Rees. Her proofreading of a subject she's not too fussed about sorted out all the blundering errors I had made!

As for the illustrations, I come to Steve Welsh first, who turned my rather complicated book cover into a beautifully constructed piece. It sells the book for its look alone. Next,

I give my thanks to Josh Clifford, who added a great style to the final product with an excellent portrait illustration of each player to begin their segments. I must also give a big thanks to Paine Proffitt. His truly unique artwork for the older generation of players dotted around the book adds to that special nostalgic feel for those players.

Finally, I would like to give a huge thanks to those who have helped me secure much needed accuracy for the book. Steve Amoia, publisher of soccertranslator.com from 2008 to 2015 and worldfootballcommentaries.com since 2006, was a valuable help as he gave precise translations of certain quotes used throughout. Next up we have Emanuele Giulianelli, who discussed his interview with Kurt Hamrin to help me give a more detailed outlook on the Swede's career path.

I would also like to give thanks to Bo Berglind for his fantastic help discussing with me his website and current ongoing project at gunnar-nordahl.com. With Bo's help, I was able to write about details in Nordahl's life that not many have seen before, including quotes from his own book.

The archives of *La Repubblica*, *La Stampa*, *La Gazzetta dello Sport* and *Corriere della Sera* were vital as research points throughout the history of calcio and without them, there would be no book. The Storie di Calcio website was just as important, giving a great rundown of the older generations of players. Although I may not be able to thank the above publications personally, I am forever indebted to them for their help.

Honestly, I couldn't have asked for a better set of people to have worked with.

George Rinaldi

FOREWORD

HAD Friedrich Nietzsche been born a century later, he might have found a home in calcio. Or, at least, empirical evidence of some of his ideas. And maybe none more so than his oft-quoted maxim, 'That which does not kill us only makes us stronger.'

The Italian game's capacity for self-harm over the years has been near limitless. And it's particularly true when it comes to forwards. No footballing culture has made life more difficult for the men charged with scoring.

Gianni Brera, Italy's most celebrated football chronicler, famously described the perfect game as one that finishes 0-0, in which the two sides' technical, tactical and mental prowess leads to no mistakes and no goals.

That's right. Because the underlying assumption is that if you do your job, if you don't make an error, your opponent won't score. Every goal is a product of a mistake because every goal can be avoided.

When unstoppable force meets immoveable object, the result is a stalemate. Or, put another way, the immoveable object wins.

Those are the conditions that – with some exceptions – historically defined the Italian game. And that's what yielded not just the stifling tactical approaches, cynical, in-your-shorts defending and *primo non prenderle* – above all, don't get beat – mentality, but also the risk-averse mentality of fans, media and coaches.

To succeed in that environment you need to produce something truly exceptional. And Italian football has, time and again, succeeded in doing that. In a footballing culture usually so focused on the collective as a defensive weapon (at least until Arrigo Sacchi), it was perhaps inevitable that the Italian game would need forwards who could create out of nothing, who would not need to rely on service and schemes or who were blessed with unusual strength and athleticism or who simply had that indefinable quality to be in the right place and punish mistakes. When it's Man v Machine, you need a special man to bust the defensive machine.

And that's what calcio did. From Roberto Baggio to Francesco Totti, from Christian Vieri to Gigi Riva and from Pippo Inzaghi to Benito Lorenzi, Italian strikers have mostly fallen into one of those three categories. It's not enough to be a virtuoso blessed with superb technique. Strikers like that abound in other leagues and, on good, attacking teams, they score plenty of goals. But in Serie A, in addition to the skill you need that extra: whether it's outstanding vision and creativity, freakish athleticism or the single-minded selfishness of the natural-born goalscorer.

George Rinaldi has brought together these different figures in this book. It's a labour of love and a celebration of the legends who thrived with the odds stacked against them in a culture that still seems more comfortable with the men at the other end of the pitch. That's why, to paraphrase Jovanotti, Italian forwards are – *fiori cresciuto sull'asfalto e sul cemento* – flowers who grew up on asphalt and cement. Adversity is what made them who they are. They are Nietzschean heroes. Everything they suffered and endured only made them stronger.

Gabriele Marcotti

INTRODUCTION

DURING a tightly fought contest between Udinese and Verona in mid-December of 2014, Luca Toni netted his 300th career goal to help secure all three points for the Gialloblu. Cue congratulations from my own team, Fiorentina, applauding Toni for his accomplishment. I questioned where fans of Italian football would rank the 6ft 3in striker in Serie A history following this feat.

Research began to look at former players outside of my knowledge. Silvio Piola, the current all-time top scorer in Serie A, was my first port of call. This led on to players such as Giuseppe Meazza and Gunnar Nordahl. To scratch just the surface of what they achieved at their respective clubs was astounding and admirable. Players who had become such icons in Italy yet are failing to be recognised that often in this day and age by supporters, except by putting a goalscoring tally to their name. I for one was unaware of Piola's lack of Scudetti, Meazza's antics before a game, as well as Nordahl topping the league's top scorer chart five times – something that has never been bettered.

It led me on to discover some of the adversity many of these players felt during their upbringing and careers. From Gigi Riva's traumatic childhood to Antonio Di Natale's crisis involving team-mate Piermario Morosini. Even then, injuries sustained by such greats like Marco van Basten show that these incredible footballers are just men – human beings – like you and I.

As such, it prompted me to begin this project – to create an enjoyable easy read featuring only the very best forwards in the history of Italian football. The shortlist of players began and soon a list of over 40 attacking wizards were jotted down in my trusty notepad. The plan was to cut them down to 20 and that was nearly achieved! The chosen forwards for the book were down to my own personal preference, which did mean even though he was the reason for writing this book and is one of my favourite players, Luca Toni did miss out. Of course, there are many others who people will believe should be included and haven't, such as the overlooked George Weah, Ronaldo, Rubén Sosa, Omar Sívori and John Charles to name just a few.

The late Valentino Mazzola does not feature, but only because I believe the words that would have been written for him would not have been in any way worthy of his legacy and that of his team-mates due to the Superga tragedy. I hope many readers will wish to look further into *il Grande Torino* to truly capture his, and Torino's, brilliance in the 1940s.

The 21 chosen gave a mix of old and new, with many overlapping career-wise. I wanted people to learn about players from the very start of Serie A to the present day.

What followed was getting the help I needed to turn the project into the real deal. Emails were sent, messages exchanged and I soon had on board the very best Italian sports journalists around. They helped turn a simple idea into a fantastic reality. It was hard work, but worth it all in the long run.

This is a book filled with insight and hopefully you enjoy the content inside and learn something new about your favourite striker. The segments on each player focus on their careers only at club level in Serie A, as well as in domestic and European club competitions, such as Hernán Crespo's UEFA Cup success with Parma and José Altafini's European Cup victory over Benfica. Their national careers are sometimes briefly visited – unfortunately for Roberto

Baggio that is the case – but this is a book solely on their superb playing days in Italy.

I hope that my work provides an easy research point for many in the future to use, but also to reminisce about the time calcio was unrivalled at the top of the football pyramid. I want the reader to relive some of the finest moments their favourite forward conjured up in a match, to then head to the nearest computer and look back on some of the greatest goals calcio has seen. So dive in wherever you wish and, of course, enjoy!

George Rinaldi

JOSE ALTAFINI

'A game without a goal is like love without a kiss.'

– José Altafini's *Incredibile Amici!*

ONE of the greatest players Serie A has ever seen, José Altafini was the complete attacker. Pace, power, precision – he had it all. Time after time the Brazilian would run full pelt at the helpless defenders who were attempting to thwart his attacks. That rarely happened though, the end result was already decided – Altafini had scored. It didn't matter where on the pitch he was, he would score. From a 15-yard bicycle kick to a long-distance screamer, José gave Italy some of the best goals of the 1960s. When he wasn't making the highlights reel, Altafini was still lethal in front of goal, leaving goalkeepers trembling in their boots. Head, chest, leg, knee, foot – every body part had registered a goal for the striker. Despite the fact he provided memorable moments for both Napoli and Juventus, there was really only one club that he fell head over heels for, and the love was duly reciprocated. It was for the famous red and black side in Italy's top flight – AC Milan.

The Rossoneri welcomed José to the San Siro in 1958, having impressed not only several scouts from the Italian side, but also then club president Andrea Rizzoli during a pre-tournament friendly prior to the 1958 World Cup finals. Rizzoli was marvelling at the display of the young man during this friendly hosted on Italian soil against Milan's biggest rivals, Inter, as he managed to grab a goal for Brazil. What better way to get your possible suitors interested than with a goal against their arch nemeses. Milan were subsequently hooked and contact began with José's club at the time – Palmeiras. He had become a regular starter for his first professional team, making his debut at 17 years old, as he progressed from an attacking midfield role to a centre-forward. He'd even gained a nickname – *Mazzola* – as he bore a strong resemblance to the late, great Valentino Mazzola of Torino.

Mario Beni, president of the Brazilian side during Altafini's time at Palmeiras, informed Rizzoli that a deal looked likely with Serie A rivals Roma instead, who were keen admirers of the young man who had found the net 32 times in 63 matches. Fortunately for Milan, they would get the clinical finisher instead, as negotiations broke down with the Giallorossi. It seems the same transfer techniques of the modern day were in full swing by the Rossoneri boardroom team – they told *Corriere dello Sport* they had not signed him just a few days before his switch was confirmed. Altafini would be playing under the guidance of Giuseppe Viani at the age of 19 and he was relishing his chance to show what he could do on the biggest stage.

At a time in football where the emergence of the young Pelé was being hailed, Altafini seemed to slip under the radar as, despite only just turning 20, he helped his national side to the World Cup of 1958. Unfortunately, he soon fell out with the Canarinho as Brazil never called up players who plied their trade abroad. It made little difference to Altafini's mindset, he was now playing in Italy for one of the biggest footballing teams around.

Sunday 21 September 1958 will be forever noted as one of José's finest moments as he made his debut for the club against Triestina, finishing in a 2-0 victory to Milan. It would take only until the third game for Altafini to score his first in a 4-2 win over Bari and the striker wouldn't be stopped any longer from adding to his tally. The forward remembers what it felt like to sign for Milan fondly, and said the following about how the experience helped him change as a person:

> 'I was not even 20 years old and from that moment, thanks to Milan, they had changed my life. To be part of the Rossoneri made me learn to become a man. It was love at first sight, AC Milan is in my blood. I came to Italy from another world and I have met wonderful people and some great leaders at a fantastic club.'
>
> – Storie di Calcio

The forward went on to score 28 league goals in 32 matches, including a run of eight consecutive games with a goal. These included a strike to salvage a point against Inter in the Derby della Madonnina and he also provided an early Christmas present to Milan – a hat-trick at home to Torino on 21 December 1958. His season's tally was still bettered by Inter's Antonio Angelillo, who managed 33 in 33. Missing out on the Capocannoniere prize would only be a minor setback for Altafini as the red side of Milan acquired the last laugh, going on to win the Scudetto by three points over Fiorentina. Not a bad first season for José, securing the top prize in Italy at the first time of asking. Already the young man was becoming an idol in his new country while donning the red and black, embracing the countless amount of support that came his way. He was seen as a phenomenon around Milano – a spectacle both on and off the pitch.

The following two seasons saw trophy success take a downturn for Milan as they failed to gain any silverware. Altafini clearly wasn't to be fazed as his goalscoring record just kept improving with 42 goals in 67 appearances across those two campaigns. José also got his own individual achievement of note – the Coppa Italia top scorer of the 1960/61 season. Altafini acquired four goals despite being knocked out in the round of 16, the best of the tournament, alongside eventual winners Luigi Milan and Gianfranco Petris of Fiorentina.

The 1961/62 Serie A season sparked Milan back into life and Altafini was once again at the heart of their success. The now-Italian striker, who had since adopted the Azzurri as his chosen nation following his move to Milan, scored 22 times in just 34 games. José made sure there would be no repeats of the previous disappointing campaigns that had seen Milan fall way short of expectations, finishing third and then second respectively. Juventus were crowned champions on both those occasions.

Milan's eighth Scudetto would come during this season, and it was even sweeter for the Rossoneri as they finished just above rivals Inter. During this campaign, José found the net with a brilliantly skilful goal when playing host to Lecco in October. With four defenders around him, Altafini flicked the ball behind him with a clever back-heel before finishing smartly across the face of goal. As José lifts both his arms up in celebration you can see all four of the bamboozled defenders sitting on the ground, just as confused as goalkeeper Eugenio Bruschini.

If long-distance strikes are more up your alley, then 15 April 1962 would have been your day. This time Altafini lined up opposite Spal for the final game of the season at the

Stadio Paolo Mazza. With his side already a goal to the good thanks to José himself, with just over 15 minutes to go, the striker hit a ferocious shot from all of 35 yards out into the top corner. The keeper was motionless in his actions as he watched the ball fly past him at a colossal speed. The goal meant he grabbed a total of 22 for the season, making him Capocannoniere for the first time, sharing the award with Fiorentina's Aurelio Milani.

The Scudetto triumph would be just the warm-up for their major success the following season however, as José played a pivotal role in the Rossoneri's greatest accomplishment. An Italian side had never won the European Cup but at the end of the marathon 1962/63 season, Milan made history.

Altafini was key as they brushed Union Luxembourg aside 14-0 on aggregate in the preliminary round. José netted five in the first leg and picked up a hat-trick in the second to progress on to the challenge of Ipswich Town. The leading man didn't need to find the net in either match as they won 4-2 overall and began preparations for the quarter-final. Galatasaray were the opponents and more goals ensued with the striker notching up another four over the course of both matches in an 8-1 aggregate victory – one of which was a cracking first-time volley which he nonchalantly side-footed in.

The entire tournament had nearly passed with Milan safely avoiding the back-to-back winners Benfica, who had successfully ended Real Madrid's five-year consecutive run of European titles, beating Barcelona and Madrid themselves in the previous two European Cups. It remained that way with the Portuguese side drawing Feyenoord. Altafini and co. would have Dundee to overcome and although the striker didn't manage to score in either game, they came out on top with an overall 5-2 scoreline.

Along came 22 May 1963 with Wembley Stadium the venue of choice for the final. Benfica were the clear favourites due to their previous successes and 19 minutes in the ever-

ALTAFINI

present Eusébio broke away from the Milan backline before lashing across goal to give them the lead, which they still held at half-time. The second half would be José Altafini's proudest moment as a Milan player as he did what any aspiring football player has dreamt of – score the winning goal in a cup final. They needed to equalise first and the moment would come in the 58th minute when a blocked strike fell kindly for Altafini on the edge of the box.

The clear striking instinct of the man saw him quickly swivel to meet the ball and fire it low into the bottom corner. Sensing blood, Milan began putting Benfica under immense pressure and a loose pass in the centre-circle allowed Milan to capitalise.

Altafini led the charge in a one-on-one situation with Benfica goalkeeper Costa Pereira. In spite of Pereira's best efforts as he foiled Altafini's first attempt, the striker made sure with the rebound as Milan took the lead for the first time.

The Italians held out and made history not just for their own club but for the country as a whole, with Altafini the man at the centre of it all. The brace from the forward up front meant he finished the tournament with a total of 14 goals, creating a new record for the competition. It was only beaten during the 2014 UEFA Champions League by Real Madrid's Cristiano Ronaldo (17). Altafini closed out that historic day by saying:

> 'If I hadn't have obtained cramp I would have scored a third! I owe everything to Milan as I could have gone elsewhere with more money, but this club gave me two league titles and this European Cup. They taught me everything.'
>
> – Storie di Calcio

As for matters in Serie A, José also scored another superb goal to add to his collection. It just so happened to be versus

Spal, a side he'd found the back of the net against with a wonder-goal the previous season. This time they were at the San Siro on 5 May 1963 where the forward netted the third in a 4-0 win.

The goal itself falls into the category of pure and utter brilliance, if that is a category, that mere words can barely convey. The ball was played into the feet of Altafini at a striking pace, yet he simply lofted it over the defender with his first touch, while having his back to goal. He spun the humiliated centre-half before unleashing a right-footed volley into the bottom corner. Think Dennis Bergkamp's 2002 goal for Arsenal against Newcastle United, only better.

It would sadly prove to be the height of José's Milan career as relations with the Rossoneri's technical director Viani worsened. Viani had changed role from coach to technical director at Milan after a short stint at the head of the Italian national team in 1960. Altafini's demand for a better contract was not met and the striker wanted to leave the club. Alongside this, Altafini was struggling to find game time due to the signing of Amarildo, another Brazilian striker who had left Botafogo in 1963, which had led to his state of mind at the time. The previous four seasons had seen him score no less than 20 league goals in each but he only managed 11 and 14 respectively following the European triumph. The forward ended up returning to train with Palmeiras until he had his contract demands met and despite Viani's stubbornness, president Felice Riva reinstated the forward back into the red and black shirt.

José's final half a season proved to be a disappointing one as Milan slipped up late on to their biggest rivals and handed the title to the Nerazzurri due to a 5-2 Derby della Madonnina defeat. Altafini only scored three times in 12 appearances since his return from Brazil during the season, although did score probably his finest in a Milan shirt, and considering some of his past exploits in front of goal, that's quite something.

This one is well worth trawling various clips for, with José netting the winner in a 2-1 away victory against Torino. The goal itself was breathtaking as he guided a lofted ball into the box with a volley that nestled in the bottom corner of the goal. Not only that, but he did it with the most ridiculous bicycle kick you're ever likely to see in the 1960s. Altafini is already floating in the air waiting to make contact with the ball – time almost standing still. It was also around 15 yards out, if you're not already impressed. It was the perfect send-off as the time had come for José to draw the curtains on his time at Milan and thus wave farewell to a seven-year stay. A time consisting of highs and lows had come to an end as he moved to the newly promoted Napoli in the summer of 1965.

Altafini would lead the line alongside another new signing, Omar Sívori, who had joined from Juventus, and José had clearly found his new partner in crime as the two went on to fire the Partenopei to a third-place finish in the 1965/66 Serie A, with Altafini notching up 14 league goals altogether. His goalscoring exploits continued in the coming seasons – 16 and 13 scored – before the downturn occurred.

In the past seasons he had guided Napoli to a runners-up place in Serie A behind his former side Milan but his age was catching up on him. At this stage, José was 30 and wasn't the player he once was. Even though he had also helped his side to the 1972 Coppa Italia Final, in which Napoli were defeated 2-0 by Milan, the goals had dried up substantially, scoring a total of 28 from 1968–72. It also meant Altafini would be without a trophy over his seven years in Naples. At 34 years old, it seemed the decline of the prolific forward would ignite the start of his retirement but instead a part-time offer had appeared on Napoli's doorstep – Juventus had come calling.

The Bianconeri were prepared to keep Altafini at the top level even if he wasn't to be a regular starter. He would prove vital in his first season in Turin, as he once again won the Scudetto at the very end of the campaign. Milan led the standings by a point over Juventus but with José's former club failing to register a result against Verona, Altafini himself scored in a 2-1 turnaround victory over Roma to secure them the title. It proved to be the only trophy they'd win despite Juventus reaching the Coppa Italia Final and European Cup Final, losing to Milan and Dutch side Ajax respectively. He did however close out the year with nine goals from 23 league games which decreased to seven in 1973/74.

Two more seasons were left of his professional career in Italy, capped off with nine goals in 30 games across them both – picking up one more league title in 1974/75. This one was just as special as the previous season, but instead of gaining a bittersweet success over his first club Milan, this time it would be against Napoli. With just a few games remaining of the season, José grabbed a late but valuable equaliser against the Partenopei, who were also in contention with the Old Lady for the Scudetto. The goal had spurred Juve on, with the side from Naples succumbing to the Bianconeri in a 2-1 defeat.

It wasn't the first time Altafini had hit back against his former side – scoring the opener earlier on when they saw off their rivals with a thumping 6-2 win. They ended up finishing just two points above Napoli, a point's difference that was won thanks to José Altafini's goal just a few weeks prior to draw them level. Coincidence? Unlikely.

Although the ageing forward was only seen to be good enough to start games on the sidelines, the fact he wrote himself into the history books for his goals at Juventus made him the surprising protagonist in their Scudetto-winning seasons. He wouldn't see it that way – he always knew he was the centrepiece – the main attraction even.

As Juventus finished runners-up in 1975/76 to Torino, Altafini decided to end his time at the club. The striker sits joint fourth in the all-time scorers' table for Serie A – 216 goals in 459 appearances to his name – showing he is more than just a man with an impeccable goalscoring record. He loved the sport, the teams he played for, and of course the adoring support that never left his side during his 18 years in Italy. In 2013, when commentating for Rai Sport on a Confederations Cup game, Altafini was quick to compare the current state of football to his playing days. There were no longer any hard-hitting tackles, or simple celebrations with a solitary arm held above the head. He would draw a fitting comparison between what he had endured during his career, and what the sport has become today:

> 'Football is becoming a game about excessive athleticism with no poetry. So for this reason when I see someone who can recite football as if it was, I let myself go in the moment. Modern footballers are machines.'
>
> – *Corriere della Sera*

ROBERTO BAGGIO

INTRODUCED BY DOV SCHIAVONE

'I have just one image I would like to cancel from my life – that penalty.'

– Rai 1's TG1

WHEN people think of Roberto Baggio, their minds are immediately drawn to 1994 and a fateful afternoon in Pasadena's Rose Bowl.

That penalty has defined the career of *Il Divin Codino* – The Divine Ponytail for many, but he was much more than that. A genius, gliding past defenders as if they were mere shadows. A man who, and still is, an inspiration.

The magnitude of what Baggio means to calcio fans can be summed up by one episode in Genoa.

A friend of mine went to see Baggio play for the Italian national team at the Stadio Luigi Ferraris, but the only shirt with Baggio's name on the back happened to be that of Brescia – a team hated by the local Genoa fans.

While making his way to the Curva, he was stopped and told to remove the Brescia shirt, or he would not be making it to his seat. Confused, our Baggio disciple turned round and said, 'But it is for Baggio.' He was allowed to pass by the now appeased and apologetic Ultra.

That incident, for me, is an example of how Baggio was able to transcend club rivalry. Like Raymond...Everybody loves Baggio.

Baggio was one of the best I have ever seen, and definitely the best Italian player I have had the pleasure of taking in. The ability to make the game look so effortless is one held back for just a few, and Baggio was one of those.

One of my earliest memories is sitting with my family watching Italy v Czechoslovakia. I was only six at the time, but having an Italian family of 15 round to watch the match leaves an everlasting imprint, before the craziness of the day ensued due to Baggio's wonder-goal. From then on, I was always looking out for the great man's next feat.

Like Andrea Pirlo, should there have been a free kick in and around the penalty area, you knew a goal was probably forthcoming.

Renowned Italian journalist Gianni Brera deemed Baggio to be the best player he had ever seen – and who is to argue with a man who also witnessed the likes of Giuseppe Meazza, Gianni Rivera and Sandro Mazzola?

If one moment can be used to sum up the man and myth of Roberto Baggio, it is that he inspired a generation of online gamers. Those of you of a certain vintage will remember Baggio's Magical Kicks well.

Dov Schiavone

CALCIO'S GREATEST FORWARDS

Some events occur in world football that remain unforgettable. These events rear their head every so often, just to remind us all that football is the greatest game on the planet. Sometimes it's a spectacular goal, a horrendous challenge or a goalkeeping calamity. If it's not one of those, then it's probably one thing – a miss – a penalty miss. A 12-yard spot-kick to determine your side's fortunes. Tuck it away neatly into the bottom corner and all is well. Miss, and it'll haunt you forever. This is what happened to Italy's hero. This is what happened to Roberto Baggio.

He gave his all for the Azzurri, handing his national team five goals in the lead-up to the 1994 World Cup Final against Brazil. His goalscoring record in that tournament doesn't sum up his effort at all though – he seemed to be in every nook and cranny on the field when Italy were playing – constantly adapting his game to suit his team-mates. He was the reason Italy even had the chance of lifting their fourth World Cup at the time.

But what does it matter these days in football knowing how a player performed out of their skin in an entire tournament when you can simply click repeat on a video titled 'Roberto Baggio penalty miss'. It's a shame, because *Il Divin Codino* was one of the world's best on his day. He is known for striking a ball over the bar, despite being prolific in hitting the back of the net on a regular basis. It was his World Cup, and yet it shattered into a million pieces right in front of his very eyes.

> 'Unfortunately, and I don't know how, the ball went up three metres and flew over the crossbar. I was knackered, but I was the team's penalty taker. I've never run away from my responsibilities. Only those who have the courage to take a penalty miss them.'
>
> – Roberto Baggio's *Una Porta Nel Cielo*

The occurrence was devastating for him, killing the confidence of a man who ruled Serie A with Fiorentina and Juventus. Some will argue he wasn't the same after that penalty, never truly reaching the standards he once met. Those who simply watched him on a highlights reel will never forget his miss, but those who loved him will forgive him. He was the man who produced astounding moments for world football to gawp at for years to come, painting new memories for thousands of fans who were in love with calcio. He was Italian football, the penalty a mere blip on his talent. Had he not missed, maybe more would rank him up there with Pelé and Diego Maradona. And to think, this all began when he was just a small boy, kicking worn-out tennis balls into the open bathroom door.

Roberto was a shy boy, anxious even, when it came to daily activities. He struggled to really fit in, and even found flashing sirens on an ambulance frightening. His release was football. This was where Baggio came into his own – any worry or dread the young man had virtually disappearing. He didn't wish to pursue a career in accounting that he had been working toward, but instead chose the route of football and joined up with Vicenza, who were residing in Serie C1. The Italian had previously been at Caldogno, a village club, since the age of nine. Thanks to six goals in one game, scout Antonio Mora made sure his future would lie with Vicenza. Baggio cost them just £300.

His goals in the youth set-up meant he would progress on to the first team and he made his debut on 5 June 1983 against Piacenza, the final matchday of the season. Italian coach Bruno Giorgi, who was the man on the touchline for Vicenza at the time, elected to slowly ease Baggio into life at the club, picking him six times with a solitary goal to show for it.

The next year was far more 'Baggio' if that's a thing, with the attacking maestro playing in 29 games of the 34 available to him, securing 12 goals in the process. It was this season that saw interest for Baggio grow as his stock rose considerably. Two of those sending inconspicuous glances to *Il Divin Codino* were Juventus and Fiorentina. La Viola remained coy, sitting comfortably in the background waiting to make their move and did so at the last moment, securing the 18-year-old's signature on 3 May 1985.

It should have been a time for celebration for both club and player. Fiorentina had landed one of the hottest talents around while Roby was about to take the big step up to Serie A. Just two days later however, with Vicenza taking on Rimini, Baggio succumbed to a horror knee injury that saw him tear his anterior cruciate ligament. In layman's terms – it was not good news. Please make sure your seatbelt is firmly fastened, the rollercoaster ride is about to begin.

Roby learnt from the unfortunate accident though. Firstly he remained humble, considering Fiorentina elected to honour the deal and still take him on. Secondly, it meant he was able to connect with Buddhism, allowing him to recover, embrace calmness and build as a person due to the experience. *Corriere della Sera* quoted him to have gone to his friend's house soon after the injury and he was introduced to the religion. It proved to be the 'serenity he was looking for'. It taught him to learn that things happen for a reason, to learn from it, and to progress through life having experienced it.

After missing out on the entirety of the 1985/86 Serie A season, Baggio would finally end the wait to make his Fiorentina debut on 21 September 1986 against Sampdoria. Just a few days later in training, the pain returned with a problem in the knee again. With that, most of the campaign sped quickly past Baggio, with 220 stitches popped in his leg – according to *La Gazzetta dello Sport* – and Baggio even stated to *Corriere dello Sport* how he 'told my mother to kill me'.

Thankfully his mother never followed through with such demands and with rehabilitation behind him, Roby was finally ready to introduce himself to Italy's top flight properly, playing in the final few matches and guess what… he scored.

That's right, no injury could hold Baggio back from popping the ball into the net. It was 10 May 1987 when Fiorentina travelled to Naples and to the San Paolo stadium. Napoli were three points clear of Inter in the race for the Scudetto, and four above Juventus going into this penultimate matchday. If results went their way, even a loss to la Viola would mean they could lift their first Scudetto.

Andrea Carnevale opened the scoring just before the half-hour mark to send Naples into raptures. Ten minutes later Fiorentina were on the attack when a free kick was won just on the edge of the area. Cue Baggio, the once shy and skinny boy from Caldogno, to take the set piece. He steps up, caressing the ball low around the wall at pace, peering over the helpless defenders to see where his fate lay. It ended up nestling into the bottom corner. Two years of dreaded injuries hampering his career were long forgotten. His goal secured a 1-1 draw, enough to save Fiorentina from tumbling into Serie B and proved good enough for Napoli, who won the league on the same day. The Partenopei's finest moment was Roberto Baggio's. It was here that Baggio breathed new life and was born into the beautiful game, and there would be no stopping him from now on.

The next campaign on matchday two saw the Italian already creating headlines, securing a 2-0 win at the San Siro up against AC Milan under the guidance of new coach Sven-Göran Eriksson. Despite his side's eighth-place finish, Roby finished up with six goals, with the next year being the season he alerted the nation to his talent.

It began at home to Ascoli on the second matchday, taking the ball in his stride brilliantly before slotting home and racing to his adoring fans – arm well aloft. Cesena and Torino would feel the force of Baggio during the next two matches, including his first converted penalty in Serie A. He would go on to score 15 in total but he was about more than just goals, applying a handful of assists to Stefano Borgonovo.

He was a *fantasista*, the creative element of the team. One time you'd find him putting the ball in the net, the next, a sumptuous long pass would be played to his team-mates. It was what made Baggio so brilliant to watch and it was showcased during the majority of the 1994 World Cup finals. He would stay after hours with coach Eriksson practising his shooting and long balls, striving to be the most complete player. He embodied the notion of the *fantasista* – wearing the number ten shirt with pride and acting as an icon to those in the stands.

Leading on from his remarkable past year in Italian football, Roby was keeping his cool and was still improving. He scored a remarkable goal up against Napoli that season on 17 September 1989 when he beat three defenders having run from deep inside his own half – arguably the furthest back he ever was on the pitch – before leaving goalkeeper Giuliano Giuliani on the ground with a scooped fake shot. As he rounded the Italian the whole of Italy stood in awe as he rolled the ball into the empty net. For those who like the standard thumping effort, he did that two months later at home to Ascoli on 19 November.

His exploits continued in Europe with Baggio letting everyone know that he was alive and kicking, particularly in the 1990 UEFA Cup. He sent Fiorentina all the way to the final to face Juventus. The Bianconeri deservedly took the title though, winning 3-1 over two legs.

It hadn't hindered interest in Baggio, who was attracting a host of clubs clambering over one another in an attempt to sign him. Fiorentina were dealing with a financial crisis and it appeared as if Roby would be departing. One of those interested suitors were rivals Juventus, the side that had just killed their European dreams. As if that wasn't enough for la Viola to deal with, two days after the second leg, Baggio completed his move from Florence to Turin for a then world record fee of £8m. The sale of Roby had led to around three days of protests in Florence, seeing over 50 people injured and the president of the club taking refuge in the stadium so as to not lose a limb.

It was all occurring at the worst possible time, with Italy about to host the 1990 World Cup finals, and most eyes were on Baggio and what he could do for the Azzurri. With Fiorentina fans angry at the owners and Roby, who they believed had wanted to transfer away from Florence, the Italian was faring no better with the Juventini. He sat in at the press conference with black and white scarves draped around the chairs, yet refused to wear the garment during the talk.

Even after scoring *that* goal against Czechoslovakia during the World Cup finals, the tension still hadn't dropped during the Serie A season with Fiorentina preparing to welcome Juventus on 6 April 1991. La Viola led the game 1-0 before the Old Lady were awarded a penalty. All eyes fell upon Baggio. 'Great,' whispered fans of the Curva Fiesole. 'I wonder who's going to take this.' Roby elected not to, letting team-mate Gigi De Agostini get the goal. He didn't, and they lost the game. Baggio opened up about the decision, stating his mind wasn't in the right place. He probably didn't help himself when he picked up a Fiorentina scarf after his substitution to then wear it, allowing the Juventini to add another thing to the list of why they were angry at him:

> 'I just wasn't feeling right. Suppose I miss the penalty kick? People would say I did it on purpose. The Italian press blew this out of proportion. I picked up a scarf, and they bust my chops.'
>
> – *The Guardian*

His 14 goals didn't go unnoticed though, despite the fact Roberto was having a torrid time with supporters as well as the press, and his new side had gone five years without a Scudetto. Giovanni Trapattoni took over and wanted to make sure Baggio was the centrepiece, giving him some confidence following the previous events of the last few years. Injuries still tried to stop him, but Baggio wouldn't be beaten. He scored 18, his best thus far, silencing those who were criticising him. Roby even got his first Serie A hat-trick against Foggia, dispatching two penalties before curling a beauty of a strike into the top corner. It was one of his best, a gift to the Juventini and calcio fans – except maybe Foggia.

His form continued into the 1992/93 Serie A, one that ended in Baggio's first trophy. No, it wasn't the Scudetto, that prize still remained a whisker away from Roby, who again netted a ridiculous 21 goals that year domestically. For those who are probably nudging the person next to them and going, 'I bet half of those were penalties,' you'd be surprised to know that only three of his 21 efforts came from 12 yards.

His goals were simply a consolation due to another poor league season, and tensions were rising between Baggio and coach Trapattoni. Roberto was clear with his intentions, he wanted to stay with Juve, but realised, 'Every time I opened my mouth chaos broke out.' This was noted in *Corriere della Sera*, which also went on to quote Trapattoni saying, 'If Roberto is not happy, he can leave.'

Leaving behind the tensions at the top, let us refer back to the aforementioned trophy a certain Roby ran home with – the 1993 UEFA Cup. His best came in the final few games, letting fly with a rocket shot along the ground that might as well have set the grass on fire and left the white lines disappearing into a cloud of dust against Paris Saint-Germain in the semi-finals, such was its power. He got another during that first leg too – just a standard 25-yard free kick into the top corner. The Italian went on to score the winner in Paris two weeks later, sending Trapattoni's intrepid troopers into battle for the final against Borussia Dortmund.

The first leg fell on 5 May 1993, in Germany, and it was here that Roby and Dino Baggio won their side the UEFA Cup. Despite falling behind, Dino levelled proceedings before Roberto handed them a valuable lead with a poked effort from inside the box. Stefan Klos would be picking the ball out of his goal yet again in the second half thanks to a first-time shot from our *fantasista*, although he was deployed mainly behind Gianluca Vialli and Paolo Di Canio for most of the campaign. A 3-0 return leg victory closed out any Juventini doubt – the trophy was theirs.

Baggio kept his head about him, though; he wasn't going to let his first major success block his vision and stop him performing. He picked up the Ballon d'Or at the end of the calendar year, alongside the 1993 FIFA World Player award. Aside from this, the drab 1993/94 Serie A season came and went for Juventus as quickly as can be, waving goodbye to Trapattoni on the way while welcoming in a certain Alessandro Del Piero. Marcello Lippi was instated, ready to make an impact on the Scudetto-less club.

Roberto had since returned from the 1994 World Cup finals, penalty miss and all, for the upcoming season. Injuries and Lippi's tactics meant Roby saw the least amount of game time since 1987. He continued to give the biggest effort possible, helping Juventus to end their eight-year drought without the Scudetto, and also picked up a Coppa Italia along the way. With his little sack of trophies dragging behind him, just like his ponytail in the wind, it was time for Baggio to move on. Milan had slapped a deal on the table and that was that – Baggio was at the Rossoneri with Fabio Capello.

His time at Milan was short, two years in fact, but his first year brought home his second consecutive Scudetto. It was the prime example of how silverware doesn't warrant what a player actually wants, with Baggio seemingly disappointed with another injury-plagued, low-morale campaign. His confidence was still shattered from the penalty back in 1994 – you don't forget a penalty miss in the World Cup Final and you don't need to be in that position to know that. Milan wanted the best Baggio, but got a botched Baggio.

Harsh? Probably. This was the man who defined Italian football. Problems with the coaches yet again, especially when Arrigo Sacchi took charge for the 1996/97 Serie A. The two had previous from the World Cup finals and Baggio's appearances on the field began to decline. Sacchi had a torrid time at least and Capello returned, but by then Baggio was gone – Bologna his next port of call.

Bologna? Yes, you read that correctly. All of a sudden Italy's finest was at the mid-table Rossoblu. He was 30 years old, but coach Renzo Ulivieri believed in him, ready to give Baggio a chance. It was here that *Il Divin Codino* – although we can't call him that anymore – rejuvenated his career. He chopped off his ponytail, removing not only his iconic image, but the troubling past – his Buddhist roots were now shining bright. It worked though, scoring 22 in 30 games, his best in the top flight. He silenced Milan when they came to the Stadio Renato Dall'Ara, poking home the opener before dispatching a penalty. He raised his hands to his ears, cupping them to embrace the 'I can't hear you' attitude. Roby wasn't done there though, and did it again at the Stadio delle Alpi against Juventus. Baggio was reborn… again.

His solid season meant he ended up at Inter for around £2m, ready to climb the ladder of success once again. He was the wrong side of 30 though, and it proved another poor move – clearly the style of the time for Roby and Milan clubs. The two years there were average at best, meeting up with Lippi again, another coach he had unfinished business with. He was handed no favours when Lippi turned round to him and asked for his assistance on spying on his team-mates. Baggio turned it down and thus began the demise of his game time, which was no surprise.

He ended up with lowly Brescia at the turn of the millennium and relaxed into his new side, realising that this was the atmosphere he could thrive on at his age. The Italian played regularly and scored consistently during four years on the books at the newly-promoted side.

On the outside, it appeared as though Baggio was having an enjoyable time – scoring ten goals or more in all four seasons he remained at the Rondinelle. However, the game was slowly killing Roby. Injuries had plagued him for arguably his entire career, telling *Corriere dello Sport*, 'I struggled to walk for two days after each game [at Brescia],' and, 'When I got out of my car, I had to use the door to hoist myself up.'

The end finally came on 16 May 2004 when Milan welcomed Brescia and Baggio back to the San Siro. With five minutes remaining and his side down 4-2, the substitution was made. Baggio removed the captain's armband from his side, applauding the entirety of the stadium that stood to applaud the work of art that stood before them. He embraced Paolo Maldini on the way, his trademark ponytail back and better than ever flowing in the wind. He kept the tears to himself though, or at least attempted to, as he high-fived possibly all those around him.

As he headed to the tunnel with the crowd still saluting his contribution to not just football, but Italy as a whole, everyone realised they were losing an icon. As he disappeared from view, it spelled not just the end of Baggio, but the end of an era. He spoke with Sky Sport Italia following the match, closing out his phenomenal career:

> 'It was my last game, so thank you all. Today was beautiful. The Milan fans were fantastic. I received a huge manifestation of affection. The only regret of my career is the missed penalty in the final of the 1994 World Cup finals. After that mistake I wanted to stop, instead, here I am talking about a career lasting 19 years.'
>
> – Sky Sport Italia

GABRIEL BATISTUTA

INTRODUCED BY GIANCARLO RINALDI

'When I was playing football I never enjoyed it that much, I was never happy. If I scored two goals, I wanted a third, I always wanted more.'

– FIFA.com

I CAN still remember my excitement when Fiorentina went shopping for two of the starlets of Argentina's Copa América-winning side of 1991. It felt like a signal that the days of selling our best players were behind us. And, while Diego Latorre would sink without trace, Gabriel Omar Batistuta became one of the finest footballers I have ever seen in the hallowed purple shirt.

Almost from the outset there was something pretty special about the boy. It wasn't just the power, determination and eye for goal which marked him as being out of the ordinary. There was also a spirit, style and sense of loyalty which was – and still is – pretty uncommon.

Remember that he could easily have walked away from the club when they got relegated to Serie B just two seasons after he signed. It was a World Cup finals year and many players would have been tempted to keep their talents on show at a bigger club. Instead, *Batigol* seemed to feel that if he had got Fiorentina into this mess, he would have to help to get them back out.

That was when a full-on love affair with la Viola support was born. This was the real *Re Leone* – the Lion King – with his flowing mane of hair, thumping shot and thunderbolt headers. Many a goalkeeper was in danger of being carried over the line by the momentum of a strike from the Argentinian's boots.

In a city which has always idolised the individual – from Hamrin to Antognoni to Baggio and beyond – he became an incarnation of Florence on the field of play. *Guerriero mai domo, duro nella lotta, leale nell'animo* – he was described in scarves of the time. A never defeated warrior – strong in battle but loyal in spirit. And that was how we liked him.

He silenced the Camp Nou, struck stunners at Old Trafford and Wembley and gunned down Juventus. He went on a record-breaking goalscoring run at the start of one season and we thought it might never end. He won us the Coppa Italia and Supercoppa Italiana and, by God, he gave us the strongest whiff of the Scudetto we have had in the last 30 years or so.

I was lucky enough to see him in action in the flesh and can attest to just what a force of nature he was. He seemed to knock down defenders like a battering ram before drilling the ball like a missile inexorably heading towards the back of the net. When we invoked a goal with our chants of his name, he hardly ever let us down. He simply did not know how to give less than 100 per cent.

His tears when he struck for Roma against us would only cement his legend. The bond between *Batigol* and Fiorentina was more than just the average player–club relationship. We gave him unconditional love and he returned it with a ferocious determination to deliver the victories we craved. And, when he ran to the corner flag to celebrate yet another goal, our Sunday afternoons were complete.

Giancarlo Rinaldi

Lionel Messi may have all the personal accolades modern-day football can offer, yet he still sits second in the Argentina top scorers' chart. Who's the man holding the top spot? Look no further than the sensational striker Gabriel Batistuta. *Batigol*, as he was more commonly known, plied his trade in Italy from 1991 to 2003, a 12-year period which saw the striker represent Fiorentina, Roma and briefly Inter.

Gabriel was brought into this world by Gloria Batistuta on 1 February 1969 just in time for Apollo 11 to descend upon the Moon's surface. He grew into his life of fame and fortune from a modest upbringing in Avellaneda, working on a farm his family owned to make ends meet. It was here that Gabriel first realised the harsh reality of life and the world he'd entered into. He wasn't to know he'd become one of the greatest strikers Serie A has ever seen, or arguably the greatest player that Fiorentina fans have paid witness to.

He was a growing boy, experiencing the simpler things in life than a professional footballer. He met his future wife – Irena – having snuck into her birthday party at the age of 15. Gabriel was turned down at first; clearly the one present Irena didn't want was the rather overweight Batistuta. Even then, as clichéd as it may sound, his determination and drive was on full show before he was professionally kicking a ball for a living. He never took no for an answer, until finally, on 28 December 1990 she said yes at the altar.

But we're not here to pry on his personal life, or draw rather below-par parallels between his time on the pitch and his flirting off it as a naive teenager. He was a lover of basketball more than anything, mainly thanks to his height over other budding players, but as we all know, Gabriel would choose the footballing route for his future. It was a tough choice, considering his concentration on his school studies, but Batistuta would go on to sign his first professional contract at 19 years old – set to become one of the hottest and most prolific goalscorers around. Newell's Old Boys would be the first to welcome such a player under their wing, having been impressed with Gabriel in a youth cup match when he represented Platense. The losers on that day were in fact his new suitors, and probably snapped him up so as to not have to face the wrath of his striking prowess again.

It wasn't the perfect start to his footballing career however – playing out a subdued 30 minutes against San Martín de San Juan, he was then subsequently loaned out to Sportivo Italiano. It was clear he had struggled to adapt to his new life at La Lepra, but some fine performances for the Buenos Aires side meant there would be a 1989 move on the cards. Despite being a long-term supporter of Boca Juniors, a club he wished to end his career at, he signed for their biggest rivals, River Plate, one of the giants of Argentinian football.

Of course, things seemed to not be easy for him – he would spend just a solitary season there due to disputes with then coach Daniel Passarella. Passarella was adored by not only the entire country for playing a part in the 1978 World Cup success, but he was also a hero of Batistuta's. Sadly the two would never stand side by side without some sort of argument breaking out, leading to a troubled footballing life at Los Millonarios. Hatred toward another professional is entirely plausible, but Passarella insisted for many years that the striker just wasn't as good as he was made out to be. In fact, he was quoted to have said *Batigol* had 'square feet and a technique to match'. Oddly, this was a claim made during the height of Gabriel's career – the stubborn nature of the former River Plate and Argentine coach in full view.

To look back on it now, the experience clearly made Batistuta stronger and more mentally fixated on becoming one of the best. It was a shame, because Gabriel looked like he could have found a home for more than just a year at his new club, scoring four goals in 17 appearances. Even though the goal tally doesn't look impressive, it was the first time his ridiculous power in the attacking area of his game was on full show at the age of 21, bombarding defenders at any given moment.

As expected, Batistuta moved clubs yet again, not so far this time, jumping ship to play for deadly rivals and boyhood club Boca Juniors. The trend continued and the forward found life tough during the first season, mainly due to being played on the wing, but would finally find his feet thanks to the introduction of coach Oscar Tabárez. Batistuta would lead the line and form a ferocious partnership with Diego Latorre. The 1991 Primera División soon followed with *Batigol* getting the goals his nickname reflected, finishing as the top scorer in the entire league.

Potential clubs were soon intrigued by the promise Gabriel held, and at the 1991 Copa America tournament for Argentina he would soon show the world what lay ahead. La Albiceleste would secure their 13th title, with *Batigol* grabbing six in total, the tournament's best. Gabriel had caught the eye of a number of clubs – Real Madrid, Juventus and Verona to name but a few. However there was one club that were swift in their negotiations in an attempt to land the forward – Fiorentina. It began thanks to then vice-president Vittorio Cecchi Gori, who was in attendance at the 1991 tournament. Talks opened up, albeit with much difficulty due to the language barrier. However, after much deliberation, the deal was complete. La Viola had snapped up the talented attacker, as well as Boca team-mate Latorre. It would be a tale of two careers as the latter went on to make just two appearances in Florence, with the former becoming one of the greatest players to ever grace the field in Italy.

For once *Batigol* wouldn't struggle when joining a new side, despite the drastic change of scenery. The culture and language didn't faze Gabriel as he found the back of the net 13 times in his debut campaign while simultaneously guiding his new club to 12th in the table. His first of many strikes came during a 3-1 victory over Genoa, gobbling up a deflected free kick from all of six yards out to get his Serie A goalscoring under way. After goals against Cremonese and Verona, Gabriel truly won the hearts of all Fiorentina fans when he managed to help secure an impressive 2-0 victory over runners-up Juventus. Just seven minutes in, a hopeful ball was played into the box. Quick as a flash, Batistuta contorted his head to meet the ball and direct it past Stefano Tacconi. Cue the celebrations, as Gabriel leapt over the advertising hoardings straight to the rapturous *La Vecchia Guardia Firenze* in the Curva Fiesole. Constant fist-pumping, shirt-pulling and roars of approval ensued. It was at this moment the love between the fans and player was truly secured.

If that wasn't enough, he scored seven goals in his next four games including his first Serie A hat-trick which came away at Foggia. His first was something of a dying art – a well-guided diving header flying past the defenceless goalkeeper at a tremendous speed. The forward lashed his second into the net with a fierce right-footed drive before heading home to complete his hat-trick and earn a point for la Viola.

Such an impressive season would sadly be met with the complete opposite, when the club were relegated to Serie B. Batistuta's side had actually been doing quite well but the unexpected sacking of Luigi Radice saw Aldo Agroppi take his place. A shocking run of results under their new coach meant la Viola were in a relegation battle, and were confirmed to be heading to Serie B on the final day. It was a real shame for Batistuta and co. as the striker had netted 16 goals during the campaign, his best so far in his career.

Cue inevitable interest from the likes of Real Madrid, looking to snap up the Argentine to save him from second-tier Italian football. As the football world watched on, they saw an act of true decency, with *Batigol* stating he would stay and play for the club that had fallen in love with him:

> 'I just fell in love with the city and I really liked the atmosphere and I said to myself, I'm going to stay here. That was despite the fact that back then big teams from abroad such as Real Madrid and Manchester United were after me on a regular basis.'
>
> – Sky Sports documentary: *Football's Greatest*

The unexpected stay of Gabriel was shortly followed by the expected resurgence of Fiorentina – under the guidance of Claudio Ranieri they finished top of the table during the 1993/94 season, with Batistuta gaining another 16 league goals to his name. It was also during this campaign that then club president Mario Cecchi Gori sadly passed away. Understandably, la Viola were in mourning and the loss of Cecchi Gori completely destroyed the ownership stability they had built. It didn't prove to be too much for the city of Florence to handle thankfully, as they had secured a route back to Serie A.

Back in the top flight the goals were quickly flowing for the forward – bagging his first in a 2-1 opening-day victory against Cagliari in front of a packed Stadio Artemio Franchi. His late winner would prove to be the start of an incredible record-breaking feat by *Batigol* as he went on to net in every single week up until the 12th round of the season, with eventual Scudetto winners Juventus halting the prolific striker. The record would still be his though, edging out the 30-year-long one held by Ezio Pascutti. It was a run of goals that never looked like they were stopping – Genoa, Cremonese, Inter, Lazio, Reggina, Padova, Brescia, Bari, Napoli and Sampdoria – these were the victims of Gabriel's incredible accomplishment. Only the Bianconeri and Roma avoided conceding a goal that season to the Argentinian, an incredible feat. Capocannoniere was of course his, finishing off the season with a total of 26 goals, holding off a fellow countryman in Abel Balbo who got 22 while playing for Roma.

It proved the start of Batistuta's best form for Fiorentina with silverware just around the corner. The Coppa Italia would be his first port of call and he was quick to help his side in the competition, scoring in wins over Lecce, Palermo and three times across the two-legged semi-final against Inter. Then came the final, another two-legged affair against surprise package Atalanta, who had finished 13th compared to Ranieri's fourth-placed Fiorentina. Having notched up 19 league goals, *Batigol* wasn't done there. The first leg was to be held at the Franchi and Gabriel was clearly in the mood, forcing Atalanta goalkeeper Fabrizio Ferron into some important first-half saves. He wouldn't be denied for long though, as a short-corner routine in the second half saw Batistuta strike a superb dipping shot over Ferron to give the home side the advantage.

The return leg was hosted at the Stadio Atleti Azzurri d'Italia where Batistuta would score again – a hard strike into an empty net to make it 2-0 on the night and 3-0 on aggregate. It had been the dream of Gabriel to change the misfortunes of the underachieving Fiorentina and such a result had secured this. The cup success meant entry into the Supercoppa Italiana, another game *Batigol* thrived in, scoring twice to edge out Milan 2-1. The first saw him flick the ball over captain Franco Baresi before leathering it into the back of net, while his second came from a wonderful free kick from 25 yards out. To this day, it is their only success in the competition.

The previous season's finish of fourth would not be topped straight away with *Batigol*'s Fiorentina finishing ninth in 1996/97. Twelve goals were etched to Batistuta's name, falling well short of his previous tallies of 19 and 26. Gabriel would be back to his best soon after, guiding Fiorentina to fifth with his total of 21 across 1997/98. He did however score a second-half hat-trick on the opening day in Udine that included an 18-yard bicycle kick. No really, it's true – well worth searching for this one online.

The next campaign would be an interesting one, with la Viola finally mounting a real charge for the Scudetto. The key figure of Batistuta was leading the line as he did so well when donning the Florentine shirt, yet following a 0-0 draw with eventual champions Milan in early February things fell apart. The clinical finisher had already scored 18 times in 19 appearances, including a fantastic headed winner at home to Juventus. Watching back on the goal, it seemed as if Batistuta wanted to perform every celebration possible. It was everything that showcased what Batistuta was all about – driven by his passion. Even the cameraman seemed to join in, bobbing up and down frantically trying to keep up with the ecstasy oozing out of the scorer. He could have also been spurred on after being expelled from the UEFA Cup a month earlier due to a fan's lunacy of throwing a bomb at a linesman against Grasshopper Zurich. Such a driven nature was regrettably brought to a halt due to an injury in the game with the Rossoneri.

Gabriel was made to watch from the sidelines as his beloved team began to crumble. He returned just as Lazio had overhauled his side at the top of the table. The shock of the disastrous February games showed in the remainder of the season – Lazio and Milan continued to pick up points as la Viola drowned in draws and losses. A third-place finish ensued, the gluttony of goals from *Batigol* virtually diminished. It would be the club's biggest sniff at a chance of the Scudetto, which sadly ended prematurely with the injury to their prized asset.

The mismanagement at the top of the club's hierarchy was becoming ever greater and after a sixth-place finish in 1999/2000, Batistuta would no longer be in Florence. Their previous third in Serie A meant they did enter the UEFA Champions League however. After easing past Widzew Łódź 5-1 in the third qualifying round, they would meet Barcelona, Arsenal and AIK in the first group stage. *Batigol* was at the forefront of reintroducing Fiorentina to Europe's biggest club competition, netting at AIK as well as finding the net with a thumping effort versus Arsenal. How it didn't break the net we'll never know.

It took Fiorentina through to the second group stage where they met Manchester United, Valencia and Bordeaux. Even with his side missing out on qualification to the quarter-finals, he scored a truly memorable goal at Old Trafford. Within two touches, *Batigol* had made room for a shot which he duly snapped up from 30 yards out. The sheer velocity and swerve on the strike was unbelievably brilliant. Gabriel had stunned the Premier League champions.

As for his final season domestically, a true send-off occurred with the last game of the season being a home clash against Venezia – *Batigol* playing his part, netting a superb hat-trick. It would be the last time Fiorentina fans would see their forward celebrate with the ever-present showcase of an imaginary machine gun, beautifully representing the way he destroyed Serie A defences in the past nine years. He had amassed over 200 goals across all competitions since his move to Fiorentina, a truly remarkable record.

All the goals had seen little silverware on the other hand and Batistuta dreamed of the Scudetto, something he had so wished to have won with Fiorentina. After swift negotiations, he would be partnering Francesco Totti at Italian giants Roma.

Three years would be spent playing at the Stadio Olimpico, although in the first season his Scudetto dreams would be answered. Fabio Capello, then Roma coach, had also acquired the services of Walter Samuel to add to the acquisition of Batistuta. The two Argentines entered a team of Vincenzo Montella, and of course, Totti. In a season where they suffered just three losses – Inter, Milan and Fiorentina – in which all were away, Roma edged out Juventus thanks to a final-day success over Parma.

Batigol was at the heart of the victorious Giallorossi, scoring not only in the 3-1 Parma win, but also having scored another 19 times in the previous 33 games to finish as his side's top scorer for the season. It was also in this campaign that Gabriel brought tears to all Fiorentina fans as well as himself when he netted the only goal in a 1-0 win on 16 November 2000. The goal itself was typical of *Batigol* – a half-volley from 20 yards.

The pinnacle of Gabriel's career had been met and his goalscoring exploits slowly decreased – the Argentine was fully into his 30s and managed a total of ten goals across the next two seasons. It's worth noting that in 2001/02, when he scored six goals, it was the first time since his move to Italy that he had not managed double figures. A loan spell to Inter confirmed Batistuta couldn't maintain his previous level of performances in the top league and finished his career playing in Qatar for Al-Arabi. It wouldn't prove too disappointing as he made it worth his while, scoring 25 goals and breaking the league's goal record at the first time of asking.

Batistuta had enjoyed a special career, but he was not without his critics – he said the following about those who doubted him when looking back on his time playing:

> 'The fact is I never played for those people who doubted me. I've always given everything for every

team I've played for so that the ordinary fans and the people in the stadium could identify with me. I owe a lot to the fans of Roma, Fiorentina and Argentina. They were the reason I played, my inspiration. I always worked hard to improve my game, to prove to myself that I could be one of the best for as long as possible. To be honest, I couldn't care less what the others think.'

– FIFA.com

If ever there was a quote to sum up Gabriel, this was it. A Fiorentina great and a brief Roma hero, Batistuta was one of the finest in recent years of Italian football and all of Florence will never forget his long flowing hair, crazy celebrations and lethal finishes. He cried again when he was inducted into Fiorentina's Hall of Fame on 6 October 2014 – the onlooking support chanting his name as he wiped away the tears with the purple scarf. They loved him and he loved them. That was *Batigol*.

ROBERTO BONINSEGNA

INTRODUCED BY JAMES HORNCASTLE

'The Nerazzurri will always be my team, I loved my time there despite all the setbacks. I knew that as long as I ended up at Inter I would be happy.'

– *La Gazzetta dello Sport*

YOU won't find a biography of Roberto Boninsegna in your local bookshop. 'A publisher offered me a book deal,' he revealed, 'a good one. But I turned it down because if I told the truth I would have spat in a lot of people's faces and if I didn't I would only be spitting in my own. It's for the best.' Or is it a loss? Football alone would make it a great page-turner. Truth be told it's only half the story with Boninsegna.

He played under three of the wisest men in football; Manlio Scopigno, Helenio Herrera and Giovanni Trapattoni. Its greatest chronicler Gianni Brera also bestowed on him one of the game's most memorable nicknames: *Bonimba*, 'because you're a short arse and when you run you remind me of Bagonghi', a circus dwarf. It mattered little that Boninsegna was taller than Brera.

He partnered Gigi Riva at Cagliari and studied at Inter under Giuseppe Meazza, who by then was a member of the club's backroom staff and taught *Bonimba* 30 different penalty techniques. A fan favourite in Nerazzurro, he scored 14 seconds into a Derby della Madonnina. One of only ten players to finish Capocannoniere in back-to-back years, he would win the Scudetto three times and also lifted the UEFA Cup with Juventus, a treasured achievement as it came in an all-Italian team.

A nearly man of sorts, he could have won so much more. Boninsegna left Cagliari in the year they won the Scudetto. He played in and lost the 1970 World Cup Final and 1972 European Cup Final. Struck by a Coca-Cola can in Mönchengladbach, he was involved in one of the most controversial incidents in the competition's history. Even after hanging up his boots and taking a break from the game, his influence didn't stop. As a scout he claims to have discovered other great strikers like Vincenzo Montella and Luca Toni to name but two.

An exceptional career, Boninsegna's life is altogether more so. His mother, the outgoing Elsa, was so passionate about Mantova that she still insisted on going to games when she was eight months pregnant with her little Roby. Approached by a couple of concerned stewards who had every intention of turning her away at the gates, she told them, 'Not to worry boys, I've brought the midwife with me.'

Around 70 years later Boninsegna celebrated his birthday at the Burgo paper mill where his father Bruno used to work. The reason Boninsegna chose to have his birthday at the mill was a noble one. Foreclosed, its production had stopped and the redundancy pay supporting its 174 workers was due to finish. This was an act of solidarity. A blue-collar footballer, not just because he made 22 appearances for Italy, reflecting on Boninsegna's life is like listening to *Darkness on the Edge of Town*. Think of him as the Bruce Springsteen of Serie A.

James Horncastle

Boninsegna was your typical centre-forward. Strong, athletic and quite bullish in his approach for a 5ft 10in man, the Italian made life a misery for defenders in his homeland. The slowly-dying position was one the Italian mastered across the 1960s and 70s, scoring freely while his bad haircut distracted his opponents. Roberto loved his hair, though, and was quick to detail its beauty in an interview with *La Gazzetta dello Sport* on his 70th birthday. He explained immediately how his hair

> 'is natural, with no added colouring', before explaining it was proper, due to his mother who had 'died at age 91 yet still had half the colour in her hair'.

Of course, this is probably not the place to discuss the hair on the attacker's head, but it must have given him some unidentified power into the ability he held. The Italian was nimble on his feet too, leaping like a salmon over defenders which towered over him to knock home another headed effort. The attacker was christened *Bonimba* by Italian journalist Gianni Brera, with the forward basing his game on that of Inter winger Lennart Skoglund. While mainly representing Cagliari, Inter and Juventus, Roberto grew up supporting the Nerazzurri and joined the youth team set-up at 14 years old, but his road to success wouldn't be that simple.

Five years followed but there would be no advancement in the Inter ranks and thus he ended up with Prato, a side lingering in Serie B. A solitary season was spent with the Lanieri before returning to Inter where he hoped his fortunes would change. Club director Italo Allodi was quick to reiterate that they couldn't see a future with Boninsegna and for the striker to either go out on loan to Potenza, or quite frankly, get lost.

It appeared as if Roberto's love for the club he supports would soon diminish, given the way he was being treated. The striker was virtually forced to leave on loan while his beloved went on to win all there was to win in 1964/65.

Bonimba attempted to remain professional at his young age and didn't want to let the decision override his feelings toward Inter, and moved to Potenza. However he was starting to become more and more selfish. His progress was possibly hindered by this, as he was attempting harder chances rather than setting up an easier opportunity for a team-mate. As such, he remained at the club for just the one year with nine goals to his name before ending up with Serie A side Varese.

Funnily enough, and also rather predictably in the beautiful game that is football, Varese's first league match of the 1965/66 season was at the San Siro, against Inter. The home side inevitably saw out the match 5-2 with Roberto having to watch from the comfort of the bench. He did notch up his first goal a week later in front of the home support at the Stadio Franco Ossola, despite the end result finishing 4-1 in Bologna's favour. It would be a little taster session for Boninsegna, and he managed to score another four goals for the season with the Leopardi finishing rock bottom of the league.

The time at Varese proved vital, even though it did come with its controversy. In a home match against Cagliari, Boninsegna hit a shot destined to fly into the back of the net, until the opposing defender punched the ball out of play. The referee elected to give a corner, clearly acknowledging the fact the player had made contact with the ball, just not with his hand. Roberto was furious, screaming at the official to reconsider his decision, explaining what had just unfolded in front of his very eyes. Subsequently, the referee was pushed to the ground and *Bonimba* was handed a nine-match ban.

The incident had proven too much for Roberto and his team-mates to handle and they had decided that there was no better way to get the decision overturned than to push the official to the ground. Was it down to his age, inner frustration at the way he was being treated at Inter, or just a heat-of-the-moment occurrence? Only Roberto knows the answer to that and what exactly happened. What we all know however, is that he got a hefty ban from playing. But surely it meant for the young man, who was now deemed both selfish *and* aggressive, that there wouldn't be much of a future in professional football for him.

Rather unsurprisingly, the striker would soon be on the move again. Incredibly, that team was Cagliari. Boninsegna was to partner the up-and-coming Gigi Riva. The two were to work successfully in Roberto's three years at the club, and he said the following about his time with Riva at the Rossoblu and how the allegations there were problems between them are not true:

> 'Did we clash? No. All false. We were like brothers. We lived for two years in the same room and we travelled back together by car from training. True, on the field was different, but that's football.'
>
> – Tuttojuve.com

BONIMBA
INTER
Paine

It didn't take long for the partnership to begin, both of the forwards scoring in the opening league game of the season, a 2-0 away success against Lecco. After a 0-0 draw at home to AC Milan they were back to winning ways on matchday three, securing a fine 4-0 victory against Bologna. *Bonimba* got one while Riva notched up a hat-trick to complete the rout. It was a time in calcio history where two of the best strikers in the world had come together, and neither knew the heights they would both reach.

To look at it now, and see what both achieved in their careers, is remarkable. Serie A would not witness an attacking duo like Roberto and Gigi until arguably a few Dutchmen arrived at Milan, but we can all argue until we're blue in the face on that statement!

Although the former Inter man wasn't reaching the same heights as his striking compatriot in terms of goalscoring – he found the net nine times in total for his new club – every game he scored in resulted in two points. A good omen for the future clearly, as the Italian had won his side 18 points for the season. Riva on the other hand managed 18 goals as Capocannoniere and bagged the Rossoblu 17 points, meaning the two earned Cagliari 35 points for the campaign out of 40, finishing in sixth place overall. Problems? What problems?

The only seemingly bad coming-together between the two was when Gigi invited Roberto on a drive up to Villasimius in Sardinia, in which the latter only found out the car had no seatbelts on the day. According to Boninsegna in *Corriere della Sera*'s *Fifty Thousand days* – historical stories as told by Giorgio Dell'Arti – as soon as the excursion had concluded, *Bonimba* elected to 'take out life insurance' due to the fact they 'took corners on two wheels'.

Away from the death-defying stunts, his team-mate was clearly attempting to put on a show for Roberto, but things weren't as rosy goalscoring-wise for the striker. This time around it was apparent the Italian wasn't at his best, bagging just five for the 1967/68 Serie A season, while the prodigy Riva also saw a shortage of goals – 13 to his name.

The deadly duo made sure they were exactly what their aforementioned name meant again the following year though. Boninsegna's nine goals alongside Riva's 21 in 1968/69 guided Cagliari to a sensational second-place finish, just four points behind champions Fiorentina. It was the closest the Rossoblu had come to the Scudetto, the prize every boy in Italy had dreamt of night after night. It was a footballing season that had all the degrees of a rollercoaster ride for the players on the pitch, and the ever-growing support in the Stadio Amsicora. Even with Boninsegna and co. leading the way in the standings with only a couple of months remaining, things fell apart. Four matches without a victory meant they dropped below la Viola and were unable to make up the ground needed to create their historic moment. If that hadn't dampened their spirits enough, they also came second best to Roma in the Coppa Italia in the group final, just to rub salt in the wounds.

Coach Manlio Scopigno knew if the club were to progress they needed money, and as such it would mean one of the big names at the Rossoblu would have to go. The man in the dugout had a choice because only two players would attract interest from big clubs – Boninsegna and Riva. It was to be Roberto who would make way, but only if he could join the club he had always wanted to represent at this level, Inter. The deal was secure and both parties received their wishes. Scopigno and Cagliari had three new players and a cash payment with Boninsegna getting to finally play for what he described as 'his' club.

The first season, as clichéd as it may sound, proved to be an intriguing affair with Boninsegna's Inter locking horns with his former club Cagliari in a battle for the title. Inter had experience – ten-time winners at this stage – while Cagliari had only just had their best season by finishing second. During the tussle between the two teams, *Bonimba* scored one of his best goals in terms of illustrating his aerial ability, despite the fact they lost the game.

Bologna were the Nerazzurri's opponents for this one, and with only two minutes on the clock with people still getting somewhat comfy in the stands, the striker silenced the Stadio Comunale. A cross was whipped in to the far post where the Italian was already lurking, leaping into the air as if he had springs in his boots to power a looping header back across goal. It may not seem as impressive now as it did over 40 years ago, but the ability to head the ball in the opposite direction when it's coming at you like a speeding bullet in the 1970s is no easy feat.

Alas, scoring stunning goals or seeing one go in off your backside for it to nestle neatly in the corner would have made no difference to Heriberto Herrera's side's final league position. It was to be Cagliari who made history, pipping the Nerazzurri to the Scudetto by four points, detailed more in Gigi Riva's section of *Calcio's Greatest Forwards*.

Boninsegna wouldn't be too disheartened – his move had paved the way to Cagliari's instant success and he did score 13 times – his best in the top flight thus far. He wouldn't have to wait long for his own taste of glory as it really was third time lucky for Roberto, when 1970/71 would be his first success following two runners-up finishes.

Inter's Scudetto-winning season started with a bang, winning 2-1 away to Verona – the striker scoring a brace in the second half. Both goals detailed a mixture of Roberto's talent, first firing home a thunderbolt of a free kick before tapping home the winner at the far post due to goalkeeper Pierluigi Pizzaballa – yes that is really his name – spilling the ball. *Bonimba* meant business, scoring twice when playing host to Torino before another couple of goals were registered for him versus Catania.

His first against the Rossazzurri wasn't all that stunning, but he did nearly take the net off. His free-kick-taking was quite something this campaign too, smashing one right into the top corner on a snowy matchday 11 to hand the Nerazzurri a 2-0 success over Juventus.

His goalscoring exploits reached new heights in the title triumph – the Italian had overtaken his previous best of 13 when nutmegging a helpless defender before slotting home past Lazio on 24 January 1971. Goalkeeper Rosario Di Vincenzo immediately got to his feet after the ball passed him into the goal, looking as though he was about to hurl a mass of criticism toward his humiliated team-mate, but even he couldn't comprehend the skill that had just transpired, resulting in Rosario just putting his hands on his head. At the end of proceedings he had 24 Serie A goals, completely eclipsing his previous best total. The superb tally meant he finally became Capocannoniere, a personal accolade to go alongside his Scudetto achievement.

Arguably Boninsegna's greatest goal, not only in this season but in his career, came in the match that had secured the title – a 5-0 home victory over Foggia. Just seven minutes in, a whipped-in ball from the left floated perfectly in the air for Roberto to scissor-kick the ball into the top corner from all of 15 yards. Whether it was a finish that was more suited to a gymnastics event, or one that you only see once in a blue moon, it was a goal worthy of a title-clinching game and definitely worth searching for to revel in the quality strike.

Boninsegna had not only handed his former club Cagliari their historic Scudetto the previous year but had now got his hands on the trophy as well. It was a shame for both Inter and their star man up front that they would fail to retain their title the next year, finishing fifth. Roberto kept scoring however, 22 this time, and it meant he would win back-to-back Capocannonieri, something only achieved by five other players before him.

He also featured in the European Cup Final against Ajax, in which they lost 2-0 to two Johan Cruyff strikes. The competition is best remembered for an odd occurrence in a second-round match, now coined '*Partita della lattina*'

– Match of the Can – featuring Borussia Mönchengladbach and Inter. At 2-1 to the German side, in the 29th minute Boninsegna was struck with a Coca-Cola can. It was a somewhat peculiar incident and it looked as if nothing would come of it as the match continued and Mönchengladbach went on to win 7-1. Regardless of the fact the Germans won fair and square, both sides would have to play the fixture again due to the incensed Italian fans berating UEFA, engaging in a long legal case to work out that a replay would be the best alternative.

It meant that arguably one of the greatest victories for a German club was deemed irrelevant. The legs were reversed so Inter instead hosted the first game, winning 4-2 before returning to Germany at the Olympiastadion to draw 0-0 and progress. No one really knows what occurred in the infamous match unfortunately, due to no television evidence of the incident. Broadcasters in Germany were unable to reach an agreement with the club to give live coverage of what was being touted as the 'biggest match in Mönchengladbach's history' according to *Westdeutsche Zeitung,* which featured in an article recently written by Niklas Wildhagen for the Bundesliga Fanatic website in 2013.

People on the side of Mönchengladbach believe the whole debacle was created by the Italians taking advantage of the situation. Ludwig Müller, a defender on the night for the German side, stated in an interview back in 2011 with *The Rheinische Post* – a regional daily newspaper – how Boninsegna 'looked around, saw his team-mate [Sandro Mazzola] tell him to go down, so collapsed'. This was followed by the Italian going off on a stretcher from where he 'winked to one of his compatriots'. Even the referee, Jef Dorpmans, backs up this notion that it was blown out of proportion and was stunned by UEFA's choice to replay the game as the event had no effect on the final result. Roberto stayed quiet on the situation, rather unsurprisingly, and elected to concentrate on his goalscoring.

A slightly low-key 12 goals was his next Nerazzurri total before securing 23 in 1973/74. That was one short of Lazio's Giorgio Chinaglia, but in Roberto's eyes, regardless of finishing as Capocannoniere twice prior, he was unfairly denied his third:

> 'It should have been three! In that season they removed one on the final day against Cesena, the game's opening goal. They [the Italian football authorities] stated to me that it was an own goal but I know for sure it wasn't.'
>
> – Tuttojuve.com

Two more seasons were left for Roberto at Inter, helping them to finish ninth then fourth. The Italian scored a total of 19 goals across those two campaigns, taking his Inter total to 113 in 197 league appearances. At this stage Boninsegna was 33 years old and ageing but the new Juventus coach Giovanni Trapattoni took a gamble on him, and it would be three years of silverware to follow for *Bonimba*.

The Bianconeri faced a tough battle with rivals Torino, who had previously won the league, but it would be Roberto's new side that came out on top by a solitary point. He was of vital importance to his team during the final game, scoring the second goal to secure a 2-0 victory over Sampdoria, nullifying Torino's crushing 5-1 win against Genoa. Ten goals would be his seasonal total, a stat not to be chuckled at, considering his age.

A UEFA Cup triumph had also fallen into the hands of Roberto, defeating Athletic Bilbao on the away goals rule, with the striker picking up five tournament goals along the way. The silverware was stacking up as Roberto gained another Scudetto a year later and this was followed in his final season with a 2-1 victory over Palermo in the Coppa Italia – not bad for a man who only previously had one Scudetto to call his own.

So that brought to a close his third season with the Old Lady. He would drop down to Verona in Serie B, at the age of 37, to see out the remainder of his fantastic career, but he was quick to praise Juve for what they helped him achieve, even at his 'old' age:

> 'When I arrived in Turin, I never thought of winning two league titles, a UEFA Cup and the Coppa Italia. I had been conscious of my physical condition at the start and also having to replace Anastasi [Pietro], a star of Juventus. I had a duty to give it my best and the seasons went well. So much so I was offered a fourth year, but at the ripe old age of 37, it was right to move on to Verona.'
>
> – Storie di Calcio

He was Inter's child, but a hero at Juventus and even technically at Cagliari due to his exit that won the Rossoblu the Scudetto. An astounding 163 league goals in the top flight secured the Italian's name in the history books, just a glimpse of what *Bonimba* had brought to Serie A – just don't throw any cans at him.

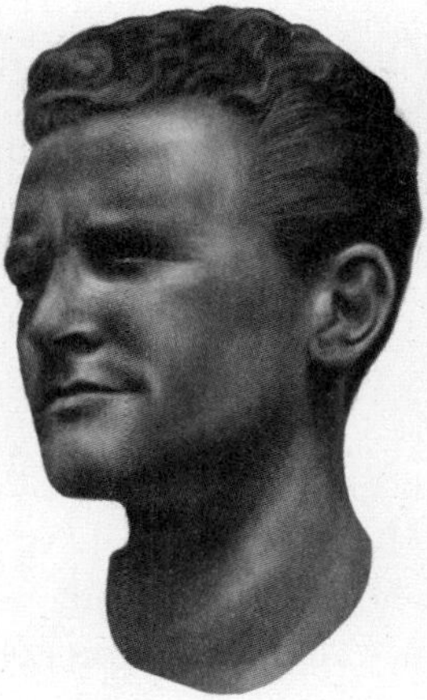

GIAMPIERO BONIPERTI

INTRODUCED BY ADAM DIGBY

'Vincere non è importante è l'unica cosa che conta.' – Winning is not important. It is the only thing that counts.

– Giampiero Boniperti

A SIMPLE phrase that has come to represent the entire outlook of one of European football's most successful clubs, and the motto of the Italian peninsula's pre-eminent team. Throughout this book you'll find storied tales of incredible goalscoring feats, of strikers who overcame adversity to break records, and even legendary tales of them wearing wrong-sized boots in order to enhance their feel for the ball.

Giampiero Boniperti – the man who uttered that now-famous phrase – did nothing like that. He was born in Turin and became a member of the local club's youth system. His ability saw him graduate to the first team where he scored goals with incredible regularity, notching 112 in his first 184 games for the club.

As a young man he was the embodiment of the future of the Bianconeri, helping Gianni Agnelli establish the famous *Stilo Juve* as he maintained a dignified, professional air at all times. His is a legacy as the golden boy of calcio, a role he picked up from Giuseppe Meazza and Valentino Mazzola before passing it on to the likes of Gianni Rivera and Roberto Baggio. That position as the game's favourite son runs intrinsically throughout its history, continuing into the modern era with Roma captain Francesco Totti.

But if those first six seasons gave birth to his legend, what followed created a legacy for Boniperti that lives on even today, the club captain and home-town hero sacrificing personal glory because to him, winning truly was the only thing that mattered. It is repeated by Juventini to this very day and is found stitched inside the latest version of those famous black and white striped shirts.

He learnt to play an entirely different role in midfield, allowing Juventus to bring in two more iconic strikers – John Charles and Omar Sívori – as they became known as *La Trio Magica*. He still scored of course, retiring as the club's all-time leader in both goals and assists, but he would eventually become club president too.

Boniperti oversaw yet more Bianconeri glory – including nine Scudetti – endearing him to a generation of fans too young to have watched him on the field. One of his last acts as president was to sign a young striker named Alessandro Del Piero, who would eventually go on to break those aforementioned records, which had stood for over 40 years.

As his goal tally was surpassed in 2006, the elder statesman spoke with typical class when *La Stampa* spoke to him about the publicity generated by the head-to-head.

'To find myself famous once more, at the age of 77, is incredible,' Boniperti told them, but very few men have had the deep, wide-ranging and lengthy impact on Italian football that he can proudly boast. He remains a loyal and humble servant of Juventus even today, long after his incredible playing career ended and as he rapidly approaches his 90th birthday.

'Juve aren't just the team I love,' he once remarked, 'they are my love.' Thanks to what Giampiero Boniperti did for La Madama, millions of others feel exactly the same way.

Adam Digby

Giampiero Boniperti *is* Juventus. A bold statement to make at first, but the Italian dedicated his life to the Bianconeri and he never regretted it for one moment. Born in Barengo in 1928, the young Italian fell in love with the beautiful game when he played for amateur side Momo. It was here that the major teams in Italy began to sit up and take notice of Giampiero.

One of those was Juventus and after some swift negotiations between the two clubs, Boniperti was soon to be in black and white. Just under 18 years on from his birth on 22 May 1946, the Juventus faithful caught a glimpse of their new hero for the first time as Boniperti scored all seven goals in a 7-0 victory over Fossano.

Some praise must fall to then club doctor – Dr Egidio Perone – who saw potential in the young player after it seemed he wasn't up to the standard expected to represent them. If it had not have been for Perone, Juventus and Boniperti could, and possibly would have missed out on some of the greatest and most successful years the club has ever seen. Giampiero opened up about his love for Juventus, and how he had always wanted to represent the Bianconeri:

> 'Juve was the dream of my life. I had only one desire – to play a game in Serie A with Juventus. My destiny was in the hands of Dr Egidio Perone, friend of Felice Borel, who was player-coach at the time. Perone telephoned him – here is a guy who would be good for Juve. Answer – bring him Thursday.'
>
> – *Corriere della Sera*

From that moment on Giampiero never looked back. He was placed in the starting XI at 19 years old against AC Milan, a 2-1 defeat, and he showed brief glimpses of his ability. It wouldn't faze him as he kept working hard, scoring a brace in a 3-0 success over Sampdoria at the Stadio Luigi Ferraris. Coach Renato Cesarini elected to keep the striker in at the deep end and it paid off – grabbing his first with a simple yet composed finish after being set up by Vittorio Sentimenti III – the third of five footballing brothers.

The young man's confidence was set at boiling point, adding another later in the game to wrap up the successful match. Moments like the above truly make a player what they become. Had Cesarini decided instead to keep Boniperti on the bench after his mediocre first performance who knows what that would have done to the morale of the soon-to-be 20-year-old. Some might argue that with the talent he held it wouldn't matter how long he remained out of the first team, while others will point out this was the defining moment in his career.

It's a great thing to deliberate and only Giampiero, alongside the brilliance of hindsight, can attempt to answer such a question. All of a sudden the young man had found his scoring boots, adding another three, which came once in a 2-0 victory over Venezia and twice in a 3-3 draw with Lazio, to take his total to five, bringing to a close a satisfying end to the season where Juventus would finish in second. The official Juventus website sums up his quick run of goalscoring by simply saying, 'He would not stop for a long, long time.' They weren't wrong.

It was also during his early years Boniperti would find his nickname – *Marisa* – thanks to his opponents mocking his blonde curls and also Benito Lorenzi, his Azzurri team-mate, who insisted on referring to him via his new name due to looking 'pretty, blond and almost adolescent' as reported by *Corriere della Sera*.

Compared to other strikers, the next season was quite astounding for Boniperti and to all calcio fans. At the age of 20, the Italian scored 27 times to become Capocannoniere, finishing above the much publicised Valentino Mazzola by two goals. His first, coincidentally, came against Sampdoria, the side he scored his first league goal against, and he then proceeded to bag two away at Genoa and the solitary winning goal against Atalanta. Boniperti secured his first hat-trick on matchday ten thanks to a thumping 6-1 triumph over lowly Livorno, completing his best achievement at the time while also finishing with an appearance in all 40 league matches.

The Italian's tally would drop considerably the next campaign, 15 would be his total, but for the young talent it was merely just a warm-up for the next and most important stage in his career. Before reliving the moment Giampiero had arguably dreamt of as a child, let's take a moment to quickly look back on the Superga tragedy.

The deeply saddening incident occurred due to a plane crash involving *il Grande Torino* – the unstoppable Turin side of the 1940s – when the aircraft carrying the side from Lisbon following a friendly with Benfica hit the back of the Basilica of Superga. Those who lost their lives included the truly astounding Valentino Mazzola, who'd have been an absolute certainty to feature in *Calcio's Greatest Forwards*, but the words that would have been written wouldn't do justice

BONIPERTI
1946
1961
JUVENTUS
la Vecchia Signora
PAINE

to his brilliance or his team-mates during their unstoppable spell in Serie A. This brief remembrance should hopefully send all readers out there to read more on *il Grande Torino* and on Mazzola – they were everything that is beautiful about Italian football in the 1940s, and may they forever be remembered.

The 1949/50 Serie A season would be the start of the silverware won by Giampiero, with his goals alongside the Dane John Hansen, seeing the Bianconeri lift their eighth Scudetto. The Italian got the ball rolling with the first in a 5-2 opening win against Fiorentina. Don't be fooled by the amount conceded at home – new in the first team, Giovanni Viola was just getting to grips with playing in goal for one of the greatest teams in the world and would go on to play for the club until 1958. His shot-stopping ability, matched with the combined 49 goals of Hansen and Boniperti, the latter gaining 21 of those, saw many goals scored for Juventus and few conceded. They registered more than four goals at home a total of six times across the season – the only blip being a 7-1 mauling handed to them by Gunnar Nordahl's Milan.

Losses such as that mentioned didn't faze them, going the opening 17 games unbeaten and experiencing defeat on only three other occasions, 2-1 to Lucchese and Lazio and 1-0 to Roma. The 22-year-old was on fire, completing three hat-tricks over the campaign versus Novara, Como and the ever-present Sampdoria, who at this point were probably already adding his name to the scoresheet prior to kick-off on the final day as the title-winning marathon came to a close.

Milan would be the top side for the following season however, Juventus and Boniperti having to make do with finishing third. Goals never seemed to be the problem as previous times had showed and during 1950/51 the Old Lady scored 103 times, only four less than both the Rossoneri and Nerazzurri above them. Boniperti got 22 of those including a hat-trick away at Atalanta and a brace over deadly rivals Torino.

The Scudetto would be back with the Bianconeri thanks to new coach György Sárosi, a former Hungarian footballer. The new man didn't need to tinker with the free-scoring strikers but aimed to strengthen a defence that had let in over 80 goals across the past two seasons – Viola being key in stopping that total from increasing. Sárosi did just that in improving the backline as they would only let in 34 goals while cruising across the finish line for the club's ninth league title.

Giampiero of course played his part, amassing a 19-goal haul, while John Hansen managed an impressive 30. At this stage, Juventus were seen to not be as strong in depth as Milan and Inter, yet Sárosi's men were more consistent and deserving of their title.

Boniperti was key in the season's most important match when Juventus hosted Milan in early May. Juventus were already five points clear but the Rossoneri had won their last four including a 2-1 derby victory over Inter. The match would end 3-1 to Juventus, Boniperti managing to get the second goal in the comfortable win that saw Nordahl silenced for a full 90 minutes. Even though they then went on to win twice in the final six games, the Old Lady would be champions again. What the Juventus faithful weren't aware of was the growing tension in the boardroom and the club would soon enter a transitional period resulting in a dry spell from any silverware.

As such, the next Serie A season was one of pure disappointment for all associated with the Turin side as rivals Inter regained a stronghold on the league, holding out to topple Juventus by two points. Giampiero managed a measly seven league goals, not for his lack of talent, but he had yet to perfect playing on the right of the midfield. It showed how much the Italian was willing to sacrifice for his club, his team-mates and the fans. He would rather learn the ropes of his new position and supply assists, than take the central role and go for goal himself.

The trend continued the following campaign, again losing out to Inter, this time by a single point. Despite missing out on the title, the season showcased one of Giampiero's finest goals. On 16 May 1954 with Inter and Juventus both locked on 46 points, Atalanta hosted the Bianconeri at the Stadio Atleti Azzurri d'Italia and raced into a 3-0 lead. Boniperti and co. would go on to lose, but in the 78th minute with the score at 3-1, a hooked ball into the box saw the Italian hit a first-time bicycle shot from a tight angle into the bottom corner.

Many supporters never seem to revel in a goal such as this anymore, and maybe it's due to the massive difference in modern-day football compared to just over 60 years ago. For a player to hang themselves in the air and make such a brilliant connection with the ball to not only direct it toward goal, but to also place it so accurately, is art in itself. Come on now, how many of you could replicate that at the first time of asking in the park? Unless you're Trevor Sinclair, probably none. It was a goal which should have been worth levelling the game instead of the consolation that it ended up being.

Inter were held 2-2 away from home against Palermo yet the point proved vital in the final standings. Aside from the inadequate scoreline, it was a goal to savour and Boniperti himself once jokingly spoke about the beauty of such goals, as seen here:

> 'The most beautiful shots occur when you don't think about it. Or when you make a mistake but the ball still goes right into the top corner!'
>
> – *La Repubblica*

Aside from the jokes, things were still far from rosy at Juventus with Boniperti's right-hand man John Hansen leaving for Lazio and Helge Bronée arriving as his replacement from Roma. Giampiero managed nine goals with the team slumping to a seventh-place finish. The troubles occurring between the presidents were clearly affecting Boniperti, who was the captain, the rest of the team and the Juventini. The Old Lady flirted with the relegation zone for much of 1955/56 before ending up in ninth at the close, their worst finish. After another ninth-place season changes were afoot.

Umberto Agnelli entered the boardroom and was quick to open negotiations for new additions. Omar Sívori and John Charles were soon donning the black and white strip. Agnelli was all smiles and so was Boniperti, who had patiently played through the past few dismal seasons. The 1957/58 season was the one of the revived Bianconeri, with a shiny gold star heading to Turin. Boniperti, Sívori and Charles became known as *La Trio Magica* – the Magic Trio – and were one of the best striking trios in Italian football history.

At 30, Giampiero was still trying to get used to his new position on the right of midfield, designed to provide as well as score. It all seemed to click into place almost immediately – the opening game of the season seeing all three players get on the scoresheet in a 3-2 success over Verona. As clichéd as it may sound, it really was a sign of things to come as they went storming off with the Scudetto. The Italian got eight, and was significant in being the final part of many flowing moves of the Bianconeri – Charles ending the season with 28 goals, Sívori 22.

Boniperti opened up about the Magic Trio and just what difference the Welshman and Argentinian had brought to Juve:

> 'With these two ahead of me, and after eight years as a striker, I was finally comfortable with the move I had made. I am now happy as a midfielder. The midfield director is a role I invented myself to

> dictate the play in an attacking sense. Sívori was the leading attacking midfielder/inside-forward [*mezzala di punta*] and Charles was a magnificent central striker. He fought the battles that I had previously.'
>
> – Juveternamore.blogspot.co.uk

There was a halt on the title success the following campaign, finishing fourth, but a Coppa Italia would prove sufficient. The Old Lady knocked out Alessandria, albeit after extra time, before easing past Fiorentina and Genoa to set up a final with Inter. It was quite the final, especially since it was to be played at the San Siro. Nothing would faze Boniperti and co. as they ran riot over the Nerazzurri in a 4-1 win. Inter coach Aldo Campatelli opted to substitute his starting goalkeeper, Enzo Matteucci. Both keepers still conceded two and a 17-year drought had come to an impressive end.

The blond hair of Giampiero flowed in the wind as he made many a darting run on the wing during the game, tormenting the defence. He seemed to move so gracefully, with such elegance, and he was doing all this at the tender age of 31. That's just the type of player the Italian was. Age was simply a number, and although he wasn't as quick as he used to be, Giampiero gave his all for the club. His passion was something no one could knock – a player who wore his heart on his sleeve and spoke wonderfully about everyone and everything surrounding him. Everything that is right about football, about Juventus, and about the sport as a whole was because of Boniperti. Deservedly, more title triumph was on the horizon.

The 11th Scudetto was soon Boniperti's as they romped to victory in the 1959/60 Serie A season, as well as gaining their fourth Coppa Italia, again at the San Siro. This time it was Fiorentina who had to succumb to the deadly trio in a 3-2 win for the Bianconeri. He also scored another beauty of a goal against Genoa on 10 April 1960 – finishing off a brilliant passing move before drilling the ball back across with a first-time left-footed volley in a 6-2 triumph.

The Italian's career was about to come to an end and it finished on a high in the 1960/61 season as they once again conquered the league. The highlight was a truly phenomenal 9-1 demolition of Inter. Such a scoreline had occurred due to protesting from the Nerazzurri, who had seen the previous game, which they were leading 2-0, abandoned, and were asked for it to be replayed due to a pitch invasion. They opted to stand up to the Federazione Italiana Giuoco Calcio (FIGC) – whose president at the time was Juventus's Umberto Agnelli – by fielding their youth team, resulting in the complete annihilation with Omar Sívori scoring six times. It was also Boniperti's last game for Juventus as well, reiterating that this game would be his final flourish by stating how he wished his boots to be put away for good.

So that would be that; after 444 appearances and 178 goals, Giampiero closed out his Juventus adventure. He would go on to become president, cementing his legacy at the club. Mr Juve will never be forgotten, and to conclude, in the words of the great Boniperti as we began his segment:

'Vincere non è importante è l'unica cosa che conta.'

HERNAN CRESPO

'Once upon a time all the best players wanted to come here [Serie A]. Now Ronaldo and Messi don't dream of putting a foot in Italy. We have to change that mentality.'

– *La Gazzetta dello Sport*

THE number 15 is placed alongside the shirt number of a certain Argentinian's 11 on the sidelines, signifying the change is to be made. The 29-year-old begrudgingly exits the pitch to make way for Jon Dahl Tomasson with just five minutes of time remaining.

Hernán Crespo's UEFA Champions League Final had come to a disappointing end. It began so positively, grabbing Milan's second and third goals of a lethal first-half display, yet ended on possibly the worst and most unexpected note. It would be his best and only chance of lifting the trophy but it is not something that will stop Hernán being remembered by both sets of Milan supporters, Lazio, and of course Parma for his time in Italy. *Valdanito*, a nickname gained due to his resemblance to Jorge Valdano, managed 153 Serie A goals in his professional career. You do not score that many times without being held in the highest regard by those around you.

River Plate would be his first port of call – the first step into becoming a professional footballer. His debut was made when he was 18 years old, like many first-timers, but his breakthrough season was something special. The Argentinian announced himself on the scene of professional football with 11 league goals to propel Los Millonarios to the 1993 title. He would win the league again the following year and soon Hernán Crespo was the name on everybody's lips in Argentina. A few seasons prior, a certain Gabriel Batistuta had come through to go on to greater things, and people were beginning to question where they thought Crespo's future lay. After a scintillating performance in the 1996 Copa Libertadores, in which Crespo scored twice to turn around a 1-0 deficit to beat América 2-1, it seemed his time in Argentina was up.

Serie A side Parma came calling following this incredible display and with new coach Carlo Ancelotti at the helm, the Crespo that calcio fans all love to this day was ready to bloom. However, it seemed this flower wasn't ready to emerge into the massive world of European football just yet. It took Hernán six months to score his first home goal for the Gialloblu, and he had netted just once prior to that in a 3-1 defeat at Inter in October. It wasn't a bad first goal though, sweeping home a cross into the bottom corner just two minutes into the game.

He wouldn't score again until March and finally broke his duck at the Stadio Ennio Tardini in a 3-2 home victory against Cagliari. After Lilian Thuram's flicked header opened the scoring, the home crowd finally got to see a glimpse of what was to come from their Argentinian wizard. His first occurred when he dispatched a rebounded effort into the roof of the net from all of three yards just before half-time. The relief can be seen when watching the celebration – jumping up and down, pumping his fists and pulling on his shirt. He'd finally netted in front of his supporters.

The second half soon swung around and Hernán was at it again, but this time it was more than just a tap-in. A corner had been headed down, bounced up and there was Crespo to scoop an acrobatic half-volley into the top corner. Cagliari goalkeeper Marco Pascolo was completely unmoved as the ball shot into the net with Crespo already wheeling away in delight. All of a sudden the striker had found his feet in Serie A, and at the right time too, with Parma hot on the tail of Juventus in the race for the Scudetto.

He scored the following week away at Perugia to narrow the gap at the top to five points. Crespo netted twice against Sampdoria a few rounds later before grabbing the only goal in a vital victory at the Stadio Olimpico versus Roma. After a 2-1 success over Atalanta in which Hernán also scored, the next game would prove to be the Argentinian's finest in his debut Serie A season.

Parma welcomed mid-table Vicenza to Emilia-Romagna as they looked to close up a four-point difference on Juventus. Crespo took it upon himself to make sure they'd be taking all three points from this affair and after 13 minutes he had already found the scoresheet. A low, driven ball was swept home at a striking pace from inside the 18-yard box. Hernán wanted more and this time attempted to turn provider just moments later, lifting an exquisite chip over the entire defence only for Enrico Chiesa to mis-hit his shot. The striker would decide to do it himself, and got the second in the 50th minute. A long ball from Fabio Cannavaro found an unmarked Gianfranco Zola to volley a perfect cross into the box for *Valdanito* to come flying in with a diving header that, unsurprisingly, flew into the roof of the net.

The hat-trick goal was everything that is memorable about Hernán. The forward dribbled past two players with power and determination, side-stepping the final defender with a quick burst of pace before chipping the ball over Luca Mondini and into the goal. That was the Crespo fans remember. The turn of pace he held was one of sheer brilliance and this, coupled alongside his clinical nature, was what made Hernán one of the world's best.

From six months without a goal at home to netting every other week was a miraculous transformation. It begs the question of what could have been for Parma that season had Crespo begun his scoring from the start, as they then went on to miss out on the Scudetto by just two points. His final goal of the season came in the last match, a 2-1 win over Verona, but the title challenge was already finished. Crespo ended his first Serie A campaign with 12 goals from 27 appearances – 11 of those strikes coming after March, the final two months of the season.

Despite the disappointment, it had meant Hernán was ready to get scoring right from the start of the 1997/98 season. It was an odd campaign however, with Ancelotti's side failing to build on the previous season's impressive second-place finish, and ended up coming sixth.

The UEFA Champions League saw no difference in fortunes for Crespo's team as they were knocked out in the group stages. Their luck in the Coppa Italia also ran out in the semi-finals after losing on away goals to AC Milan. Even though the 1997/98 campaign is one to mull over on a regular basis by fans, Hernán still went about his business in front of goal and scored 12 times again. He netted a brace in the third game of the season, at Piacenza, as well as against Udinese, Juventus and Napoli. He completed home and away goals against all of the above except Juventus and finished 15 goals off of Capocannoniere winner Oliver Bierhoff.

A rather subdued season you could say, with nothing major really coming to the forefront for Crespo. He'd already had his debut season, scored a few great goals and got a glimpse at what it could be like to lift the Scudetto. Crespo didn't see it like this. Every match, every minute and every second was a learning curve for the 23-year-old. Ancelotti was relieved of his managerial duties when the season closed out but the Italian brought a lot to Hernán. He gained tranquillity, humility and a capacity to always be harmonious with his team-mates. Heaps of goals and trophies wasn't what the striker needed at this stage. *Valdanito* was like a schoolboy, learning the ropes and understanding the game in Italy without being incapacitated by the surroundings. With Alberto Malesani in place to lead the striker and his compatriots into the 1998/99 Serie A season, little did they know it would be one of the most successful in the club's entire history.

The team had not undergone any major change and the competent squad that featured such names as Gianluigi Buffon, Fabio Cannavaro, Dino Baggio and Juan Sebastián Verón was ready to hit the ground running right from the off. It wasn't the thrilling start a supporter of the beautiful game would expect for what was to come, with the Gialloblu drawing their opening two matches 0-0 to Vicenza and Venezia. As results started to pick up all eyes were back on Hernán, who hadn't managed a goal in the opening six games in the league. Along came Fiorentina to the city of prosciutto and cheese and Crespo must have snuck in a few slices prior to kick-off as he was rampant against la Viola. A diving header, that was becoming quite the forte of Crespo's, gave the game its first goal ten minutes ahead of the break before he released a sumptuous effort at the near post to put the game beyond a side that featured international counterpart Gabriel Batistuta. Hernán was off the mark.

The goals began to flow again and Udinese felt the full force of an in-form Crespo two weeks later with a hat-trick.

Funnily enough, one of those goals was indeed, a diving header. A lost art it seems in the current day and age of football, but Crespo knew how to connect his head with the ball. A technique so enjoyable to see pulled off and there was a 23-year-old doing it week in week out.

It is worth mentioning that during this time Malesani's men were progressing in the Coppa Italia and UEFA Cup. The former saw comfortable wins over Genoa and Bari with the latter being a bit more of a task, coming from behind to knock out Fenerbahçe 3-2 on aggregate before dispatching Wisla Kraków in the second round. Crespo did his duties, scoring across both competitions as Parma continued to make a steady advancement. Unfortunately for Udinese they would have to face up to Crespo again, this time in the Coppa Italia quarter-finals. It was an enthralling first leg with Hernán scoring but Parma fell to a 3-2 deficit. The return fixture was much different and the Gialloblu hit four past the dejected Zebrette – Crespo scoring two.

A successful aggregate win over Inter going into March saw Parma book their place in the Coppa Italia Final and they were gearing up for their UEFA Cup quarter-final with Bordeaux, having defeated Rangers in the previous round. At 2-0 down in the first leg with the tie seemingly coming to a disappointing end in France, a low ball was driven into the box for Crespo to score. Of course, this wasn't just a simple tap-in. Crespo took it upon himself to guide a delicately flicked effort with his heel into the far corner. It was a finish executed with such grace from a man who had by then the look of someone made of pure strength. He was much more than just a machine.

In mid-March the second leg was to be played and Parma needed a win. The fans began to become restless. Cue the Argentinian to work his magic. Shortly before half-time Paolo Vanoli was played through behind the French side's defence before squaring the ball to Crespo to do the damage. He ran to celebrate with Vanoli, pumping his fists in gratitude before passionately embracing one another. Chiesa added a second before the whistle went and the Gialloblu were in the driving seat for the first time in the quarter-final. The first period had pretty much destroyed Bordeaux's confidence and Parma were free to add more goals to their tally. *Valdanito* got his second and his side's fifth midway through the half. A knocked-down ball sent Crespo into the area, taking one touch to control before finishing calmly with his second. The game ended 6-0 in the Italians' favour, gaining them a place in the semi-finals with Atlético Madrid.

Following a 3-1 away win against Atlético in early April, just two weeks later would be the first leg of the Coppa Italia Final. Their Serie A season had still been going at a good pace, with Crespo on 16 league goals – the tally he would complete the campaign with. The first leg took place on 14 April 1999 with Crespo's opener cancelled out by his Argentinian colleague Batistuta. Hernán was juggling the two competitions at once – scoring in the first leg of both matches. He failed to net in the second leg against Atlético but his side still managed to pull through and book a place in the final against Marseille on 12 May.

The Serie A season was three weeks away from finishing and it was now time for the Coppa Italia Final second leg. It was Crespo's first piece of major silverware as he scored with an exact replica of his goal against Bordeaux, guiding the ball with his heel into the far corner. The match itself would end 2-2, giving Parma the trophy on away goals, with Crespo gaining the golden boot with four strikes in total. But there was no time to celebrate just yet with the UEFA Cup Final looming large.

Crespo's seasons of being coached by Ancelotti had paid dividends. He was more aware of his surroundings as a player, stayed calm on the pitch and was passionate when the time was right. A few of his team-mates knew what the final was like, having beaten Juventus in the same competition back in 1995. On 12 May 1999 Hernán Crespo exited the tunnel on to the pitch at the Luzhniki Stadium in Moscow ready for his moment.

Marseille made a quite reluctant start to the game, sitting deep in their own half, and they paid the price 26 minutes into the game. A poor headed back-pass from Laurent Blanc was gobbled up by, you guessed it, Crespo. He closed down the defender, anticipating the mistake, then seized his chance by guiding a first-time lob over the head of Stéphane Porato. Vanoli added the second before Chiesa completed the emphatic victory. Crespo played his part in the final goal too, producing a clever dummy to deceive the Marseille defence before Chiesa unleashed an unstoppable strike into the goal. Game over.

You can see the absolute delight on Hernán's face when he collects his medal. It is one full of complete and utter joy as he proceeds with a fist pump as all calcio fans had become accustomed to. A quick embrace with Vanoli followed before Crespo looked back down at his medal then let out a roar of approval. He claimed the man of the match award for the final as well, completing a marvellous season for himself.

It was the high point of Crespo's Parma career and he spent just one more season at the Gialloblu. Following the 1999/2000 Serie A season where his goalscoring tally hit 22, making him the all-time Parma top scorer in the process, he was also a winner in the Supercoppa Italiana against Milan. However, the time was up for Crespo and Lazio came calling with a world record fee – £35m. The new chapter had opened for the striker and Parma was to become a memory. Crespo said the following about the club that had welcomed him to Italy:

> 'It's my second home. The city embraced me at the age of 21 and made me grow up. I decided to live here. The fans elected me the player of the century for Parma. I couldn't be in a better place.'
>
> – *La Gazzetta dello Sport*

Crespo was ready to launch his new adventure and it started brightly, scoring the opener in his second game for the club when Perugia came to the Stadio Olimpico. A glancing header from a corner just before half-time was the goal in question. Typical of Crespo, and the celebration was just as expected – a pull of the shirt and a massive fist pump ensued – kissing the ball as the pandemonium finally came to an end. The kiss sparked a beautiful relationship between player and ball for the Serie A season as he became Capocannoniere for the first time with 26 goals, two better than the previous year's winner Andriy Shevchenko. It was predominantly down to his antics in front of goal during the later stages of the campaign, scoring in each of their last six games against Bari, Napoli, Udinese, Inter, Fiorentina and Lecce.

After Lazio completed the season by finishing in third place, *Valdanito* began to feel troubled. He had never been properly injured in his professional career thus far and started to endure a niggling muscle problem in his right leg. Lazio were in no better a position and were suffering heavily with financial difficulties. Even though Hernán made a somewhat speedy recovery against Milan in September, spectators could see that the Argentinian was being overused by new coach Alberto Zaccheroni. Crespo made it through to the end of the season intact with 13 goals and was ready to be on the move again. He closed out his time with Lazio with one success, the 2000 Supercoppa Italiana. For now, he was to join another Italian side – Inter – for a fee of around £14.5m.

It was an average opening season for Inter, scoring seven times before again having to deal with a thigh problem picked up in early 2003 against Modena that saw him out of action for the next four months. He switched clubs again, leaving Italy for England to join Claudio Ranieri's Chelsea for £16.8m. Hernán was starting to bounce around teams and in 2004 joined AC Milan on loan. He grabbed ten league goals and a Supercoppa Italiana triumph during that solitary season for the Rossoneri, but is remembered for the two goals he scored in the 2005 UEFA Champions League Final.

Hernán put the ball past Jerzy Dudek twice in quick succession before the interval to put Milan 3-0 up. His first was a tap-in at the far post before a brilliant pass saw the striker in on goal again and he wonderfully lifted the ball over the helpless Polish goalkeeper. Of course, as all football fans know, there was to be a miraculous twist that saw Liverpool return from 3-0 down to level the game before winning on penalties. Crespo was heartbroken – he'll never forget how much pain that game brought to him:

> 'I watched my two Champions League Final goals a couple of months ago for the first time [nine years later]. I simply didn't have the strength before. It still hurts me.'
>
> – *La Gazzetta dello Sport*

After another season in England, the striker was loaned back out to Italy to rejoin his former club Inter for two years. He was 31 years old at the time and was beginning to feel the strain his muscle problems gave him throughout his career.

Aside from his injuries, Crespo actually enjoyed a successful spell at the Nerazzurri. He won his first Scudetto in the 2006/07 season, netting 14 times on the way to the title. A Supercoppa Italiana was also brought home, beating Roma 4-3 at the San Siro. Hernán scored the second as Inter fought back from a three-goal deficit at the interval. *Valdanito* stooped to meet a whipped-in ball to get his team back on track for the cup.

The 2007/08 Serie A season saw his second Scudetto success, ousting Roma by just three points. He did only gain four goals that season and his first team action continued to dwindle going into 2008/09. He signed a one-year deal to stay at Inter and work with the newly appointed José Mourinho. His fifth Supercoppa Italiana win followed as well as a third Scudetto, but Hernán played a very small part in these successes.

When his contract ended in 2009, he moved on to Genoa and performed to an average degree, which wasn't unexpected. Five goals was his total come January before returning to his beloved Parma, full of emotion and gratitude towards his old club. A single goal against Livorno marked his entire scoring for 2009/10. After an improved 2010/11 season where he scored nine times, including five in three during the winter period, the Parma faithful were ready to hear the news that Crespo was retiring. It took an extra season, and it wasn't until a lack of first team opportunities arose that the forward wanted his contract terminated. The time was up for the brilliant Argentinian, ending his career where it began in Italy. The boots were hung up and he would go on to become coach at Serie B side Modena ahead of the 2015/16 season. Tears were shed during his final press conference prior to his retirement. Little did he know the perils Parma would soon face, but he concluded his career with this:

> 'I'm sad, I would have preferred not to do this but I had to for the Parma fans. It is not easy for me today to put a full stop at the end of my Parma adventure and 19 years of football at the top level. I wanted to return home. Today the side is in tranquil waters and they have shown that they can survive without me. I leave calmly and with the club in the right place. That is why I took this decision.'
>
> – Hernán Crespo, 2 February 2012

ALESSANDRO DEL PIERO

'I knew in primary school that I wanted to become a professional footballer. I had to write my future dream on paper but I couldn't write football player – that's not a job, is it?'

– *Football Italia*

ALE had it all. Serie A was won numerous times, the Coppa Italia secured as well as lifting the UEFA Champions League, but for some reason, becoming Capocannoniere was just kept out of the 5ft 7in man's reach. Fifteen years it took from his debut against Foggia in 1993 to win the individual award, gaining the prize he had craved for so long. It was a great battle with long-term team-mate David Trezeguet, one that wasn't sorted until the final game of the 2007/08 season against Sampdoria at the Stadio Luigi Ferraris.

The quick, dancing feet of Del Piero were on show, earning a penalty midway through the second half. Stepping up, he stutters, letting the goalkeeper do all the work as he then caresses the ball into the opposite corner. Ale sprints off, tongue out in jubilation. Goalscoring was the norm – another one to add to the list. This one was that little bit sweeter for Del Piero though, with the knowledge he was now finally Capocannoniere.

But let's rewind a bit, 41 years to be precise, to Conegliano, where the future Juventus legend Alessandro Del Piero was born.

Bruna Del Piero was the woman who brought Ale into the world, and also denied him the chance to join, of all teams, Torino's youth academy. According to her son, she didn't want him too far away from home. He enjoyed his childhood, living in San Vendemiano, and was proud of his father, an electrician. The constant thought was always in young Ale's head – football, football, football. He used to play with a tennis ball in the garage in the early hours of the morning and was only stopped, in his own words, by being 'dragged to bed'.

Bruna always kept a watchful eye on her youngest son and even made sure he would play in goal where he wouldn't have to run around a lot to avoid getting ill. Stefano, Ale's older brother and a former footballer himself, knew his sibling had the qualities to play up front, and convinced their mother to make the switch. On 10 November 1987 at 13 years old, the recently-turned forward was successfully scouted by Piero Aggradi. Then, on 18 August 1988, Padova coach Adriano Buffoni came calling to give the young man his first giant leap into professional football.

At Padova, he remained in the youth set-up with a number of other keen youngsters, sharing a flat during the days while venturing out to take to the field on matchday.

He liked a dance as well, and wasn't afraid to show off his moves at a later date with senior team-mate Angelo Di Livio after taking ballroom dancing classes. It was one of a variety of hobbies Ale had and looking back on his career now, the Italian probably added 'goalscoring' and 'winning Scudetti' to that list.

Although his life was leaving the terminal and speeding off into the distance, he was still a teenager who was separated from his family for the first time. Everyone has felt it: the initial excitement of being independent away from your roots for a while, followed by the sudden realisation you've left the one place you feel safe in. Panic ensues and you wonder just what is in store or around the corner. He recalls this moment of understanding and knowing that now, he was growing up:

> 'San Vendemiano is only 77km away from Padova, but for me it seemed to be a very long journey. Now when I think back, I realised that those 77km were the exact distance between the child I no longer was and the man I was becoming. For the first time in my life I was far from home, always following the ball, that has never ever left me alone.'
>
> – Alessandrodelpiero.com

It all culminates into a sea of emotion, something Ale most definitely felt, and it was that drive and determination from deep down inside that spurred him on to become the player and person he is. On 15 May 1992 Alessandro Del Piero entered the fray to make his first professional appearance for Padova against Messina in Serie B.

He got his one and only professional goal in Italy away from Juventus the following season in 1992/93, scoring with a low shot when trouncing Ternana 5-0. Serie B drew to a close on 13 June, Padova narrowly missing out on a play-off spot for a chance to get promoted to Serie A. It wouldn't matter for Ale though as he was about to get his own promotion to the promised land, with 22-time Scudetto winners Juventus.

It was Giampiero Boniperti, a president of Juventus, who sealed the deal pretty much as soon as Padova had played their final match. He took the 18-year-old around the trophy cabinet and stadium, making the young man consume all the brilliance the Bianconeri hold dear to them. It was then Ale fell in love with his new club – he was ready to add a Del Piero-shaped memoir into the history of the Old Lady.

He spent his first full season at Juve jumping between the Primavera, Serie A and the UEFA Cup, picking up goals and trophies along the way. As for his league contribution, Ale made his Serie A debut four games into the season against Foggia on 12 September 1993. He came on with 16 minutes remaining for goalscorer Fabrizio Ravanelli. What are the odds supporters at the Stadio Pino Zaccheria on that day thought, 'That Del Piero is going to become one of the finest strikers of the next 20 years.' But those who paid witness to such a momentous moment in Ale's career have a little piece of history to remember. That's exactly what Del Piero did, leaving a lasting memory on all those whose eyes fell upon him. Be it with one of his trademark slalom runs, a delicately placed free kick or celebrating his goal versus Bari after his father's death, Ale left a trail of wonderfully crafted moments for football fans to revel in.

The next week saw Juventus host Reggina, and with goals from Ravanelli, Roberto Baggio and Andreas Möller, Giovanni Trapattoni's side were cruising to their third win from five at the start of the campaign. With just ten minutes remaining, an exact replica substitution from the previous week was made with Ale entering the field for striker Ravanelli. It took just a minute of time – 60 seconds, just 60,000 milliseconds – for the world to see the 18-year-old score his first goal in black and white.

A lofted ball from the centre-circle found the on-rushing Del Piero who would let the ball fall over his shoulder before striking first time with his left foot. The connection was sweet, easily beating Andrea Sardini in the Reggina goal. The first of 188 top-flight strikes was on the board. The smile beamed across Ale's face as he was greeted by his team-mates with hugs and high fives galore. He was fitting in – becoming one of the family.

How many goose bumps do you get reading that, Juventini? The connection Del Piero has with the fans is quite incredible, sending them through every emotion possible during his 19-year stay at the club. He continued to impress for the youth team, helping them win the 1994 Torneo di Viareggio by netting the winning penalty in extra time against Fiorentina. He was only just getting started, and back in Serie A he managed another nine appearances and four more goals to his name. Those wouldn't arrive until mid-March as Genoa and Parma felt his force.

The game against the Gialloblu also is worth noting due to the fact a certain someone picked up a hat-trick. His first was simple, a rebound smashed home from a corner to put Juve up 1-0 going into the break. The second was a low shot in the corner, something Ale specialised in among 101 other qualities. It's worth noting his celebration as he leaps into the air in jubilation, gaining about another foot to his rather small exterior. Whether he had springs in his boots no one will know, but he was bouncing yet again when he got the fourth of the game and his third. Ale thumped the ball home before nonchalantly pointing to the man who provided him with the goal.

It almost seemed as if he knew this sort of thing would happen a lot in the future, and if so, he wasn't wrong. Aside from his growth as a player in his first year at the Bianconeri, the club themselves had a poor campaign, finishing second to AC Milan. Change was afoot: Marcello Lippi was hired as coach as well as the introduction of a new team of directors by the names of Roberto Bettega, Antonio Giraudo and Luciano Moggi. The fun was about to begin.

The 1994/95 Serie A season saw the Scudetto finally return to Turin with Ale playing a vital role in his team's success. He found himself in the starting XI on a regular basis due to an injury sustained by Baggio, and Del Piero scored one of the finest goals in his lifetime in December. It is hard sometimes to put into words the beauty of a goal, and to feel the sheer euphoria a Juventino might have felt when this one hit the back of the net, but words can lay out a story for everyone to immerse themselves in. The goal occurred on 4 December 1994 when hosting Fiorentina and was all the sweeter as it secured a 3-2 win with Juventus having trailed by two at the interval.

Three minutes remained before a long ball was played into la Viola's box. The ball dropped over the shoulder, reminiscent of his first in black and white a year before, but this time something truly superb happened. As the ball came down, Ale stuck out his right boot, connecting with it like a magnet, lofting his shot over the helpless Francesco Toldo. Baggio? Who's Baggio? The artist had been to work, finishing off his first masterpiece. A piece of brilliance from *Il Pinturicchio.*

This nickname was bestowed upon Del Piero later that season in 1995, by Gianni Agnelli of all people. Pinturicchio was a painter but a lesser-known artist compared to such greats as Raphael, whose name was given to Baggio by the club owner as well. It was to resemble the difference between the two – the master and the apprentice. Some could say it's a shame Ale got stuck with a nickname resembling a man who lived in the shadow of perceived better painters, but Del Piero did a bit of research on Pinturicchio, and he saw that he'd left his own mark on the history of art, something he wished to do at Juventus. Although it was the end of Baggio at Juve, Ale had some important words to say about the two of them:

> 'At the end of the season, Baggio left and Juventus was now meant to be mine. My only regret is that I couldn't have played with him a bit more, but I never agreed with those who said that he and I didn't get along. For me, Baggio had always been the example to follow: a great champion. That's why it was a real honour for me to take his place and his number for my shirt.'
>
> – Alessandro Del Piero's *Giochiamo Ancora*

Prior to the season's conclusion, Ale had been one of the stand-out performers as he aided the Bianconeri in their successful quest for the Scudetto. He concluded with eight goals altogether, and also won his one and only Coppa Italia with a 3-0 aggregate victory over Parma.

The 1995/96 season was solely dedicated to the UEFA Champions League success for Ale. Juventus lost in the previous year's UEFA Cup to Parma but were ready to tackle Europe's biggest club prize that had eluded them since 1985. The road to Rome was where *Pinturicchio* played his part, scoring six times in total as Juve made it all the way to the final. The 21-year-old found the back of the net in five of the six group matches, missing out during the final game away at Steaua București.

Ale also opened the scoring during the quarter-final second leg against Real Madrid, curling home what would soon be a trademark free kick in front of 63,000 fans. Although he wouldn't score in the semi-final victory over Nantes, Juventus progressed to the final at the Stadio Olimpico, ready to take on holders Ajax. The Bianconeri would win on penalties and even with Ale not contributing to the victory with a goal, his performances leading up to the final made him a hero in just his third year at the club.

The forward could not be stopped and superlatives were already running out for a man who still had a lengthy career ahead of him. In 1996/97 there was success in the

UEFA Super Cup, scoring three times and assisting in a 9-1 aggregate win over Paris Saint-Germain. The goals may not have been coming in bucketloads but Del Piero's contribution on the pitch was impeccable. Another Scudetto was secured having finished as runners-up the previous season – Ale gaining eight goals in the league despite the muscle injuries attempting to hold him back. Again they made the UEFA Champions League Final, this time taking on German side Borussia Dortmund. The forward missed out on a starting place due to an injury but a stupendously brilliant back-heel with his left foot after coming on as a substitute put Juve back in contention. Alas, they would go on to lose 3-1. Ale even said how such a beautiful goal, as well as winning the Scudetto, would not comfort him after the loss. It was their second of three consecutive finals in the competition.

Del Piero was still performing out of his skin across the 1996/97 and 1997/98 seasons, and even finished fourth in the running for the 1996 Ballon d'Or midway through the former. The latter was just as good for Ale, although the finale mirrored that of 1997, in that all Juventini wished to forget it.

Looking to the league first and the Italian's time on the field, it would be his most successful goalscoring season, scoring 21 in 32 appearances. Three of those came in a 5-2 home victory over Empoli in which the third exemplified everything that Ale was as a forward. A great first touch followed by the close control that saw him round the goalkeeper with ease, before slotting home calmly. Away from what would be his third Scudetto, Del Piero had been the key figure yet again in the UEFA Champions League. Five goals in six appearances across the group stage earned Juve a second-place finish behind Manchester United, and a quarter-final with Dynamo Kyiv. After dispatching the Ukrainians, Juventus were to host Monaco in Turin on 1 April 1998. Ale turned on the style to score a wonderful hat-trick. His first was the one to watch over and over, scoring arguably his best free kick in a Juventus shirt. From all of 25 yards out, *Pinturicchio* curled the ball over the wall with both power and accuracy, leaving Fabien Barthez stunned. It's surprising in itself that the French goalkeeper managed to even get his fingertips to the ball, as it flew into the top corner.

While we all go back and look up this goal to reminisce, there might be another video in the recommended section showcasing Ale's brilliance, this time in Monte Carlo for the return leg. A lofted ball to the back post was perfectly set up for Del Piero to score the sweetest first-time volley you're ever likely to see. But the performances against Monaco were sadly just a mere consolation for Ale as Juventus fell victim to another defeat at the final hurdle, this time to Real Madrid. The Italian ended his most successful individual club season with 32 goals across 47 games, and the top-scorer award in Europe.

The next campaign was also one to cast one's mind back to, but for all the wrong reasons. On 8 November 1998 Ale was in tears. He had never undergone a bad injury in his five years of success and contentment at the Old Lady, but in Udine it was time to suffer. A stretch too far meant a serious knee problem would occur and it kept the forward out for the remainder of the season while Juventus went on to finish a terribly disappointing seventh. Del Piero opened up about the injury, but believed it was fate, and as such made him a better player:

> 'Even today, I still ask myself, why did I have to run after the ball that was going off the pitch. I paid dearly for the useless effort. I call it "the injury", as if it's the only one. It was the watershed of my career. However, I came back stronger following the rehabilitation, physiotherapy and of course the hard work. After scoring my first goal back, I

> realised why I chased the ball. It helped me change, both as a man and a player.'
>
> – Alessandrodelpiero.com

Carlo Ancelotti had since taken over at Juve when Ale was back to full fitness, and the striker played in all 34 league games of the 1999/2000 Serie A season. He was finding it hard to score however, especially in open play, and by February he'd gone 70 weeks without a goal other than from the penalty spot. Team-mate Filippo Inzaghi wasn't making it easier for him by taking on harder chances in a game versus Venezia rather than putting it on a plate for Ale. This is looked at in more detail in Inzaghi's segment of *Calcio's Greatest Forwards*.

The 2000/01 season was mediocre at best for Juventus but it included a touching moment from our little attacking wizard. Ale's father Gino Del Piero had sadly passed away and just four days after the funeral Juventus would play Bari. Ale would come on from the bench with 25 minutes remaining and, as expected, he looked out of sorts. With the game seamlessly heading to a bore draw the striker found the net with a beautifully executed chip. He could hold it in no longer, letting out a scream full of pride but also one of utter desperation. He may have netted more valuable goals, both in terms of quality and importance in a competition, but that strike had meant the most to Ale. It is only at these moments you realise football is but a minor footnote in the grand scheme of things and how life affects us all. It was moving, beautiful and revealed that Ale is not just a player, but is a man.

The following season saw Del Piero record his fourth Scudetto success and he had begun forming a decent partnership with David Trezeguet following Inzaghi's exit, with Lippi back at the helm in replace of Ancelotti. The goals flowed throughout – Del Piero got two at the start to secure his 100th and 101st strikes in black and white.

Juventus owner Gianni Agnelli sadly passed away later in the season, with Ale dedicating his goal against Piacenza to him. In his memory, Juventus went on to remarkably pick up the Scudetto on the final day due to a slip-up from Inter, and the new duo up front had even left behind John Charles's and Omar Sívori's goal record for a season.

The trophies kept coming and Juventus won another league title, their 27th, and a Supercoppa Italiana in 2003. They also made the UEFA Champions League Final again only to lose out on penalties to national rivals Milan. After Juventus finished third in 2003/04, Del Piero enjoyed Scudetto glory under Fabio Capello in 2004/05. Ale provided one of the best assists you're likely to see when somehow delivering a bicycle kick cross for Trezeguet to head home at the San Siro to secure the 2004/05 title. In 2006, he also became Juventus's leading goalscorer, overtaking Boniperti after scoring a hat-trick against Fiorentina in the Coppa Italia.

In the summer of that same year, the scandal known as *Calciopoli* broke out and Juventus were punished by being relegated to Serie B. Ale remained at the club he loved, helping them secure promotion back at the first time of asking with 20 goals. He also got his 200th club goal during his time in the second tier, against Frosinone. He dedicated the achievement to himself, and rightly so, alongside all of those who had cherished the previous 199. It was then he would become Capocannoniere back in Serie A for the first time, scoring 21 in 37 games.

After a consistent couple of seasons finishing in the top half of the table, while also receiving a standing ovation at the Bernabéu in 2008 during the UEFA Champions League along the way, Juventus and Del Piero finally put the scandal behind them by lifting the Scudetto once again in 2011/12.

During that season he became Juventus's record appearance-maker by leapfrogging Boniperti, and also scored in his final Serie A match, against Atalanta. He was substituted with 30 minutes remaining, receiving rapturous applause from the home and away fans. The captain waved to the crowd, issuing a thank-you, but also a goodbye. The love could really be felt between player and Juventini as Ale took a lap of honour during the match. He played his final game for the club in the Coppa Italia Final defeat to Napoli. Juventus even wanted to retire the number ten shirt in respect of Ale's legacy at the club, to which he said:

> 'I hope that the player who will wear it, will have an even more extraordinary career. This is the reason why I didn't want the club to withdraw it: every child must have the right to dream about wearing this shirt.'
>
> – Juventus.com

Unfortunately there are not enough words in the world to discuss just what a player Alessandro Del Piero was during his time in professional football. Ale finished as the all-time top scorer for the Bianconeri – 290 to be precise with 188 of those coming in Serie A. He wasn't just a goalscorer however, but a role model. He isn't just one of many players to have represented the Bianconeri – but became part of the Juventus family. No one will ever forget or dispute that. All Juventini lived part of their club's history with Ale at the forefront. He isn't just family – Del Piero *is* the centrepiece of Juventus.

ANTONIO DI NATALE

INTRODUCED BY PAOLO BANDINI

'I would like to get to 205 Serie A goals alongside Roberto Baggio, and I also wish to reach 200 goals for my father, as at this moment he is not doing too well.'

– *Corriere della Sera*

I WAS covering the Wimbledon tennis championships on the day that Italy were eliminated from the 2010 World Cup. As the Azzurri stumbled toward a 3-2 defeat to Slovakia, I found myself huddled together with a small group of Italian journalists who had commandeered a TV in the media centre to watch the game.

Among my most vivid memories of that day is of my companions raging against Antonio Di Natale for missing a golden opportunity. They accused him of being a provincial player and lacking the nerve to thrive in big games.

Such criticisms would be repeated in the following day's newspapers. *La Gazzetta dello Sport* gave Di Natale 4.5 out of ten in its player ratings, saying he 'had been crushed by a stage that made him small'.

Di Natale's performance had been far from perfect, but the entire team was dysfunctional that day and somehow nobody else was accused of lacking big-game mettle. This condemnation was unique to Di Natale and it had less to do with his performance than a widespread refusal to accept the fact that such a talented player could content himself with playing his club football at Udinese.

He has, at different times, had the chance to join Juventus, Milan or Liverpool. That he always turned down such opportunities has been portrayed almost exclusively as a character flaw.

The reality might be the exact opposite. Di Natale himself has always asserted that he stayed at Udinese because he knew that he and his family were happy where they were.

That footballers have a life beyond the pitch is a fact that we too often refuse to acknowledge, even knowing full well that most of us work to live rather than the other way around.

We will never know the full thought process that Di Natale went through before rejecting those various transfers – what conversations he held behind closed doors with his wife and young children. Personally, I choose to believe him when he says he was not scared, telling *Sportweek* magazine, 'I fear death, not football.'

It has never seemed to me that he was overawed by the biggest games of his career. This is a man who found the net within moments of being sent on in Italy's first Euro 2012 meeting with world champions Spain and who scored a brilliant looping header to drag Udinese level in their 2011 UEFA Champions League play-off against Arsenal. Most of all, though, the one thing I can say with certainty is that I have loved seeing Di Natale play. His timing, his touch and his finishing are exquisite but it is the joy, the grin, the childlike enthusiasm for chasing a ball that make him such a pleasure to watch.

Di Natale plays like a man who knows he has the best job in the world. Or perhaps we should say second best, just behind those of us who have been paid to watch him do it.

Paolo Bandini

It was 29 May 2014 when Antonio Di Natale made the call to do a complete U-turn on his retirement from professional football. The 36-year-old had looked set to call it a day and leave Udinese after ten years, having joined the club back in 2004. His father was battling a long illness and the striker was failing to score the goals expected of him. He appeared rather sluggish, a shadow of his former self. It was here he announced his retirement midway through the 2013/14 Serie A. He remarked to Sky Sport Italia that it was a shame, considering he had 'scored more goals for Udinese than had dinners with my wife'. However, with the fans and his family truly behind him, *Totò* was to change his mind and push on to help achieve his father's aim of 200 Serie A goals.

Six months later, on 29 November, during a drab game with Chievo, he netted the memorable 200th goal for his father, who was watching him from the heavens alongside his mother. Antonio Di Natale is a man who showcased that there was more to life than simply football, but also displayed to the world how to be a professional and a role model for all who watched him.

Antonio was brought up in Naples before moving to Empoli to begin his footballing career having been scouted at 13 years old by Lorenzo D'Amato, who ran the San Nicola football school. Despite being a few years older than the crop of hopeful youngsters at the school, Empoli youth team coach Maurizio Niccolini decided to give *Totò* his first major step to achieving his dream.

The move away from home was a worrying time for the young man, realising that he was no longer a child. One night it all seemed too much for Di Natale as he decided to attempt to run away back home to his parents. He missed the home comforts and the safety his family brought him, remembering the best times in his life thus far. Despite all this, one man managed to salvage Antonio before he made the wrong decision – Vincenzo Montella.

At the time, *L'Aeroplanino* – The Little Aeroplane – as he would become known, was at Empoli in the senior team and was also a role model of Di Natale's. In an interview with *Corriere dello Sport*, the forward spoke of the night he ran home, but also when he had dinner with Vincenzo a few days later, and the support given to him from his idol:

> 'Montella had told me that when he was a boy, while in the Empoli youth team he also was homesick and wanted to escape. He convinced me to stay. I was very young and I was remembering life back at home with my parents, family and my city. Both Vincenzo and the president helped me a lot. In that period, Empoli were my family.'
>
> – *Corriere dello Sport*

The words of his idol and those around him meant Antonio stayed on and even managed to make his first team debut during the 1996/97 Serie B season, in which they were promoted. From here, *Totò* was to be loaned out to a few different clubs, including Viareggio. During his time at the

Tuscan club he scored his first goal in a 3-0 win over Novara before securing a superb hat-trick over Biellese at the Stadio dei Pini. Di Natale was seen as a second striker during this time, with rapid pace and an eye for goal. It may seem a little odd to some readers to acknowledge the association between *Totò* and the word 'pace' but the forward was once, as much as we dare to deny it, a young man.

Those at the head of Empoli were closely monitoring the progress of their young man and elected to bring him back to try him out for the senior team ahead of the 1999/2000 Serie B season, having been relegated previously. Antonio would have to wait until the third game to be picked, with coach Elio Gustinetti electing to change up the style of play to a 4-3-3 to accommodate him. They welcomed Sampdoria to the Stadio Carlo Castellani on that day with the match ending 1-0 in the Azzurri's favour. Who scored? Correct – Antonio Di Natale.

It was a defining moment for *Totò*, who had scored his first for Empoli, and after another two years his side were promoted back to Serie A for the 2002/03 season.

It was to be Di Natale's first proper year in the top flight of Italian football and he made sure he left his mark. He announced himself on to the scene on 14 September 2002 when they visited Como. With Luca Saudati opening the scoring, *Totò* would soon have his first goal in the promised land. Things wouldn't slow up for him either, inflicting pain upon Perugia, Roma and Brescia before adding a hat-trick at home to Reggina in November.

It took just three minutes for Antonio to get his first on the day, lofting a first-time lob over the despairing Luca Castellazzi. The striker wheeled away before spreading his arms out to celebrate, just like his idol Montella. It was rather fitting and his replication of the celebration showed a clear parallel between the two men, as both players and professionals of the game. A whipped-in ball just before half-time saw Di Natale secure his second, drilling home after some poor defending from the initial cross. The hat-trick was obtained in the final minute, side-footing home at the back post with the Reggina defence all at sea.

If ever there was a game that illustrated just the type of player Di Natale is, this was it. A delicate lob, a hard-hitting shot and a tap-in exemplifies Antonio and his footballing career. He could go from scoring the most elegant of goals to nearly breaking the net, before simply being in the right place at the right time to slot home à la Pippo Inzaghi. As incredible as Pippo was as a striker, Di Natale brought a lot more to his game than simply seeing the ball kindly land in front of him from all of six yards. He had the ability to create the chances himself, always giving the opposition defenders something new to think about every matchday.

Even though he had hit the ground running in 2002/03, the next year would be one to forget for Di Natale as he managed just five in 33 appearances and Empoli were relegated back down into Serie B. It was a real shame to see, considering the previous season's exploits. He had been scoring freely and even earned his first call-up to the Italian national team after his memorable hat-trick.

With his current team back in the second tier, it was inevitable *Totò* would want a move to revitalise his career and to progress in football. Udinese came calling, wishing for Di Natale to become their new hero in an attack that already had the likes of Vincenzo Iaquinta to possibly partner. The deal was soon settled; Antonio was at the Zebrette.

This was an exciting time in Antonio's life. It was his second professional club and it brought about new team-mates, new fans and a new city to ply his trade. He was joining a side that had been placing themselves in the top ten for the past couple of seasons, and knew he would have to assert himself in the early stages of his career in Udine.

Ahead of the new 2004/05 Serie A, *Totò* was given the number ten shirt for the first time, having had to settle for the number nine at Empoli due to striking compatriot

Francesco Tavano. He was able to put his foot down early on, as was expected, scoring the opener on matchday two at home to Parma. Antonio ended with seven to his name, including a hidden gem of a goal many forget about. They may have lost 3-1 to Milan at the San Siro but Di Natale showed off his brilliant technique and ability to score the game's opening goal.

Just seven minutes in, a ball was played into his feet from Iaquinta around 20 yards out. In one touch he flicked it with his left foot to gain height on the ball, before spinning and hitting the sweetest of dipping volleys with his right. Goalkeeper Dida remained completely rooted to the spot as he watched the ball sail into the top corner.

With a first full season under his belt for his club, at the time, many would have expected a hoard of silverware to come Antonio's way. As all calcio fans know, however, this is not the case. However, Antonio Di Natale was a player who needed no trophies to prove himself as he was more a man than many footballers of the modern era. Let's fast forward a little bit to clarify this statement.

During his time at Udinese, Antonio came across players from all different backgrounds and nationalities. One of those was Bergamo-born Piermario Morosini. The midfielder had joined the Zebrette in 2005 but struggled to find a place in the team, leaving in 2007 to join Vicenza, but he went back to Di Natale's club in 2009. Despite the return, he was subsequently loaned out a number of times during his second spell at the club and in 2012 found himself at Livorno.

The match between Livorno and Pescara in Serie B, one that many would dispel as a nothing game between two second-tier teams, took a disastrous turn in the 31st minute – Morosini had collapsed to the ground with no one around him. Those at the Stadio Adriatico watched on in stunned silence as he was treated on the pitch before heading to the nearby hospital where he sadly passed away.

The death of Morosini meant his disabled sister, who required round-the-clock care, was alone. His life had already been surrounded by grief – his mother and father had both died while he was just a teenager before his brother, who was also severely disabled, had ended his own life. Without the financial support of Piermario, his sister would be unable to cope. That was until Di Natale stepped in. *Totò* decided to take matters into his own hands and insisted Udinese took care of her no matter what, and would look after her by himself if he had to:

> 'We know the situation of his sister and we as a team, the club, and Udinese for Life have decided to help her because she is in real need. It is essential to stay by the side of Piermario's sister for her entire life. She needs us and we want to help, both for her and for Mario.'
>
> – Udinese.it

Such a story goes to show that this isn't about just detailing the incredible strikes and mountains of trophies these superb forwards won. It's about showing the man behind the greatness, revealing to us all that they are only human. If anything, the kind of man Di Natale was is worth 100 Scudetti alone.

The Scudetto was something that Antonio hadn't lifted and looked unlikely to by that stage of his career. Udinese's finish of fourth at the end of 2005 was the best there was to come in terms of league positions.

Antonio was still creating moments of brilliance, bringing about an odd record, as he became the first Italian footballer to score in every single competition he played in across a single season – eight in Serie A, three in Coppa Italia, two in the UEFA Champions League and a solitary goal in the UEFA Cup. His goalscoring exploits continued and were growing at a significant rate as the striker became captain of the club. He secured 40 across 89 appearances in the next three Serie A campaigns. It was 2009/10 when Di Natale's goalscoring fortunes took a huge turn for the better. Going into the new campaign, *Totò* was 32 years old and had lost his partner in crime Fabio Quagliarella to Napoli. Antonio himself had been targeted by English side Liverpool, about whom he revealed in an interview with *Sportweek* magazine in 2014, 'The only other team I would have loved to have played for due to the atmosphere of Anfield, was Liverpool.' It came to nothing, and something those in the Curva Nord will be joyous about, considering what occurred in the following seasons.

Looking first to Serie A in 2009/10, *Totò* proved that age was just a number, dispelling all calcio supporters who believed he would become just a bit-part player, as he secured the Capocannoniere prize for the first time in his career with 29 goals in 35 appearances – a goal every 0.8 games.

He sprung into action right from the off, netting a brace at the Stadio Friuli in a 2-2 draw with Parma. The aeroplane celebration was on full display after scoring from the spot before salvaging a point late on with a wonderful effort. The clock was ticking down and it seemed inevitable the Zebrette would be leaving the first game with their tails between their legs. A badly-hit cross ended up on the edge of the box which just so happened to be where the Italian was. The cross itself was so poor that the bounce bamboozled the defender, who let the ball squirm from under his foot and over his head before landing with *Totò*, who thumped the 18-yard volley home. The world's worst assist and one of Antonio's best finishes. Football eh?

From then on it was goals, goals, goals and he added a hat-trick to his name on matchday three, ousting Catania 4-2. He did it again in February, this time against Napoli as he secured the win with two goals in additional time. Di Natale made sure it was done in style – a scissor-kick gave them the lead in the 91st minute. It was wrapped up when Antonio broke through with the Partenopei leaving men forward in an attempt to try and bag an equaliser. Annoyingly, Napoli's Gianluca Grava ruined the celebrations when he ran straight over to the striker and pulled at his shirt, before pointing to the Udinese player on the ground. Di Natale was quick to make the same gesture toward the defender, telling him that if his side had wanted to put the ball out of play, they would have done so.

If that wasn't enough, he scored in each of the last seven games, making doubly sure that Diego Milito wouldn't catch him in the race to become top goalscorer. His strike against Cagliari two weeks from the close of the campaign secured his 100th in the colours of Udinese – another success ticked off his list. Antonio's goals meant more than just an individual accolade however – he scored over half his team's goals that year – earning them 22 points. They finished 15th in the end, but the Zebrette would have ended up rock bottom without him.

His achievements didn't go unnoticed after the marathon campaign, with Di Natale being awarded the Italian Footballer of the Year prize. Alongside this, he was also nominated for the *Miglior gol* – best goal of the season – for his effort against Napoli the following year. Napoli were probably sick of the sight of him, not only for the fact he was scoring wonder-goals against them but they always came in threes. This incredible finish was one of his best, hitting a swerving ball with pretty much no backlift from around 25 yards. Your reaction will be the same as the commentator on the day, 'Mamma mia!' If goals like that don't impress you, he scored from a corner in the second half should that be more your thing.

In that same year he also became the first player since Giuseppe Signori, another of our *Calcio's Greatest Forwards*, to win back-to-back Capocannonieri, this time netting 28 times. This was a remarkable feat for a man who was then 34 years old, having scored 57 in 71 games. On 22 May 2011, before a match with Milan, he was presented with the *Pallone d'argento* – the Silver Ball – an award given to a player who has, according to *Legaseriea.it*, 'shown good sportsmanship throughout the year as well as acting as a role model off the pitch for those both young and old'. If ever there was an award that summed up *Totò*, this was it.

His antics in front of goal continued, scoring 23 times in each of the next two years, a period that included his FIFA Puskás nomination when he notched a left-footed beauty, volleying home from a tight angle. It's very much like Francesco Totti's 2006 strike against Sampdoria, which is better, but we'll keep that quiet.

With the 2013/14 Serie A season coming to an end, it seemed as if calcio fans were waving goodbye to *Totò*. As previously noted, this wasn't to be, as he would soldier on for the new season, producing a touching moment as he made sure his father would see him score 200 goals from the heavens. He did so in 400 league games too, a stunning ratio. Antonio went on to meet his own target – to better Roberto Baggio's 205 top-flight goals – doing so with a clever flicked finish against a side he was used to scoring against, Chievo, on 3 May 2015. He ended the season with 207 to his name.

The Italian will remain at the Stadio Friuli for 2015/16, in which if he was to replicate his tally of 14 from the previous year, he'd leapfrog both José Altafini and Giuseppe Meazza in the all-time table. He won't care if he doesn't though. Antonio Di Natale is a man who cares not for trophies and accolades, but for finding a family in football, something many professionals are without:

> 'The truth is that I've found my natural home in Friuli and I've never thought about leaving a team, a town and a family who have adopted me like a son.'
>
> – FIFA.com

KURT HAMRIN

'I remember my first visit to Turin. I could see the Alps from the hotel. Nordahl [Gunnar] told me, "If you are lucky enough to come to Italy, stay there."'

– *La Repubblica*

'THE Flying Bird' read the headline of Florence's daily newspaper *La Nazione*. It was a striking headline, attracting a gluttony of readers to part with their hard-earned money to find out who this 'Flying Bird' was they spoke of. One of those interested individuals was Kurt Hamrin. The Swedish footballer had moved to Florence to further his career, having already starred at Juventus and Padova, to join Fiorentina during the tail-end of the 1950s and into the 60s. He picked up the paper, puzzled by the odd yet intriguing headline. The striker elected to purchase a copy, opening up the pages to find the report by journalist Beppe Pegolotti. It stated, 'Hamrin runs down the wing like how a little bird flies.' It was then Kurt realised who Pegolotti was referring to. It was him. He was the 'little bird'.

The Swede grew up in a busy household with four other siblings, fathered by a man who was a painter with Kurt himself electing to work at *Dagens Nyheter*, a daily newspaper published in Stockholm. Hamrin told *La Repubblica* he decided to take the job because he 'liked the smell of ink'. He kept his education going too, taking zincography – for those wondering, it means a printing process using zinc plates – to keep his options open as in Sweden, football was yet to be a professional career.

He was a keen player though, representing amateur side AIK Solna, dreaming of the day he could follow the likes of Nils Liedholm, Gunnar Nordahl and Lennart Skoglund to Italy. His technical ability was always on show, illustrating his agile movement and speed on the wing before dribbling inside to unleash an inch-perfect shot into the top corner. In 1954, at the age of 20, he managed to become the top goalscorer for his side, grabbing a remarkable 22 goals in 21 games.

The Little Bird was clearly progressing at a fine rate in football, and had even been picked for Sweden's national team a year prior to the recently mentioned goalscoring heroics. Hamrin had notched up eight thus far for the Blågult – the blue-yellows – and as such interest was building up from professional clubs outside of his homeland, one of them being the Old Lady – Juventus.

What follows is a rather peculiar way of scouting a player, but one that clearly worked for the Bianconeri. Fiat Sweden, which was part of the Agnelli family's car manufacturing company based in Italy, had hired a man to keep an eye on any sporting talent in the surrounding area. The Swedish attacker spoke of such an occurrence and detailed exactly what unfolded in an interview with Emanuele Giulianelli:

> 'They [Juventus] had been following me through Fiat Sweden in Stockholm. In every international branch, Fiat had a man who was interested in sports appointed to follow the local championships in order to discover new talents to bring to Italy. One of the observers followed all my matches in Sweden and sent the reports back to Turin. During a match with Portugal in Lisbon we won 6-2 and I scored. Sandro Puppo, who was the coach there, asked me to come and play. It was my dream to be a professional player.'

So with that, Hamrin was based in Italy, ready to show the Juventini exactly why he had been signed as Kurt was one of only two foreign footballers at the club – Argentinian Raoul Conti the other player in question.

This wasn't as strange as you might think, as Italian rules meant only two foreign players could play at a team at one time.

It wasn't Juventus's best season, not by a long shot, but it helped Hamrin get acquainted with the type of style needed to be successful in one of the world's best leagues. He made his debut on the opening day, 16 September 1966, away at Lazio, scoring a brace in the second half. The perfect start continued, netting on matchday two at the Stadio Comunale in a 2-0 triumph over Spal. It was extraordinary for a 22-year-old, who had been playing amateur football back in Sweden just a few months ago, to be scoring like he'd been in Italy since birth.

Everything just flowed for Hamrin, not letting the change of location or incredibly steep step-up in quality on the pitch affect his game. Inter and Udinese felt his full force when he bagged a goal in each of those games, before succumbing to an ankle injury. It was here that things began to take a bad turn.

His explosive start to life at Juventus was halted with this unfortunate injury, and it plagued him throughout the course of the season. Juve were desperate to get him back on the field and after two weeks on the sidelines Hamrin entered the fray once more. The Bianconeri were rushing him, not letting Kurt have time to properly heal and recover, and it proved costly as he suffered the same problem more times through the year. The celebrations of the strikes against the Nerazzurri and Zebrette were memories long in the past for the Swede.

Juventus went on to finish ninth, and the perceived glass ankles of Hamrin meant an early exit was on the cards. It was confirmed in the summer of 1957, prior to the new Serie A season, when John Charles and Omar Sívori signed – a Welshman and an Argentinian. Because of that two-foreign-player ruling, Kurt was sent out on loan to Padova which at least gave him a chance to rejuvenate a professional career that had started so promisingly.

At his new side, Hamrin was put under the guidance of coach Nereo Rocco, and the Italian made sure his new signing played his part by putting the number seven in his favourite right-wing position. He joined up with two other forwards, Sergio Brighenti and Enore Boscolo, in an attacking 4-2-3-1, with Boscolo and Kurt pushing up to help the lone forward. It was daring but it paid dividends and at the Stadio Silvio Appiani on matchday one when they welcomed Lazio – who were probably realising Hamrin was to become their Achilles heel – they secured a 3-1 win with the speedy Swedish winger grabbing the opener.

Bad ankles or not, he wasn't showing it. He secured a hat-trick the week after over Genoa and produced the same heroics at home to Torino on 20 October 1957. Padova were producing some incredible performances in Serie A and found themselves locking horns with Juventus for the Scudetto. The Little Bird decided to make Genoa his new team to torment when he fired in four, all of which came

FIORENTINA
Paine

in the first half to get his team on course for a 6-3 win on 2 February 1958.

The Biancoscudati began to curtail in mid-March however, and soon found themselves six points adrift of top spot. A 6-1 final-day loss away to Fiorentina meant they'd have to settle for third, which by no means was an easy feat for a club that finished 11th the season before. Even with the dream coming to an end, the year at Padova was valuable in Hamrin's development. He was no longer the young lad who played for AIK gaining 50 crowns – around £4 – for a win or a draw. He was constantly learning, growing stronger and more able to brush defenders aside. Those at Padova made their players walk and cycle everywhere instead of driving, always taking a brisk stroll from the station to the stadium on matchday. Kurt was becoming a seasoned expert in Italy's top league. The goalscoring didn't seem to be a problem either, having ended with a total of 20, the fifth best in the division.

As such, it led Sweden into the 1958 World Cup finals, which they hosted, with plenty of optimism knowing they had Hamrin to hand. In spite of the fact we're only detailing the football played in Serie A by these great forwards, it's hard to not include a brief mention of this tournament as it featured one of Kurt's best goals.

The nippy winger had already acquired a tally of three for his country going into the semi-final with West Germany. With the hosts 2-1 to the good, Hamrin, with his trademark socks as low as his ankles, produced magic worthy of a stage show. He collected the ball on the wing, slowly edging forward as the clocked ticked down and Sweden looked set for a final in their own backyard. A rather agitated German came gallivanting at Hamrin from behind, only for the winger to sprint away, leaving a cartoon-like trail of dust behind him. As he entered the box, Kurt beat the next man like he wasn't even there, before lifting a delicate chip over Fritz Herkenrath.

Moments like these are valuable to reflect upon in short because it clearly boosted the morale of Hamrin, who was probably still a little disappointed his former club Juventus had toppled Padova and gone on to win the Scudetto. That coupled with the fact two of the players who netted more league goals than him were Charles and Sívori, whose introduction basically pushed him out of the club. But as this shows, it didn't affect his reputation on the pitch.

Hamrin can always remember the fact his goal sealed the game and sent his country to the final of the biggest footballing competition in the world, although it appears his favourite goal for the Blågult was when they drew 2-2 to the mighty Hungary in Budapest back in 1953. Marianne – his wife – described it in *La Repubblica*'s 2014 interview by saying how she was 'sat watching the match with our cat in my arms' before 'seeing Kurt score, I then jumped in celebration only for the cat to end up attached to the chandelier'. She was probably used to her partner scoring by that point, it was etched into her head, and so all feline friends of his wife can rest easy.

His antics both for Sweden and Padova meant The Little Bird would be migrating again, this time to the team who just leapfrogged them into second on the final matchday – Fiorentina. His Florentine adventure began in the Coppa Italia and coincidentally it was a clash with Padova. Despite Fiorentina going a goal down, Hamrin found the back of the net and his side progressed on to the challenge of Bologna, which they met with a 4-2 win. The final was to be played at the Stadio Olimpico, where they would meet Lazio, and a solitary goal from Maurilio Prini – a diving header – meant the Swede would narrowly miss out on his first piece of silverware.

Hamrin had joined Miguel Montuori up front for the upcoming Serie A campaign and it started positively, with Kurt's new team earning a 3-1 win over Vicenza. It wouldn't take long for the Swede to get his first in the league either, netting in a 4-1 away triumph over Alessandria. The confident start by player and club meant there were faint whispers being heard from those in purple – Scudetto anyone? Going into matchday ten on 30 November 1958, Milan and Fiorentina were at the top end of the table with la Viola just a point above the Rossoneri. Hamrin would travel to Milan on this day, full of optimism and enthusiasm – his side were yet to lose in the league. After a steady first half it all seemed to crumble, with José Altafini dealing the killer blow to seal a 2-0 win.

Kurt wasn't knocked back and he went on to score four goals in the next four games, three of which ended in ridiculous scorelines – against Genoa (7-1), Udinese (7-0) and Torino (6-0). The incredible goalscoring kept Fiorentina right alongside Milan, keeping their horns well and truly locked in battle. Hamrin was enjoying himself, speeding past perplexed full-backs who were left scratching their heads, as well as getting a face full of dust when Kurt breezed past them. It really must have been like watching a cartoon – the defenders representing the unfortunate figure of Wile E. Coyote trying desperately to thwart the Road Runner that was Hamrin. It's rather fitting considering his nickname The Little Bird – he really did fly down the wing.

With his first season entering what is best described as the 'business end', things took a turn. Again it was Milan who were ready to spoil the party. The Stadio Artemio Franchi watched in stunned silence as they fell to a 3-1 defeat, despite Hamrin's best efforts that saw him on the scoresheet. From that moment on the Scudetto dream faded away. Milan had leapfrogged Kurt's Fiorentina into top spot and they wouldn't budge from the perch they had claimed. Losses to Spal and Udinese confirmed la Viola would have to make do with second place yet again, even with Hamrin bagging his second hat-trick against Torino, thus continuing the trend of the year considering they also finished as runners-up to Lazio in the Coppa Italia. It all appeared too familiar for

Fiorentina, having finished second the previous two years. Kurt's 26 goals weren't even enough to see him become Capocannoniere, a prize he'd never earn.

Hamrin would go on to spend another eight years at Fiorentina, with the Scudetto constantly just a fingertip away from his grasp. His lack of trophies didn't stop his passion and drive to perform, though. The next year he again proved ruthless up front – another 26 to his name. As he put it in his interview with Emanuele Giulianelli, it was a 'spray of gunfire'. It proved that a gluttony of silverware wasn't the reason players wished to remain at their respective clubs, it was because they loved the name on the front of their shirt.

In that previous year they again came second, this time to Juventus, even with Hamrin scoring a sublime chest-and-volley effort to defeat the Bianconeri, as well as losing out in the Coppa Italia to the same team. The Swede was still tearing up defences, letting his Stanley Matthews and Lennart Skoglund influences run wild, due to the fact he based his game on them. In the 1960/61 season things would finally change in terms of success for Fiorentina and Kurt. The Scudetto was a distant memory, finishing seventh, but one trophy proved to be the best moment of Hamrin's career in Florence – the European Cup Winners' Cup.

It was the first year the competition had been introduced so for Fiorentina to take part in the inaugural edition was pretty special for the club and the city of Florence as a whole. Rather ironically, la Viola hadn't actually won any cups the previous season, having finished second best to Juventus on both occasions. But they still joined the likes of Rangers, Dinamo Zagreb and Wolverhampton Wanderers who had all successfully won their respective domestic competitions. Hamrin and co. entered into the quarter-finals of the tournament, drawn to face Swiss outfit FC Luzern. The first leg was to be played away from home for Fiorentina on 23 November 1960 – Hamrin netting a hat-trick in a 3-0 win. He was on the scoresheet twice more in the return fixture to complete a 9-2 aggregate victory. They progressed on to the challenge of Dinamo Zagreb, and even with Kurt unable to find his shooting boots, the Swede's assists proved vital as they went on to win 3-0 and 2-1 to set up a meeting with Rangers in the final.

Along came 17 May 1961 at the Ibrox Stadium, the first leg of the most captivating 180 minutes Hamrin would ever play in a Fiorentina shirt. La Viola boss Nándor Hidegkuti had all the players he wished to have at his disposal for this one – Luigi Milan, Enrico Albertosi and of course Hamrin. Rangers however were without Jimmy Millar, their top scorer, meaning beating someone as good as Albertosi would prove a tall order.

Some 80,000 supporters would be in attendance for the first leg, including many Scots-Italians who were based in Scotland but came from Italy. One of those was Loreno Rinaldi, then a 17-year-old Fiorentina fan who lived in Dumfries, a lucky individual to have attended such a game. In an interview with BBC Sport that focused on the first European Cup Winners' Cup Final, Rinaldi reminisced about the match, saying, 'It was a bit scary to be in the ground, especially because Fiorentina won 2-0,' and adding, 'A winger called Hamrin was running up and down the wing giving the finger to the crowd!'

The most important note of that was the fact Hamrin's Fiorentina won the opener 2-0. With the match starting off rather heated, it was Kurt's boys who got the ball rolling just 12 minutes in. Milan pounced on a poor error in the midfield before slotting the ball across to Gianfranco Petris, who somehow managed to squirm the ball back to his team-mate. Harold Davis, a defender for Rangers, attempted to clear the danger but failed miserably, leaving Milan to tuck home past goalkeeper Billy Richie. A penalty was later awarded to the Scottish side only for Eric Caldow to put the ball wide. Milan got his second with a cool finish just before the game ended, putting Fiorentina well in the ascendancy.

What is great to see, in the rare footage of the match, is a number of Rangers players lining up at the tunnel to applaud their opponents off the field, even though they had just succumbed to a 2-0 defeat. They fared no better in the second leg and this time it was the Swede's time to shine. Having provided the assist for Milan's opener, with the score perfectly poised at 1-1, The Little Bird cut in from the right, darting past two despairing defenders before lifting the ball delightfully into the goal. It was typical Hamrin but a not so typical Fiorentina, who had secured their first major silverware for over four years. If that wasn't enough, they wrapped up the Coppa Italia on 11 June 1961 with a 2-0 win over Lazio.

It was his proudest moment while at Fiorentina, and the high point too. He went on to score 150 goals for them, revealing to Emanuele Giulianelli just how amazing his time in Florence was before preparing for his brief spell for Milan:

> 'I spent nine years there – all wonderful. In my later years in Florence, I was like a hen for the young talents of the new generations. I was almost 35 when I went away to Milan. The one who wanted me at all costs was Nereo Rocco, my coach from the Padova days. He insisted that he wanted to bring me!'

It was here at the Rossoneri that Kurt's Scudetto prayers would be answered, lifting the precious trophy in his first year at the club, 1968. He also won the European Cup Winners' Cup but it didn't have the same meaning the success at Fiorentina did. In his 36 games there he scored just eight times, picking up the European Cup in the process. He later moved on to Napoli for a couple of years, winding down his career before returning to Sweden to end his long journey.

The club he loved never forgot him though, with Fiorentina welcoming him back in 2012 during the unveiling of the top five scorers in their history to go up on museofiorentina.it – the online Fiorentina museum. Hamrin topped the list, just above Gabriel Batistuta. They had already opened their arms to their star man in 2009 when he turned 75, and greeted him at their doors yet again in 2014 when he was presented with a shirt by coach Vincenzo Montella and manager Vincenzo Guerini for his 80th birthday. With that year's crop of players having autographed the shirt, he turned to the camera holding the garment as if he was the club's new signing as it read 'Hamrin 80'.

As he walked around taking in the new sights and sounds of the bustling Florentine club's training centre, shaking hands with all who followed him, those who watched the presentation – available at it.violachannel.tv – could see the emotional attachment he has with the club. On that day, he spoke of his time at Fiorentina, and when he knew his life was destined to be lived in Florence:

> 'The best memory I have of my time at la Viola was when we won the Cup Winners' Cup Final against Rangers. I loved Florence ever since I saw the change coming from Padova. It was here that I established both my life and my love.'
>
> – it.Violachannel.tv

PIPPO INZAGHI

INTRODUCED BY SUSY CAMPANALE

'The fact is I live for scoring. Goals are a positive drug and I've never been able to get enough.'

– *FourFourTwo*

FILIPPO 'Pippo' Inzaghi was a very easy player to dislike. He seemed to be constantly diving, straying offside, arguing with the officials or celebrating a tap-in from six yards as if he'd just won the World Cup. What most people don't realise is that these are the precise characteristics that made him the best player to have in your team. Super Pippo was annoying because he appeared to have few genuine skills and almost all his goals were scored from ten yards or closer.

Sir Alex Ferguson famously said Inzaghi 'was born offside'. The label haunted him ever since, but the statistics in reality do not bear that up. It's just that when he was flagged, he would argue until he was blue in the face that it was a terrible decision, even when replays showed him to be clearly in the wrong. The boy who cried onside.

These drama-queen tendencies were fuelled by almost pathological self-belief; he just would not give up. When the rest of the squad had long lost hope he'd carry on harassing defenders and officials, using that dogged determination that covered a multitude of technical deficiencies, behaving as if every chance could be the one to change the game.

The quintessential Inzaghi goal was one that isn't on his CV. In the 2003 UEFA Champions League quarter-final, Milan were drawing 2-2 with Ajax at the San Siro, a result that would see the Dutch side progress on away goals. Deep into stoppage time, when all seemed lost, a long ball was nodded on into the box by Massimo Ambrosini. Inzaghi moved quicker than defender and goalkeeper, stretching up a boot through sheer willpower to flick it over them. As the crowd was already screaming his name, Inzaghi watched the ball dip at just the right moment for Jon Dahl Tomasson to tap in from a yard. It was going in anyway and is every inch the classic Inzaghi goal, but the history books have the Dane on the scoresheet. Milanisti, however, will never forget the real hero.

Inzaghi would celebrate every goal as if his life depended on it. One assumed if he ever scored in the World Cup finals, his head would literally explode and shower spectators in joyful goo.

Want to know how important Inzaghi and his infuriating/inspiring attitude really was? He didn't play in the 2005 UEFA Champions League Final where Milan threw away a 3-0 lead against Liverpool. He did start the

2007 edition and scored both goals as the Rossoneri took the trophy and revenge. Coincidence? Not a chance.

Susy Campanale

There are no 30-yard screamers to cast our minds back to when we think of Pippo's exploits in front of goal. This was a man who had set up camp in the six-yard box, toasting marshmallows while waiting for some form of chance to fall his way. When it did, he gobbled it up. Inzaghi was a goalscorer, always letting his feet do the talking. He helped his team win countless trophies – domestically and in Europe – and no success would elude him. The Milanisti loved him, constantly breaking out into a chorus of, '*Pippo Inzaghi segna per noi!*' – 'Pippo Inzaghi scored for us!'

There is, however, always that form of frustration a fan holds to a player when they can't hold their run and therefore are flagged offside. The difference with Pippo is he knew that for every offside claim called against him, there was one that wouldn't be, and it would lead to a goal. Who knows how he scored so many goals, living off of just pasta in tomato sauce and air-cured beef according to his father Giancarlo?

He got his first of many in Serie A for Parma when facing his home-town and former club, Piacenza. The emotions ran through him when he scored that goal, lying motionless on the floor – it was his Piacenza. Those tears fell for the club who raised him 25 years ago.

Inzaghi joined the club as a naive 18-year-old, making two early appearances – one as a 90th-minute substitute versus Casertana and the other with 30 minutes to go in the final game against Taranto. Pippo was loaned to Leffe in Serie C1 and propelled them to a fifth-place finish by scoring 13 times, just two off the top goalscorer for the season, Cosimo Francioso of champions Ravenna.

The Italian was on the move again in 1993/94, this time to Verona in Serie B where he once again amassed 13 goals. Pippo had started to pick up the pace in front of goal and subsequently attracted interest from possible suitors. Piacenza managed to hold on to the youngster for another season in the second tier of Italian football, but once he had completed the campaign with 15 goals to his name and by helping them to win promotion, it was time to move on.

Forty-one goals in 96 matches over the previous four seasons meant that in 1995 Pippo moved to Parma, joining the likes of Gianluigi Buffon, Dino Baggio and Gianfranco Zola. Aside from his winner against his former club, Inzaghi only scored once more in his debut season in the top flight, in a home victory over Bari. The striker had clearly not had enough time to adapt to his new club under the watchful eye of coach Nevio Scala. He was unable to change the style of his game in the lower leagues as quickly as the man in charge wanted, and it meant a partnership with Zola or fellow new arrival Hristo Stoichkov never took off.

It wasn't a failure that the passionately-driven Pippo would dwell on. Even with football fans across the globe still unaware of this up-and-coming talent, including those in Italy who were still marvelling at the likes of Roberto Baggio and Gabriel Batistuta, it was in the 1996/97 Serie A season that everyone finally sat up and took notice.

Emiliano Mondonico, coach of Atalanta, decided to take a gamble on Pippo and the striker picked up a brace when the Nerazzurri welcomed Fiorentina to the Stadio Atleti Azzurri d'Italia in the second game of the season. His first came from the penalty spot to put his side back on level terms. The celebration could seem subdued in hindsight for what was to come in the future from Pippo, with simply an arm aloft and a high five to boot. His second goal meant the fans got to see more of the Pippo that all calcio-lovers enjoyed for many years. After hooking in a right-footed volley, Inzaghi ran to the fans, both arms to the side, showcasing what would be his trademark celebration. A roar of satisfaction and a tug of the shirt ensued. Serie A, meet Pippo – Pippo, meet Serie A.

He would score in the next three matches, cementing himself in the first team for the rest of the season. Inzaghi wasn't just the typical six-yard-box finisher many see him as during his solitary season in the black and blue of Atalanta. The eighth match saw Pippo cut inside brilliantly before smashing the ball into the roof of the net to put his side 1-0 up against Milan at the San Siro while a trip to Bologna two weeks later produced a wonderful 20-yard free kick into the top corner.

Unfortunately there was to be no release of ecstasy from Pippo, with his side 3-0 down before the magic occurred. It was a shame as had Inzaghi known it would be his only goal direct from a free kick in his entire career, he'd have probably set up a gazebo full of party supplies at the corner flag.

Every type of goal just seemed to be happening on the field when Pippo played – he was just always in the right place. He completed the season with 24 goals, making him Capocannoniere – the biggest individual prize in Italy for any striker. His goals averaged out at around one every 119 minutes and he also became the Serie A Young Footballer of the Year, the first winner of the award.

His heroics for Atalanta meant former club Parma and Scudetto holders Juventus were interested in Pippo's services. The latter tabled an offer of around £7m to prise him away from Bergamo. Inzaghi was set to join the biggest club in the land, boasting the likes of Alessandro Del Piero and Zinedine Zidane.

The 1997/98 Serie A season, his first at the Bianconeri, would be one filled with silverware. The season began just how Pippo would have dreamt it, scoring twice and assisting Antonio Conte in the Supercoppa Italiana over Vicenza. *Corriere della Sera*'s headline the next day read 'SuperPippo gives the Super Cup to Juventus'. There was more success to come for Pippo right around the corner, this time in

Serie A, scoring the opening goal in a 2-0 home win over Lecce by bundling the ball home with six minutes to go. He went about his first celebration in black and white in typical fashion, arms flailing about like something only a contortionist could replicate.

It was the kick-start Inzaghi needed for his four years at the club and he formed a quite formidable partnership with Del Piero in the first season. He managed 18 goals across the course of the title-winning campaign, including his first Juve hat-trick, in the penultimate game against Bologna, and helped earn his side 19 points. A truly valuable asset considering they only won the Scudetto by six points over Inter. It was also the season Pippo was introduced to arguably his greatest love in football, the UEFA Champions League. Although it culminated in a final defeat against Real Madrid, Pippo scored six goals including an away hat-trick in Ukraine.

Away from the jubilation and celebration of the impressive first year at Juventus, Inzaghi and the Bianconeri took a downturn in fortunes. In 1998/99 they finished seventh, mainly down to the absence of Del Piero, who had suffered a bad knee injury. Pippo scored 13 times and again grabbed six in Europe, only to see his early brace in the semi-final second leg against Manchester United overturned as Juventus were knocked out.

Their poor Serie A campaign meant Carlo Ancelotti's side entered the 1999 Intertoto Cup. They won it however, thanks to the goalscoring exploits of Pippo who contributed seven. Despite the summer success, things were no better domestically – quite literally. Inzaghi's partner in crime Del Piero was back from his injury and had struggled to find the net from open play, and Pippo wasn't making this any easier for him.

However, 20 February 2000 soon rolled around with Juventus visiting the Stadio Pierluigi Penzo, home of Venezia. The away side were a goal to the good thanks to Del Piero tucking away a first-half penalty and with the game entering the final 15 their playing partnership began to take a turn for the worse. With just over ten minutes remaining, Pippo stole the ball off of a defender before electing to round the goalkeeper instead of popping it across to an onrushing Ale. No harm done one would think, as it was just a goalscorer simply wanting to get himself on the scoresheet.

Five minutes later Pippo was played through, again deciding to go for goal – which he found – leaving striking compatriot Del Piero motionless in the box. His third and final goal was one that clearly illustrated the fact Inzaghi must go by the famous 'there's no I in team, but there are five in individual brilliance'. Pippo pretty much chose to dart in front of Ale to get the goal instead of his struggling team-mate. Del Piero was clearly frustrated by what had unfolded on the pitch that day, later stating to the Italian press how it was 'lucky he scored' before deliberating over whether he would pass to Pippo in the future, saying, 'Only if the moment was right.'

With David Trezeguet joining the ranks ahead of the 2000/01 Serie A season it seemed Pippo's time at Juventus was up. An impressive haul of 89 goals across 165 games was not enough to keep him in contention and he was sold to the club many fell in love with in the decade – AC Milan.

The Rossoneri paid a fee reported to be around £25m for Pippo, and at least wouldn't miss out on UEFA Champions League football, something he needed. His 42 per cent goals to shots on target ratio prior to him signing for Silvio Berlusconi's team speaks volumes. It was here that Inzaghi would win his beloved Champions League twice, as well as two Scudetti and even a Coppa Italia. On signing for Milan, Pippo was clear on what he wanted to achieve at his new side:

> 'I've signed a five-year contract here at Milan and considering my age this is further proof of a mass amount of respect and trust. As for my aims during

> this time, I want to win trophies both in Italy and Europe and I also hope to add to my memories. I have five years in red and black ahead of me so I want to do better.'
>
> – ACMilan.com

His opening season with his new club saw them finish fourth, with his first goal coming at home to Fiorentina – stealing in on a defensive mix-up to tap home from close range. Pippo added another nine to that goal in what had been a steady first year at Milan. The 2002/03 season was one to savour as Milan won the UEFA Champions League and the Coppa Italia. The latter was a 6-3 aggregate victory over Roma, with Pippo picking up a goal during the second leg.

Quite surprisingly, the goal came from around 20 yards out with the forward hitting a first-time shot into the corner. It proves quite comical to watch over, as it's clear Pippo is in an area of the pitch he rarely frequents, but his shot was well taken, swiping the ball home with his left foot. As for the former, this is where Pippo really shone. He got two in the group stage opener against Lens before netting a hat-trick away at Deportivo La Coruña. He capped off the group games with another three goals, giving him a total of eight with Milan progressing as Group G winners.

On the route to the final, Pippo picked one more up against Borussia Dortmund before grabbing the first goal in the 3-2 quarter-final win over Ajax. After seeing off rivals Inter in the last four they would meet another Italian side in the final – Juventus. After 120 minutes of brilliant yet goalless football, Andriy Shevchenko stepped up to give Milan their sixth title with the crucial kick in the penalty shoot-out.

It was Pippo's first success in Europe and he loved every minute of it, even if it was against his former employers. As for his time in Serie A, he also scored 17 goals that season as well, as if his exploits elsewhere weren't enough.

Following on from such a triumph, Milan and Pippo would then go on to win the Scudetto in 2003/04. Disappointingly, Pippo played little part in this victory, scoring just three times in an injury-plagued season. Typical football. The man was playing the best he'd done in his career but a head injury sustained against Perugia kicked off two seasons of time spent largely on the treatment table. He also suffered from a severe knee injury and broken hand.

Pippo never gave up hope though, even after not finding the net at all in 2004/05. I'm sure that had he been more persuasive to the physio, he could have been wheeled on and just sat in the six-yard box ready to swing his leg out at any passing ball. He made his comeback the following season, scoring 12 in 23, and was starting to manage more than four games in a row.

Even though his performances had dipped in Serie A due to his previous injury struggles, Pippo showcased how he was always in the right place at the right time in the 2007 UEFA Champions League Final against Liverpool. He scored the game's opening goal by deflecting home Andrea Pirlo's free kick past Pepe Reina with his shoulder and added his second when he rounded the Spaniard. He ran straight to the corner flag, grabbing it with one hand as he let out an unquestionable amount of emotion. Where he stored it no one will ever know, but as he dropped to his knees you could see how much this meant to Pippo. This was his trophy.

Eleven goals was his total in 2007/08 and during 2008/09 he reached a superb career landmark – 300 goals – by scoring twice in a 5-1 away victory over Siena in the second half of the season. Pippo was thrilled, reiterating how he felt like a kid again following his achievement:

> 'I didn't sleep. But then again, after the goals in Athens I didn't sleep for ten days. It's just the way I am, I like to play as if I were 20 years old, I steal the balls at the end of the match. I stole two in one

> week: the one of the hat-trick and the one of my 300th goal as a professional. On the way home, Alessia [his partner] told me, "You're like a child." She's right, but I think that's the spirit that led me to here.'
>
> – *La Gazzetta dello Sport*

As the seasons wore on it was clear there was not much time left on the field for Pippo at Milan. In 2009/10 he scored just twice, the same total he would acquire in 2010/11. The latter provided a mix of emotions for Inzaghi. He scored twice against Real Madrid in a thrilling 2-2 draw in a Champions League group stage match. The first came from a poor Zlatan Ibrahimović cross that Iker Casillas could only parry into the air, which he gleefully headed home. Pippo ran straight to the touchline, knee-sliding some distance in the process. Even at 37 the celebrations were still the greatest thing about Inzaghi. He immediately got up to congratulate Ibrahimović on his fortunate assist before being given a shirt that read 'Inzaghi 69' as he became the all-time top scorer in all European competitions.

The second goal was a typical Pippo goal – running off the back of the defender before poking home. Oh, and he was offside. Either way, his two goals at 37 years and 85 days saw him second on the list of the oldest goalscorers in the history of the competition, something only surpassed by Ryan Giggs and more recently Francesco Totti.

An injury the following weekend put Inzaghi out of contention for the remainder of the season, one that saw Milan lift the Scudetto for the second time in his career in red and black. The 2011/12 Serie A would be his final campaign in professional football and it proved a poignant end with the Italian getting on the scoresheet in his last match at the San Siro against Novara. In the 67th minute, it was time for Massimiliano Allegri to make the change all Milanisti wanted to see. Antonio Cassano made way for their true love Pippo Inzaghi. A banner was raised in the Curva Sud – '*Pippo: per il tuo cuore e la tua passione. Non basta uno striscone*' – 'For your heart and your passion, a banner is not enough'. He gave the fans the perfect goodbye in return as he chested down a ball from Clarence Seedorf before smashing a volley past Alberto Fontana. Pippo embraced another veteran, Alessandro Nesta, by the corner flag with pure emotion etched upon his face. The perfect send-off.

In the months following that final game, Pippo took over at Milan's Primavera before finally getting his chance to coach the senior side in the 2014/15 Serie A. Unfortunately it was not a season to remember, finishing tenth before being told he would not be taking the team any further during 2015/16.

It wouldn't taint his 11 years at the club as a player however. The Milanisti will never forget his passion and the success he achieved for them. One thing is for sure, the fans will always reminisce about his goals. The Italian had successfully broken the offside trap yet again. You know the rest – '*Pippo Inzaghi segna per noi!*'

ROBERTO MANCINI

'The number ten is that player who surprises and excites, wrong-foots everyone with a piece of skill perhaps he's not even fully aware of. This number was my destiny right away.'

– Robertomancini.com

IN 1991 a little club based in Genoa wowed Italy and took Serie A by storm. The Blucerchiati had been steadily progressing over the years. A Coppa Italia here, a European Cup Winners' Cup there – there wasn't a shortage of trophies heading Vujadin Boškov's way yet the Scudetto just remained a dream. For years those who occupied the Gradinata Sud longed for their first league title, constantly living in the shadow of their rivals Genoa, who had already won eight prior to the inaugural Serie A season in 1930. A long divide continued between the two sides, each hoping they could enter the new era with the biggest prize of all. And 61 years later the call of the Scudetto was answered, not in favour of the Grifone.

Step forward Sampdoria, the club that hadn't even been born until 1946 and the home of one Roberto Mancini for 15 years. Many know *Mancio* as the man in the dugout, leading Manchester City to their first Premier League title, while later coaching at Galatasaray and more recently Inter. But there was a time that the Italian wasn't shouting instructions from the touchline, wrapped up in a scarf on a cold, wintery night in Stoke.

His hair tells the story – short and grey resembles his life now, conducting from the touchline for the Nerazzurri. There came a time when the luxurious locks beamed light brown, golden even, reflecting just the type of player he was. He led the line of attack for the Blucerchiati alongside Gianluca Vialli, and the two crafted pure poetry on the pitch – the Shakespeare and Whitman of the footballing world. When Luca Pellegrini lifted the Scudetto that year, it was then Mancini knew he had made history. It had been what he wanted to do since he was just a boy, even if it did interfere with his classwork.

Roberto always had football on his mind. Each school day would be a torturous wait until he could kick a football again. It was as if he was deprived of food and water, the satisfying sound of leather against boot easing his woes. His teacher, Ms Bevilacqua, was once furious when her pupil Mancini had failed to do any work, as revealed in Luca Caioli's book *Roberto Mancini: A Footballing Life*. The inevitable tattletale we all experienced as a child stepped up, 'Roberto couldn't do his homework because he was playing football all day.' Bevilacqua's response was rather expected, responding with, 'What are you going to do with your life, if you don't study? Are you going to be kicking a ball around all day long?' If only she knew at the time what great powers of understanding she had of Mancini's future, she'd have left teaching and gone into psychic stage shows.

However, there really was only one man who produced the magic week after week to his adoring support. For Roberto was to be a footballer, receiving an early 14th birthday present from his father, Aldo Mancini, who allowed his son to move to Casteldebole due to Bologna wanting to welcome the 13-year-old in with open arms. He had played just 40 minutes of a practice game before the club's hierarchy called Roberto in to sign a contract. His dad completed the honour, signing the paper on his behalf, putting the footballing journey of his son into second gear, initiating the dream Roberto always wanted:

> 'I loved playing football; it was what I wanted to do, and then it became my life. I have had the chance to travel the world, to meet people and, above all play football. Bologna will be in my heart forever, because I was 13 when I got there, and I found a club and many extraordinary people who stood by me. It was the first step I took on my way to becoming a footballer.'
>
> – Luca Caioli's *Roberto Mancini: A Footballing Life*

His time at the Rossoblu was vital, growing into the player so many cherished during the 1980s and 1990s. At a time when such names as Diego Maradona and Paolo Rossi were ruling the roost, Mancini still managed to stand out at Sampdoria, creating brilliance that even *El Diez* and *Pablito* would be proud of. Bologna built Roberto into part of the man he became, the one who spent 15 years in Genoa. At this stage he was still in his teenage years, mingling with girls, kicking a football and enjoying life without limits. He was getting paid the incredible sum of 90,000 lire a week, or in simpler terms, £34. Roberto didn't care though, stating in his own words he was 'puzzled by the fact I was getting paid to play football and have fun' more than anything else.

The youth system worked its charm for Mancini, helping to make him understand what it meant to be a footballer and what you needed in order to become one for life. His determined attitude, hard-working nature and having that drive to succeed brought about his debut on 13 September 1981 against Cagliari. Mancini always had that sort of motivation though, remaining quietly confident of his ability but staying humble from the outset.

Tarcisio Burgnich, a former centre-back and five-time Scudetto winner, was the man who gave the young Italian his time to shine. Mancini was meant to have been in Rimini playing for the youth team but Burgnich had other ideas, installing him into the squad to host Cagliari. With 17 minutes left the flowing hair was already on show as Mancini entered the fray for Giuliano Fiorini. It culminated in a 1-1 draw and just a month later, on 4 October against Como, Mancini bagged his first goal.

Their opponents were leading 2-0, reflecting the disappointing start the Rossoblu had made in Serie A that year. Along popped Danilo Pileggi to reduce the deficit before Herbert Neumann split the Como defence like a comb through hair. Bad similes aside, the finish itself was far from a poor one. Roberto was through on goal, chasing down the ball that had landed in the box. As the Stadio Giuseppe Sinigaglia held its breath and prayed for goalkeeper and rather rhythmically-named Giuliano Giuliani to reach the ball first, Mancini delightfully lobbed it over the advancing Giuliani before the ball nestled into the net. One arm was held aloft, then two, then one again. It was evident the young man had no idea what to do with himself – he'd just scored his first professional goal though, and that's all that mattered.

It propelled Roberto on to another eight goals that season, ending the campaign as his club's top scorer with nine. It is a stat many would laugh at on first mention until remembering that the Italian was only 17 years old. All 30 games that year came and went for Mancini, playing in every single fixture under Burgnich and later Francesco Liguori. All appeared rosy in March 1982 when the Rossoblu sat on 21 points and in ninth place. Six games later, and they were 15th and hurtling toward Serie B.

The relegation prompted interest from a few clubs eyeing up young Roberto, and it was Sampdoria who made the first move. While the maturing *Mancio* went off on his holiday for the summer, the Blucerchiati had laid out a truly sumptuous offer for his services. Those who were really riled up by the news of Roberto's exit began small-scale riots, all while their baby-faced star lay on a sandy beach in his pants.

As news trickled through to Mancini of the interest surrounding him, including from Udinese and Juventus, he had to make up his mind. The Genoa-based club were quick with Bologna director Paolo Borea's move to Sampdoria making the decision a lot easier for Mancini. After discussions were held in a quaint little restaurant by Borea with father and son, he was persuaded to join them. 'Paolo Mantovani is building a great team, and you can become the main attraction,' Borea told Mancini as mentioned by Storie di Calcio. It clearly worked, and Roberto was on his way.

Four players headed in the direction of the Rossoblu as well as a rumoured 2.5bn lire – close to £950,000. At this time, prior to your transfer fees of around £80m, it was a substantial amount to be spending, bearing in mind Diego Maradona had just been bought by Barcelona for £3m. Regardless of the amount, Mancini was under the guidance of coach Renzo Ulivieri, but more importantly, club president Mantovani.

Mantovani left a lasting impression on Roberto, killing the supposed divide between player and president. He wasn't a man who'd walk into the dressing room and undermine the coach *cough* Silvio Berlusconi and Pippo Inzaghi *cough*. Mantovani connected with those he worked with at Sampdoria, firing up his troops when speaking. It was evident each word he uttered was chocked full of emotion and passion. Roberto virtually became like a son to Mantovani and *Mancio* opened up about the president on his official website:

> 'He was a dream, a man too great to be true. He used to speak once a year, but when he opened his mouth he was fulminating, two words were enough to get to the heart of the players. I met the president for the first time when I was 16 years old but the understanding with him was immediate, he was a man who did not need to raise his voice to be heard.'
>
> – Robertomancini.com

With Mantovani, it was to be the start of something special for *Mancio* and his new club, yet he wasn't to know what sort of heights they'd reach in the coming years. He joined the likes of Liam Brady, an Irish midfielder who had lit up England at Arsenal during the 1970s, and fellow front-man Alessandro Scanziani.

During that first season with the Blucerchiati, Ulivieri attempted to do something not many coaches aim to – build a player. As a player you grow into what you want to become. Of course there are guidelines set by each coach, but what the Sampdoria man tried to do was make Mancini what he was not – a goalscorer. Forwards don't have to be known for their goals. Take Roberto Baggio for example. Even with all his special strikes, he was the team player every single club wanted. He adapted to suit his own surroundings, much like Mancini in his coming years. This is not a tale of thunderous piledrivers and 20 goals a season but a story of a player who produced moments of brilliance that won his team vital trophies. If he wasn't scoring, he was assisting.

Crashing home a superb volley at the San Siro on matchday two and then squeezing one into the far corner a week later at home to Roma meant Ulivieri was adamant Mancini was an out-and-out centre-forward. Roberto's pleas to play the performing role of the second striker, or as it can also be referred to, the number ten role, fell on deaf ears. *Mancio*'s idol was Roberto Bettega, a man who became just that type of player when at Juventus. Ulivieri was blinded by his own arrogance and tried to turn him into Gunnar Nordahl. He scored four goals that year, and eight the following campaign. The 1984/85 season saw Sampdoria welcome Gianluca Vialli, Mancini's saviour. They would grow to become *Gernelli del Gol* – the goal twins – during their spell up front together. Had it not been for Vialli, it was likely Roberto would have returned to Bologna.

A three-league-goal season that also included Mancini winning the Coppa Italia, with three goals to his name in that tournament too, allowed his side entry into the 1986 European Cup Winners' Cup. It made no difference to Roberto's decision – they had lost out in the European competition in the fourth round and then given up their domestic trophy to Lazio in the final – he wanted to go back to the Rossoblu.

Cue Mantovani, the brilliantly balding president. He sat *Mancio* down and spoke to him. Ulivieri had since gone, with Eugenio Bersellini taking the reins, and he hadn't endeared himself to Roberto either. Mantovani wanted *Mancio* to stay. He wanted the young man to help rebuild the club, his way. Whenever there was a problem he would invite you round for dinner, probably rustling up a pizza in the process, and everything would be okay. With that, Bersellini was gone and in stepped Serbian Vujadin Boškov. The fun was about to begin.

The feeling inside the Blucerchiati camp was that something was bubbling up to fruition. A sixth place and then a fourth-place finish in Serie A at the end of the

1988/89 season sparked unrivalled optimism. Mancini had lifted two more Coppa Italia trophies and things were finally coming together.

Boškov wasn't holding *Mancio* back, allowing one of his most prized assets to roam free in the number ten role, understanding that keeping a player happy means good performances and therefore good results. A mentally aware coach first, a tactician second. As Paolo Brera put it in an interview with Luca Caioli, 'He [Boškov] was first and foremost a psychologist.' Mancini later mentioned how the 'barracks of Bersellini's training were broken' with Boškov 'bringing fun to training' and that 'the old fox would surprise us every day'.

Along came their biggest triumph thus far – the 1990 Cup Winners' Cup. Things were going well for Sampdoria in the league, sitting in the top five for the majority of the campaign, with European football trundling along at a constant pace. Norwegian side Brann had already felt the force of the goal twins, losing out 2-0 at home to the deadly duo before being defeated 1-0 at the Stadio Luigi Ferraris. Then along came Borussia Dortmund, ready and waiting to send Mancini home. At 1-0 down and with two minutes left to go, Roberto stepped up.

A long punt forward sent him through on goal. He delicately lobbed the ball over the goalkeeper, dropping it perfectly into the net in front of the travelling support. It was almost identical to his first goal in professional football yet it had occurred on the European stage. 'Ulivieri! Bersellini!' cried all of Genoa. 'Come have a little look at what you never believed in!' Boškov's side went on to win the tie 3-1 on aggregate and with Grasshopper and AS Monaco brushed aside, all of a sudden they were lining up at the Ullevi in Gothenburg for the final against Anderlecht. The game went all the way to extra time before Vialli gobbled up a goalkeeping error to put his side a goal to the good. As the clocked ticked down, Roberto delivered a cross with every last bit of energy left in his legs right on to his partner's head. Vialli had two, Sampdoria had two, *Mancio* had the European Cup Winners' Cup.

The momentum never seemed to drop from that moment on and all of a sudden the main course was ready to be delivered after the European appetiser – the Scudetto.

It all came as a surprise, considering Sampdoria had never managed to finish above fourth. The squad themselves never doubted their ability though, and had formed an unbreakable bond during the lead-up to the dreamlike season. Gone were the days of Ulivieri and Bersellini with the shackles well and truly off the players. They played out a near perfect campaign – scoring the most and conceding the second least amount.

For a side to conquer to likes of Milan, Inter and Napoli, seeing off players such as Marco van Basten and Diego Maradona, was nothing short of incredible.

The results began to hit calcio fans in the face like the Monty Python's Fish Slapping Dance – the goal twins were unstoppable. The opening-weekend victory over Cesena was expected, as were the following successes over Bologna and Atalanta. What followed was a 1-0 away win over the Rossoneri, and all of a sudden people's heads began to turn.

Then came Napoli, the home of *El Diez*. The Partenopei took a deserved lead then conceded four times. Vialli and Mancini were the centrepiece, the great three-tiered cake you licked the icing off of every now and again at a party to avoid drawing attention to yourself. The performance that ensued after falling a goal down was superb – someone must have eaten a whole tier of the sugary treat.

Two dreadful attempted clearances allowed two crosses to fall into the box. Vialli volleyed one, Mancini met the other. At 3-1 up, Roberto smacked home one of his finest goals. A long ball to the back post was pumped in where *Mancio* had set up camp. With his right foot he hooked the sweetest of volleys in off the post – the type of strike you try in the park that ends up residing in a bush, or swimming with the ducks.

Everything was working well. Too well. Vialli was fed by Mancini, who was fed by Attilio Lombardo. The 24-year-old Vialli wasn't blessed with incredible technique, or for that matter much hair, but his ability to pick a pass and cross a ball was more vital than ever. The following matchday brought about the Derby della Lanterna with Genoa. As typical as football can be, they lost their first game of the season, 2-1.

A period of only two wins from eight came during those torturous two months until Mancini and co. hit five wins on the bounce. Milan were dispatched 2-0 to complete a deserved double against Arrigo Sacchi's side before replicating their 4-1 victory over Napoli.

Along came 5 May 1991 with Inter hosting Sampdoria at the San Siro – only three points separated the sides with four games to go. The match was everything all calcio fans wanted it to be. Inter went at Sampdoria right from the off, the Nerazzurri knowing they *had* to win this game. They registered 24 shots that day to Sampdoria's six. The end result? A 2-0 Sampdoria victory.

It is advised to listen to this selected commentary of the goals from that incredible game of football here – *http://doria.altervista.org/1991/radiocronaca.wav* – while you read the outline of the game.

Gianluca Pagliuca could be thanked for that result, making a stupendous amount of saves during the first 45 minutes. *Mancio* only lasted that long, sent off for 'handbags' with Inter's Giuseppe Bergomi. Along came the second half with Vialli leaping on to a loose ball before playing it off to Giuseppe Dossena who leathered it home from 20 yards. Inter were soon awarded a penalty, with Lothar Matthäus handed the honour of recording his side's leveller. Instead, Pagliuca parried it away, and disaster ensued. Vialli wrapped up the win, somersaulting in joy, and the Scudetto was virtually Mancini's. *Guerin Sportivo* – an Italian sports magazine – ran with the title 'Samp Via Libera' – 'All Clear'. It summed up the match, the season, and Sampdoria as a whole. A 3-0 win two weeks later at home to Lecce completed all formalities but to Roberto, the Inter victory was what won them the Scudetto:

> 'We wanted to be the history of that club. I clearly remember the moment when I realised that it was our year. On the plane during the flight back from Naples to Genoa right after the 4-1. The Napoli fans were standing to applaud us at the end of the game. The Scudetto "formally" came in the penultimate matchday of the season versus Lecce, but "substantially" in the third-from-last matchday against Inter – where Gianluca Pagliuca saved everything – which ended with a 2-0 win. To me this was the crucial game of that first Scudetto. It was the victory of friendship and everyone's work – the president, the coach, the team and the loyal Sampdoria fans.'
>
> – Robertomancini.com

As *The Guardian* described the season in an article dated 25 June 2009, it really was 'one of football's great modern fairytales'. Mancini ended that year with 12 goals to his name, completing a truly spectacular achievement. His suspension saw him out of the win over Lecce and during the after-party, where many players donned a new hair colour, he remained true to his glorious locks. He later celebrated the acquisition of the Scudetto dressed up alongside Vialli as the band Europe though – he wasn't getting away with it that easily.

It proved the pinnacle of his career, with a European Cup Final loss to Barcelona rearing its ugly head a year later, spelling the end of Vialli's time at the Blucerchiati as the Italian moved to Juventus in 1992, along with the exit of Boškov to Roma. President Mantovani's death two years later destroyed *Mancio*, a loss to both player and club, with his son Enrico taking charge. Tensions mounted with Enrico telling Rai Sport that their 'relationship broke when I treated Mancini like an adult' before referring to Roberto as 'a spoiled brat'.

Roberto's goalscoring exploits improved under Sven-Göran Eriksson before the pair moved on to Lazio. The Italian closed out his career with another Scudetto at Lazio but it wasn't the same as the story of Sampdoria. That was what made the Genoa club as respected as they are to this very day. Mancini was everything to the Blucerchiati, and long shall Roberto be remembered as the dazzling and daring number ten, than his managerial persona. Or so we hope.

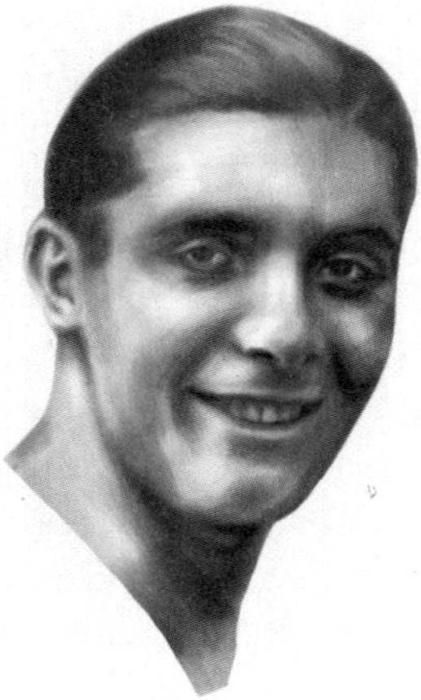

GIUSEPPE MEAZZA

'I have only two loves – my mother, and goals.'

– *La Stampa*

THESE were the words of Giuseppe Meazza, fitting for one of the finest strikers in calcio history. *Peppe*, or even *Il Balilla*, as he became more commonly known thanks to team-mate Leopoldo Conti referring to him as a 'boy scout' when starting out at Inter, was not just recognised for his goals and love for his mother however.

Flamboyant on the pitch and a hit with the ladies off it, Meazza would fit in quite well with today's footballers. He liked the champagne lifestyle – the bright lights that surrounded and consumed him and, of course, the odd cigar now and then. He was a man who would not look out of place in the Mafia with his slicked-back hair and suave dress sense.

He did his talking on the pitch however, predominantly for Inter, but also featured briefly for the red side of Milan and Juventus.

Football was the dream for Giuseppe but unlike most naive schoolboys, who enjoyed kicking a ball around the streets they inhabited, it was slightly different for him. Having grown up in a less-than-privileged family he had to make do with a ball of rolled-up old rags. A passer-by had seen the young lad running around the streets of Milan with his rags and not a care in the world. A passer-by who just so happened to be connected with the Nerazzurri.

It sounds like a scene from a predictable Hollywood blockbuster – a poor boy is whiling away the hours in the backstreets of where he lives and all of a sudden he is spotted by someone who can change his life forever. However, it is true, and Inter were fast to act – signing up Mezza at just 14 for their youth system. Cue the dramatic music playing behind Giuseppe as he prepares for his first match in Inter colours with tears in his eyes. He was of course a Milan fan, but that would not faze him. He did not waste time in stamping his authority on to the club, playing in a small tournament that Inter were participating in, making him catch the eye of coach Árpád Weisz. His debut was just around the corner and on 12 September 1927 the 17-year-old was gracing the fields at a professional level. It proved a successful game too – a 6-2 triumph in the Coppa Volta against US Milanese.

It was to be the start of a beautiful relationship between club and player, despite the odd quarrel with the directors due to his outgoing lifestyle. Meazza was thrown straight into the first team squad for the 1927/28 Division Nazionale season.

He notched up 12 goals across 33 games, only bettered by two other players at Inter – Fulvio Bernardini (17) and Enrico Rivolta (13) – who were four and five years older than Giuseppe respectively at the time. The Nerazzurri would go on to finish third in Group B and seventh in the final classifications.

The 1928/29 season would see Inter merge with US Milanese, the side Meazza made his debut against, creating Ambrosiana-Inter. A drastic increase in his goals occurred and this time around he scored 33 in 29. The goals were vital as they lifted Inter into sixth place, gaining them a spot in the newly-formed Serie A which would begin in 1929. It is worth noting however that Meazza's 45-goal haul of the past two seasons are therefore not registered as Serie A goals. Had the league been formed just two years earlier, he could have been far closer in the all-time scorers' table to Silvio Piola, who made his debut in 1930.

Serie A was thus born – the league that is still loved by millions to this very day was in full swing. The newly formed Ambrosiana, led by Meazza, won the first title by finishing just two points ahead of Genoa. Arguably it was the goals of Giuseppe that secured the Scudetto thanks to his stunning haul of 31 across 33 appearances – ten goals more than the next highest scorer in the league, Rodolfo Volk of Roma, as well as 16 more than team-mate Pietro Serantoni. It is still the record haul in a debut season for any player in Serie A, a statistic that only goes to reaffirm what the Italian achieved in that first campaign.

Ambrosiana collected some impressive results along the way in their successful season, including thumping home victories over Brescia (5-1), Livorno (6-2), Modena (5-1), Padova (6-1), Pro Patria (8-0) and Roma (6-0).

The game against the Giallorossi was a significant and memorable occasion. It was the first time Roma would play in Milan and the scoreline was one to savour for the Nerazzurri. Meazza was at the helm yet again, scoring four times.

He bagged a hat-trick of goals within three minutes – scoring in the first, third and fourth minutes of the game. It was nothing short of incredible.

He headed home the first thanks to a smart cross from Umberto Visentin before finishing off a swift move between Visentin and Serantoni. His incredible feat was completed when a whipped-in ball was turned home by the Italian. Antonio Blasevich then netted a minute later but it was ruled out by the officials.

Meazza grabbed his fourth soon after, leaving Roma goalkeeper Bruno Ballante dumbfounded. The man between the sticks had rushed out to meet Giuseppe for his first three goals despite being beaten every single time. He elected to stay on his line when Meazza was sent through again, but the outcome was still the same. *Il Balilla* had scored again. Incredibly, Giuseppe's four goals were beaten by two other players – Italo Rossi of Pro Patria and Giovanni Vecchina of Padova, with both scoring five in a single match during the campaign, but the focus will forever be on his brilliance against the Giallorossi.

He was also of great importance when they came up against Genoa in the 32nd game of the season. The Rossoblu were leading 2-0 but Meazza had other ideas, striking a sweet shot low into the bottom-right corner to get the Nerazzurri back in contention. They quickly fell two goals behind again only for *Peppe* to produce some more magical moments. He added to his opener with a curled effort before grabbing a wonderful goal. Early in the second half, Meazza collected the ball from the left, evaded a tackle from an oncoming defender, and skipped past the centre-half before hitting a terrific shot across the face of goal to bring his side level. The goal that secured his hat-trick helped keep Ambrosiana four points above their opponents. The superior goal difference of Meazza's team meant it was the result that all but secured the title.

Unfortunately, the superb game of football that took place is marred by injuries sustained by the spectators. Around 30 minutes before kick-off, with the stadium filling up, it seemed too many fans had been let in to watch what

was a sold-out match. A railing attached to the main stand gave way and over 50 supporters were reported to have fallen from a height of around four metres. The end result saw over 130 wounded but thankfully there were no fatalities. The game eventually started an hour after the proposed kick-off time and Meazza made sure his team would be going home with a point.

His 31 strikes, seeing him become Capocannoniere, were well over a third of Ambrosiana's total of 85 goals amassed over the 34-game season. Alongside this early accomplishment, the striker had also been progressing in the national team by making his full debut aged 19 against Switzerland in Rome, scoring twice. Meazza went on to become arguably the Azzurri's finest player during his playing career, although Gigi Riva may have something to say about that. His coach Vittorio Pozzo – a man who led Italy to two World Cup triumphs with Giuseppe – said:

> 'Having him [Meazza] in your team means you start every game 1-0 up.'
>
> – FIFA.com

Vittorio was not wrong and the 1930/31 season saw Meazza do what he did best – score goals. He found the net in the opening-day 5-1 victory over newly-promoted Casale. Despite Meazza's goal tally for the season ticking along at a constant pace, Ambrosiana were not as lethal as in their previous campaign. They were taken apart 6-0 by Torino in late October and then lost 5-0 to Triestina a week later. They did record a superb 4-1 victory against Milan in March – Meazza netting the fourth to round off a game which Serantoni shone in.

Meazza completed the season with 24 more goals to his name in 34 games, meaning he managed to appear in every single match that took place. Ambrosiana's fifth-place finish was less than satisfying for Árpád Weisz and his team, but Meazza still pulled out all the stops to be content with his own accomplishments. Roma's Volk denied Giuseppe a second successive Capocannoniere honour with 29 goals, but the real winner was Juventus's top scorer Raimundo Orsi, who despite only scoring 20 across the season helped his side lift their third Scudetto.

Such titles would be hard to come by for Ambrosiana and *Peppe*, aside from their earlier achievement. The 1931/32 Serie A season again saw a mediocre finish of sixth, coming below even the Rossoneri who improved on their previous finish. *Il Balilla* kept his consistent run of scoring going by notching 21.

The following year brought a bit more joy to Ambrosiana, finishing as runners-up to Juventus who claimed their third Scudetto in a row. During the season, while training with the Azzurri, team-mate and Bianconeri goalkeeper Gianpiero Combi was stunned to see a beautifully executed bicycle kick fly past him thanks to Meazza's brilliance. Combi reportedly turned round to *Peppe* and bet the young man be could not perform such a feat at domestic level against the Old Lady. This wager was also matched with another – that Meazza could not side-step him to score. Combi believed no player could do this.

So 25 May 1923 soon reared its head for a game between Meazza and Combi's respective clubs, which ended in a 2-2 draw in Milan. Did Meazza win the bet? Well, sort of.

Meazza was the supposed scorer of two quite incredible goals against Juventus but there are contradicting reference points to these claims. Meazza did net a fantastic bicycle kick just 15 minutes into the game. This incredible goal and exact replica of his training-ground strike has not been disputed, but the official stat website RSSSF (Rec. Sport.Soccer Statistics Foundation) has team-mate Felice Levratto as the goalscorer for the second. Sticking firstly with the much-publicised fact that Meazza did in fact score both, the rounding of Combi was one of pure brilliance.

The forward managed to dribble past numerous defenders before rounding Combi and passing into an open net. Apparently the goalkeeper got to his feet immediately to shake Giuseppe's hand, a gracious and outstanding moment.

However, going with the statistical side of the story, Levratto had scored the second with a delightfully brilliant free kick. Meazza has 20 goals registered to his name for the 1932/33 season and that is the undisputed figure. This is true only if Levratto did indeed score the second goal. If not, and the side-stepping goal story did occur, Meazza would have 21 goals for the season. This again means that if the story was true and he had scored both and registered 21 goals, his Serie A all-time total would sit at 217. This is one more than José Altafini, who shares joint fourth with Giuseppe in the record books on 216.

There are various versions of Meazza's brilliance in front of goal, as well as his off-field antics that preceded games. He was getting incredibly wealthy as he was growing older and becoming a national icon. This was the man who was advertising toothpaste and brilliantine when he was a mere teenager. The same man who then went on to smoke 60 cigarettes a day after spending the night out partying – followed by a flock of fans wanting to catch a glimpse of him.

His life outside of football did soon affect his life in the game however. According to some stories, on one matchday *Peppe* had awoken in someone else's bed just minutes before kick-off, only to race back home in his pyjamas to get ready in time. It is said Meazza stated the following referring to the story:

> 'Luckily I lived near the stadium, and I managed to get there in a rush. My team-mates and the coach looked at me disapprovingly. It was only five minutes before the kick-off, so I quickly changed and joined the team on the pitch. I could hear the Inter directors saying, "We'll deal with him after

> the match. We'll find out what he's been up to."
> Luckily I scored a hat-trick so afterwards no one said a word!'
>
> Giuseppemeazza.it

Meazza's quite remarkable stories have come to the surface from various journalistic sources so his extraordinary career in places must be taken lightly. One thing is for sure, his goalscoring exploits on the pitch were incredible.

They continued in 1933/34, again scoring over 20 goals to prepare himself for the World Cup that was to be hosted in his home country. Meazza retained the Golden Ball as well as becoming a World Cup winner. He scored 18 in 1934/35, guiding Ambrosiana to their third consecutive runners-up position as it seemed they would just never topple Carlo Carcano's Juventus. They did finish above the Bianconeri the following season but ended up completing the campaign in fourth with Bologna lifting their third title.

It was still a memorable season for *Peppe* as he managed to acquire his second Capocannoniere with 25 goals, his most in a season since 1930. Meazza was on hand to grab a late equaliser to secure a draw against Milan two games into the season and got his first hat-trick two weeks later in a 4-0 home victory over Palermo. His finest performance of the season came against Napoli with Ambrosiana coming out 4-2 winners. Giuseppe bagged an impressive brace including a superb turn and shot that left goalkeeper Vittorio Mosele stunned. The goal tally dropped suddenly in 1936/37 with only 11 scored but they were quickly forgotten about when Meazza and Ambrosiana would win their second Scudetto together.

The 1937/38 season would be a fascinating one due to the many stories that unfolded in Serie A involving Meazza. He scored his first goal on the opening day in a 3-3 draw with Lucchese and added a brace against Fiorentina soon after. The main attraction occurred on 9 January when Ambrosiana played host to Bari. Meazza was simply astounding, and arguably no superlatives could capture his brilliance that day. Ambrosiana ran out 9-2 winners with *Peppe* scoring five of those. Meazza bagged his first and his side's third inside the opening 20 minutes, finishing off a move started by team-mate Nicola Ferrara. He gained an assist two minutes later and scored his second and Ambrosiana's fifth in the 34th minute. They ended the half 5-2 up.

Meazza scored a second-half hat-trick to complete his own haul with Antonio Ferrara also getting in on the act. The incredible result saw Ambrosiana sit four points clear of Bologna, Genoa and Juventus who were all hot on their tail. Meazza also scored a hat-trick the following week against Lucchese, in case anyone missed his heroics of the previous game.

Ambrosiana were keeping themselves just above the chasing pack and in early February they met reigning champions Bologna. It is likely this is the match the story regarding Meazza's lion tale relates to, as opposed to the supposed game against Juventus it was said to have been. Apparently *Peppe* had spent the previous night partying and was yet to arrive at the ground with kick-off fast approaching. Two members of the backroom team supposedly searched for Meazza and found him in his home fast asleep. He was dragged to the ground, getting changed on the way while telling his saviours about feeling like a lion during his night's escapades. He went on to bag a brace in the game, securing a vital two points to keep them a point above Genoa.

Many seem to believe this story is combined with Ambrosiana's 2-1 win over Juventus. Unfortunately this is untrue – Meazza did not play in this victory – he was suspended due to being sent off two weeks earlier against Napoli. The fact Ambrosiana finished two points above the Bianconeri in the final standings means the folk story has more depth, suggesting Meazza won his side the title despite partying heavily the previous night.

The Scudetto was successfully secured on the final day of the season with mathematically five sides battling for the title. Ambrosiana travelled to face Bari, the side they had defeated 9-2 earlier in the season. They would score seven fewer goals compared to the earlier clash but the outcome was still the same. It took until the 70th minute for Meazza and his side to find the opening – *Peppe* heading home from a corner. Annibale Frossi completed the scoring in the final minute, latching on to an awful back-pass to secure Ambrosiana's second Scudetto.

His strike in the final match also made sure he would finish with 20 goals and become Capocannoniere for the third time. Runner-up Guglielmo Trevisan of Triestina also impressed, scoring 18 across the season, over half his team's goals. Meazza had prepped himself perfectly for the 1938 World Cup finals in which he captained Italy and won the most sought-after trophy in world football.

Giuseppe had been suffering from poor fitness throughout the tournament however and it showed in 1938/39 Serie A, making just 16 appearances out of a possible 30 games.

He was also made to sit it out for 30 days of the season due to refusing to play a match against Triestina and he completed the season with just four goals. *Peppe* did at least play a part in securing Ambrosiana's first Coppa Italia – defeating Novara 2-1 in the final. Meazza played in all six matches of the tournament except the 3-1 win over Genoa in the semi-final.

Unfortunately his appearance stats are all that are pinned to *Il Balilla* for this success as he failed to find the net in any of the matches. His final goal for the Nerazzurri came a few months earlier – a penalty in a 1-1 away draw against Bologna. The record books do state Meazza was still an Ambrosiana player in 1939/40, when they lifted the Scudetto yet again, but he played no part in the team's success due to a foot problem.

There would be just five more years left in Meazza's career and for the first time he would wear a shirt that was not black and blue. Instead it would be the red and black of Milan that would be *Peppe*'s shirt for the next two years. It was the start of the slow demise of one of calcio's greatest, although he did score nine goals in his two years at Milan. Ironically, and in football rather expectedly, his first goal came 18 weeks into the season against his former club Ambrosiana – scoring with just seven minutes left in a 2-2 draw.

In 1942 he moved over to Juventus, ten to his name and again putting one past Ambrosiana in a 4-2 home win and a consolation in a 3-1 away defeat. A brief spell at Varese during wartime football was followed with a player-coach role at Atalanta, netting twice as he saw his new club finish tenth. He made his return to his beloved club, by now known as Internazionale, again as a player-coach. *Peppe* bagged two goals on his comeback in a season remembered more for his emotional re-appearance than anything, before his incredible playing career finally came to a close.

His legacy has been immortalised in the renaming of the San Siro in 1980 and a minute's silence remembering the great striker following his death in 1969. Meazza always knew his achievements would live on and his legacy would remain, apparently saying the following a year before he passed away:

> 'I was Meazza. Everyone knows me. In ten years and even in 20 years' time people attending football matches will still be aware of Meazza. They will know who Meazza was.'
>
> – *La Stampa*

GUNNAR NORDAHL

INTRODUCED BY ANTONIO LABBATE

'Nordahl was born to score goals. He could score with his eyes closed.'

– George Raynor, coach of Sweden

GIANNI Agnelli picked up the phone and dialled. He was calling the boss of Fiat's Stockholm office 2,000km away with a problem. But it was nothing to do with his expanding car empire, instead it was a footballing matter of the utmost importance. By the time that conversation ended, Agnelli had inadvertently changed the history of the Italian game.

Agnelli's request was for his man in Scandinavia to suggest a player who could be offered to Milan as an apology for Juventus's decision to hijack the Diavolo's move for Johannes Pløger. The latter, a Danish attacker, was all set to sign for the Milanese giants until Juve official Remo Giordanetti intercepted the striker at Milan's train station. A more attractive financial offer saw Pløger jump in a car to Turin and set up Nordahl's arrival in January 1949. The rest, as they say, is history.

Unfortunately, the grainy black and white images of the 1940s and 1950s simply don't do Nordahl justice. For the modern-day football enthusiast, Nordahl belongs to a generation of lost talents who played in a time which was predominantly captured by the written word and modest television coverage which was still very much in its infancy.

Nordahl is Serie A royalty. Of that there is no doubt. His goalscoring feats and his role in Milan's *Gre-No-Li* trinity – alongside Swedish compatriots Gunnar Gren and Nils Liedholm – make sure of that. Yet you look at what the former fireman achieved on the peninsula and you are always left with the same two questions. The first is how many goals he could have scored in Italian football had he moved to the country earlier than 27. The second is what he would have achieved had he come along 30 or 40 years later, when the Italian game was more tactical. There are no definite answers here but the likelihood is that we'd still be talking about him today.

While we have all rightly stood up and applauded the delicate technical brilliance of the likes of Gianni Rivera, Diego Maradona and Roberto Baggio while being brought up on bread, salami and calcio, you can't fully digest Serie A history until you've seen Nordahl either subtly exploit space or bluntly blast home in between the sticks.

There are few more satisfying sights than Nordahl unleashing a rocket. In later life the former Swedish international often spoke of how his Milan team-mates provided him with simple finishes, yet he was being modest. Sure, he was a fine six-yard box poacher, but boy could he ripple a net. Check out any of his 11 volleys from his 35 goals in 1949/50 and you'll hear the ball whoosh as it punches a hole in the air.

Nordahl spent seven goal-filled years at Milan during a spell where he announced himself as a star of the European game and one of calcio's greatest ever forwards. Pløger, on the other hand, lasted 16 games in Turin. He scored once.

Antonio Labbate

Héctor Puricelli's AC Milan headed into the final three games of the 1954/55 Serie A season just three points better off than Udinese in the race for the Scudetto. Gunnar Nordahl, the newly-appointed captain and the Rossoneri's prized asset, was also battling out his own mini competition for Capocannoniere with the Zebrette's Lorenzo Bettini. The latter was already on 18 goals, one less than the Swedish forward with just 270 minutes of league football left. Bettini would go on to get two, securing a very respectable 20 for the season. Nordahl wasn't a player from this planet though – there was something different about the striker.

He ended up with 27 that season, scoring eight in the remaining three games. Genoa (8-0), Spal (6-0) and Pro Patria (1-1) all had to feel the pain of conceding to Nordahl although pain is probably the least appropriate word. Teams in Italy were used to letting in a goal or four against him, Spal found to their cost, like it was a general occurrence. But the pain of conceding would subside almost immediately when they realised they had been breached by the Swede. Quite like when you stub your toe – a sharp pain that subsides quickly – that was what it felt like when Nordahl hit one that flew into the top corner. He was *Il Bisonte* – the Bison – using his 14st to his advantage, knocking down defenders like the battering ram he was before trying to break the net, taking the goalposts with it.

The final strike – against Pro Patria – capped off that year with a second Scudetto and he also achieved his fifth Capocannoniere honour. They also called him *Il Cannoniere* – the Gunner – for his namesake and goalscoring ability. The top scorer trophy was virtually crafted just for him.

The Swede was just a normal child growing up in his home country back in the 1920s and was one of ten children, five of which were boys who all had the same dream – to become a footballer. Only one would truly achieve that, and we all know how successful he was too. Two of his brothers – Gösta and Göran – managed to maintain some local fame in terms of the sport, turning a once poverty-stricken family into a stable one.

It was during his childhood and teenage years that Nordahl developed his humble nature, one that would serve him well during his time in Italy. His desire to become a footballer finally took flight, leaving behind his monotonous job at Ängerån's brewery for amateur side Hörnefors IF. After impressing for the youth team his first team debut was just around the corner in 1935 and he began dropping in and out of the team for two years despite scoring 68 goals in 41 appearances.

That proved enough to see him sign for Degerfors IF in August 1940 and make his debut just a month later on 8 September against Gårda. Everything was gelling for Nordahl as he began life at his new club. He was finding the net and finding love too, meeting his wife-to-be Irma Berg on a night out. A love secured when Gunnar elected to give her a free ticket to his next home match. Even at 20 years old the Swede was scoring on and off the pitch.

Nordahl kept plundering the goals for the next four years, progressing on to IFK Norrköping where he would acquire his first taste of success. Norrköping were one of the biggest clubs in Sweden and also offered him a job as

IL CANNONIERE
GUNNAR
NORDAHL

a fireman. His main love was the beautiful game yet many would have to try and put out Gunnar when he was on form – the Swede was red hot when in the mood for goals. They never seemed to dry up or fizzle out when Gunnar was on the pitch, helping Norrköping to four Allsvenskan following his move in 1944. His 87-goal return was rather stupendous given the fact he had been representing his team week in week out during the aftermath of the Second World War. He won the league's top scorer award three times while he was there, something which has never been bettered and is unlikely to be.

His success in front of goal and leaving goalkeepers either scratching their heads or in the back of the net with the ball finally culminated in a move to Italy. It was a big choice for Gunnar at the time as it meant he was ineligible to play for his nation Sweden. Nordahl had already built up a much more modest reputation than a certain modern-day star, Zlatan Ibrahimović, scoring 43 times in 33 games. He also achieved fame in London during the 1948 Olympic Games by guiding his country to the gold medal in the football tournament, making coach George Raynor utter the infamous and aforementioned quote that began Nordahl's segment.

He wasn't wrong, and it was a massive decision for Nordahl to make. The dream of turning professional and representing one of the greatest football clubs in the world was too good to refuse. His Swedish foot was now firmly in Italy, despite the abnormality of the transfer outlaid in the introduction, opening the door for more compatriots from his home country to come over. It meant that by the 1949/50 Serie A, the famous *Gre-No-Li* – formed of Gunnar Gren, Nordahl and Nils Liedholm who had lit up the Swedish national team attack – were reunited at the Rossoneri.

Let's not get too ahead of ourselves here though. Gunnar was yet to make his own debut for Milan following his move in January 1949 and after sitting in the stands for the 1-1 draw with Atalanta at the Stadio Atleti Azzurri d'Italia, it was finally time for Italy to meet Gunnar Nordahl.

When he made his debut for Milan on 27 January 1949 – a game with Pro Patria that had been moved – it was one of joy, and a surefire sign of things to come. He netted, rather unsurprisingly, to give his side a 2-1 lead in what would eventually be a hard-fought 3-2 victory. The Italian press were quick to jump on Nordahl with praise and a little joke here and there. *La Stampa* said that Nordahl 'worked hard even though he is *tondo e grassoccio* – round and plump – but despite the poor shape he is a player of class'. The striker himself opened up about his first of what would be 210 for Milan, saying he put absolutely everything into making sure the ball hit the net:

> 'Guðmundsson [Albert] went past the first opponent and then another before crossing the ball into the area. I was at full speed running into the box and I knew that I had a great opportunity to score. Everything was right – the approach, impact, direction. I had the weight, power and pure desire to get to that ball. I think it was my most valuable goal.'
>
> – Gunnar Nordahl's *Guld och gröna planer*

The debut goal had sparked Nordahl into life and two weeks later he scored twice in the Derby della Madonnina, netting from close range and a pinpoint cross. The media were still quick to criticise the Swede however, with commentators from the derby with Inter and the 2-1 win over Novara a couple of weeks later – in which he also scored – referring to him as 'invisible'. Gunnar wouldn't let such complaints get to him considering the fact he was a new player, in a new country, and wasn't even able to properly communicate with his players.

Despite all of those hurdles he knew he had to overcome, there was a tally of 16 goals to his name in only 15 appearances at the end the season, not bad for a man who couldn't speak the language of the country he resided and worked in. His goals did mean fame and fortune were soon around the corner. Nordahl was at one of the world's biggest clubs and they treated him like one of the world's best. A fully furnished stunning house in the centre of Milano was his with just the click of a finger, but he opted to choose an inexpensive place just on the cusp of the city.

Fame was not something that would ever trouble Gunnar – he was the epitome of a man, not a football player. He grew up in modest surroundings and kept it that way. When others were living the champagne lifestyle, he was signing autographs until dark. Nordahl wasn't fazed by what he could have but strived to give others what they couldn't get.

But what he did hand out in spades to those who adored him was plenty of goals. After his successful half a year with the Rossoneri he was ready to kick off the new campaign in style. Milan had finished third the previous season and had then brought in a coach the striker knew very well – Lajos Czeizler, Nordahl's former tactician from his Norrköping days. Gunnar made sure his position of authority that had persuaded club president Antonio Busini to appoint Czeizler as coach didn't go to waste, and also said they should get a hold of two attackers in the shape of Gren and Liedholm. *Gre-No-Li* would thus be the centrepiece for the upcoming 1949/50 Serie A season. With Italy still mourning the loss of *il Grande Torino* in the Superga tragedy – of which more can be read about in Giampiero Boniperti's section of *Calcio's Greatest Forwards* – the Swedish trio all started in the opening game, Liedholm the one to get on the scoresheet in a 3-1 away win against Sampdoria. Nordahl didn't have to wait long to get off the mark, opening the scoring with just a minute to go at home to Como on matchday two, only to concede with the final kick of the game.

The Rossoneri entered matchday ten ahead of the Derby della Madonnina in third place, four points behind leaders

Juventus and level with Inter. The attack of *Gre-No-Li* were doing their job, having only failed to score in two matches thus far. The focus on the forwards from Czeizler did mean he undermined the defence, seeing as they only had two clean sheets to show for it before facing the Nerazzurri. It proved costly in one of the finest derby matches the two Milan sides would ever play out.

Enrico Candiani gave the red side of Milan the perfect start, firing home twice in the opening seven minutes to give the Rossoneri a two-goal advantage. Inter man István Nyers popped up from close range to pull one back before the ever-present Nordahl did what he does best. Liedholm got himself on the scoresheet in the 19th minute, meaning that Milan led 4-1. Inter seemed as if they were resigned to the fact they would lose but goals from Amedeo Amadei and Nyers ensured they would still have a fighting chance going into half-time. Amadei was in the mood for a comeback and made it 4-4 just after the interval with Benito Lorenzi then handing Inter the lead for the first time. Carlo Annovazzi's strike brought Milan level before Amadei grabbed his hat-trick and gave the Nerazzurri all three points.

Lo Sport Illustrato – a supplement from *La Gazzetta dello Sport* – produced the headline *'Pioggia a San Siro per le Difese senza Ombrello'* – 'Rain at the San Siro for the defences with no umbrella'. It was fitting for a game filled to the brim with 11 goals, and also showcased the shoddy defensive display by both teams. It was a somewhat typical performance expected of a team managed by Czeizler – tons of goals scored and shipped.

Milan were able to put the result in the back of their minds after dismantling Bari 9-1 on 18 December, keeping in touch with the other teams racing for the Scudetto. Nordahl's finest result of the season came in February when Milan visited Turin to face leaders Juve. It was a big occasion in Italy with the match being the first to air live on Italian television. The top two would play out one of the most memorable clashes in calcio history but one side will wish to forget this torrid day. It started so well for the Old Lady too, John Hansen gobbling up a chance to put the Bianconeri a goal to the good.

It would be the last time the Juventini would be celebrating that day as Nordahl had other ideas, smashing home to level the game at 1-1. From then on, it was all Milan. Gren and Liedholm picked up two in two minutes before *Il Bisonte* got his second a couple of moments later. Pure chaos was ensuing inside the Stadio Municipale. Nordahl grabbed his hat-trick soon after, then goals from Renzo Burini and Candiani completed the 7-1 win. The main Swede didn't manage to see all of the game on the field though. Gunnar Gren, one third of the *Gre-No-Li* trio, said Juventus just fell apart, with the anger boiling over so much that Nordahl ended up going off on a stretcher and missing the remainder of the win:

> 'After John Hansen grabbed the first goal, it became our turn to score and we led 4-1 before the end of the half. Juventus began to collapse like a house of cards. The usually likeable and calm player Carlo Parola kicked out at Nordahl during the match. Gunnar had to be carried off and it was a while until he was okay again. After the match the Juventus president and Parola came into our dressing room and apologised to him.'
>
> – Gunnar Gren's *Med Grenoli i Italien*

The result humiliated Juventus, with *Corriere dello Sport* running with the headline '*Il Milan ipnotizza la Juventus e l'umilia con una clamorosa vittoria'* – 'Milan hypnotise Juventus and humiliate them with a resounding victory'. In a season full of incredible results for Nordahl to savour, the Bianconeri had the last laugh by securing the Scudetto over Milan by five points. Astonishingly, the Rossoneri bettered

Juve's goal tally by 18 and only conceded two more, but were unable to topple Jesse Carver's men. It was a tough blow for Nordahl, who was very much a team player, and even his 35-goal haul that saw him become Capocannoniere – a tally that has never been bettered – was little consolation.

As expected, *Il Cannoniere* simply dusted himself down and was ready to go again. The learning curve of the previous season paid dividends with Italy's biggest prize just around the corner.

Right from the off they meant business, thumping Udinese 6-2 to get the new campaign under way in style. *Gre-No-Li* were at their best with Nordahl netting four on matchday three in a 9-2 triumph over Novara. Heading into December the Rossoneri were sitting just a point behind Inter when they went to visit Atalanta. It was here that another fascinating game of football was played, one regularly forgotten about in which Milan ran out 7-4 winners. *Il Bisonte* barged through the defence on a number of occasions, scoring twice in the captivating game. There is an incredible photograph taken following the match of Nordahl, completely drenched in the rain and mud, signifying just how much he gave to the cause. It can be viewed via *http://www.magliarossonera.it/img195051/uff235_1951.jpg.*

The result kept Milan in touch with rivals Inter and the two would continue to lock horns until the penultimate day. If Milan avoided defeat against Lazio they were guaranteed the title, but despite Nordahl's best efforts and goal they lost 2-1. The Rossoneri would have to wait patiently in the dressing room to find out their fate. Then news came through that Inter had lost 2-1 to Torino and Nordahl had helped guide Milan to their first Scudetto since 1907.

It was a historical Scudetto win, one that was fought virtually up until the very end. The final points total of 60 was enough to better rivals Inter by just one. The title was *Gre-No-Li*'s and no one could take that away from the

Swedish trio. The trophy belonged really to one man though – Gunnar Nordahl. He had scored the only goal of a 1-0 win back in March against the Nerazzuri. Had it not been for his decision to move to Milan from Norrköping and give up playing for his country, his Swedish team-mates would never have had the chance to turn professional. The unselfishness of Gunnar meant many succeeded beyond their wildest dreams and yet he took none of the plaudits, remaining thankful for what he was lucky enough to have. He also had a second Capocannonieri to his name, this time with the aid of 34 goals.

It was the high point of *Il Cannoniere*'s time in Italy. Even after winning another Scudetto in 1954/55, it would not have anything on Milan's historic success in 1951. He'd secured another three Capocannonieri in that time too, immortalising himself into the history of the Italian game and Milan's hall of fame with 210 Serie A goals in total, a stat that looks like it will never be topped for the Rossoneri. Despite what Piola accomplished in terms of goals, Nordahl would always be first in a fantasy dream team of players you would want up front. He decided to move on from his beloved side in 1956 to Roma, where he spent two years before electing to retire.

His final game came at the age of 37 when the Giallorossi visited Genoa. They won 4-2, with Gunnar securing his final goal in the last minute of his career. It was fitting for a man who virtually ate goals for dinner.

It must have been a privilege to see such a man play, watching him find the goal in pretty much most games he participated in. Even if you were an opposition supporter it would have been hard not to stand up and applaud some of Nordahl's brilliance. His trademark was that of a thunderbolt from the edge of the area, leaving goalkeepers rooted to the spot, or carrying the ball with them into the back of the net. He was quite simply unstoppable. He was *Il Cannoniere.*

SILVIO PIOLA

INTRODUCED BY JOHN FOOT

'The man on the street looks upon you as an example to be followed. You must remain, for us, what you have always been...a superman, an idol.'

– Gianni Brera on Silvio Piola

I WOULD have loved to see Silvio Piola play in the flesh. What a physical specimen he must have been. Strong as an ox. How else could he have played for so long, on those pitches, with those defenders? How else could he have scored so many goals? How else could he have played on until he was in his 40s, scoring dozens of goals for lowly Novara in Serie A?

He scored his last goal at the age of 40. But what a player he must have been in his prime. A battering ram of a forward. He was unstoppable. A goal machine as well, the holder of what still looks like an unbreakable goal record. And all this was achieved with a career that included the war years, when it took Piola six hours to get from Vercelli to Turin by train – a journey that now only takes just over an hour. It wasn't even the time lost to war, but also the privations of that period – the lack of food, the bombings of the cities, the deportations. Many players died, or never recovered from these traumatic experiences and surroundings. Piola carried on playing, and scoring – for 21 seasons.

Today, the word 'phenomenon' is bandied about for all kinds of mediocre players. But Piola was just that, a phenomenon. He only played 34 times for Italy but he managed to win the 1938 World Cup in that time and he had a scoring record of almost a goal a game. This was a player who comes around once in a lifetime – the true definition of a phenomenon. He was a force of nature.

John Foot

Since the inaugural Serie A season in 1929, there have since been over 80 Scudetti given to 11 different clubs. During 21 of those years, a man by the name of Silvio Piola took Italy by storm, scoring a record 274 league goals that has remained untouched since his retirement in 1954. Many a Scudetto was awarded during the war-hit period of Serie A while he played out his career, and yet not one felt the grasp of the Italian. It just kept eluding him, always ending up a few spots off of the league table's summit. Six teams managed to lift the biggest prize in Italian football while Silvio stood and watched.

Here was a man who didn't need trophies to signify what he achieved in his professional career. He drew in crowds of people, captivating them with every touch of the ball. His mantlepiece may have remained empty and collecting dust during his life but Silvio's brilliance in front of goal secured him as an icon in Italy. His tally of strikes for Pro Vercelli, Novara and Lazio means his legacy will live long in the memory of all those who love calcio, and even 62 years on from his retirement, nothing seems to have changed.

If Silvio was to feature in a dictionary, his name would be mentioned as an example for every superlative that exists. He was breathtaking, astonishing and quite frankly unrivalled. Not bad for a man born a year prior to the outbreak of the First World War, as on 29 September 1913 the preposterously perfect Piola was introduced to the world and he never looked back.

Silvio began it all at Pro Vercelli's youth set-up thanks to being scouted out by a priest who loved the beautiful game, answering his prayers to become a footballer. He debuted for the first team aged just 16 in a 2-2 draw away at Bologna. Piola played out just four games that season at his young age, while Giuseppe Meazza – another of our *Calcio's Greatest Forwards* – lit up that inaugural Serie A campaign with 31 goals.

What proves intriguing is the stark contrast between Piola and Meazza. Of course, at this stage Silvio was still a young man, yet to even have the opportunity to taste the life of a footballer away from the field. During their respective careers, while Meazza was living the champagne lifestyle and awakening in strangers' beds on the day of a league fixture, Piola stayed humble and away from the limelight. John Foot describes Piola's life in his book *Calcio: A History of Italian Football* as 'reclusive' while also mentioning that 'he neither drank, nor smoked nor womanised and he disliked doing adverts'. To read about two incredible forwards at the height of their careers leading such different lives is compelling, showcasing how even though they both shared the same profession, neither led the same life at all. Silvio simply focused on his football, making no change to the mentality he had after his first campaign in Serie A.

Coach József Nagy elected to install Piola into the starting 11 following his brief showing in the previous campaign. It may have taken until 2 November 1930 for Silvio to score the first of his 274 top-flight goals but it was one he would cherish forever. It came, rather poignantly, against the club that would be his long-term home in football – Lazio. Despite being nimble on both feet and surprising defenders at every turn in the near future with the ability to shoot from distance with either his left or right foot, Piola opened his account with his head. All 5ft 10in of pure Italian brilliance leapt into the air, bandage and all wrapped around his forehead, powering home the game's first goal. It was from this very moment that everything began to take shape.

Yes, it is rather clichéd and synonymous with pretty much every other footballer with mentioning that exact 'time' in their profession when things truly came to fruition, but Piola's first goal was that valuable breakthrough moment. It symbolised the start of his incredible goalscoring feat in Serie A, the point in which Ezio Sclavi – Lazio's goalkeeper at the time – picked the ball out of the back of net, the first of a long line of goalkeepers who would have to perform such a monotonous task. No one knew just what this header signified, including Silvio himself, but in hindsight it meant the starting point of one of Italy's finest ever strikers was ticked off of the checklist.

The rest of the campaign trundled along with Piola taking no prisoners, firing past Pro Patria, Brescia and then netting three at home to Napoli in a captivating 6-3 victory. It was this game when Piola truly experienced fear first hand, having defeated the side his uncle Giuseppe Cavanna played in goal for. Piola was a young man, not yet fully an adult, so he was fully aware a spanking was well on the cards that night! He won his side 13 points that year, and also scored the joint third highest amount of goals – 13 – in the second half of the season, only bettered by Rodolfo Volk, Cesare Fasanelli and Meazza. He achieved all of this at just 17 years old while the other three were 25, 24 and 21 respectively.

He continued his meteoric rise, setting his first goalscoring record on 22 November 1931 when he scored four times at Alessandria, the most amount of goals by a single player away from home. The record stood for 33 years until Kurt Hamrin managed five away to Atalanta. By the end of 1933/34 Piola had produced 51 goals, including yet another record. Scudetti may have come and gone without Piola grasping one close to his chest, but goalscoring was a regular occurrence. In 1933, with Pro Vercelli taking on Fiorentina, Piola netted after just 60 seconds – his first of six in the game.

It was moments like this we all wish could have been captured on camera, and only our understanding of what Silvio could do on a football field can feed our imagination of what went on during that match. As such, Silvio was attracting some serious interest from a number of different clubs. One of those was Ambrosiana-Inter, the home of Meazza, but the higher authority seemed to disregard the move because of a possible unstoppable partnership of Giuseppe and Silvio, or so was the reason.

Piola dreamed of teaming up with Meazza, as at this point he hadn't done so with the Azzurri, so moving to Ambrosiana-Inter was the only viable option. Torino were also hot on the tail of Silvio, another possible option which could lead to a Scudetto. However, Lazio remained in the background watching these events unfold. The Biancocelesti housed arguably the nation's biggest supporter – Benito Mussolini.

The Prime Minister was drawn to the club due to the fact Lazio were founded by Italian army officers and as such it screamed the perfect place for Benito and his fascist regime to continue to grow in stature. At the time Mussolini was well aware of the power sport held in terms of political gain,

PIOLA
LAZIO

something he had to try and explain to Adolf Hitler, who wasn't the biggest fan of sport. The German leader tried to understand what Mussolini meant, attending his first football match during the 1936 Olympics. Germany ended up losing 2-0 to Norway and he never went again.

While Piola was engaging in his military service having turned 21, it was the best possible time for Lazio to get their man. It left Silvio with little to no choice. His questions on what had happened to the offers from the Nerazzurri and the Granata fell on deaf ears as his pen hovered above the contract laid before him. He was to be a Lazio player.

Piola would go about his business at the club as soon as possible, scoring on his debut on 30 September 1934 in a 6-1 thrashing of Livorno. Twenty-one goals in his first season was a worthy tally and it was here that he obtained his first proper nickname, *Piola-gol.* It was rather more appealing than his original *Aquilotto* – Eaglet – due to his youth and rather large nose. Paola Piola, daughter of Silvio, spoke of her father's connection with Lazio and what it meant to him to play for the Biancocelesti:

> 'He told me that the Biancocelesti was a crucial period of his growth as a man and an athlete. Leaving the small province of Vercelli for the big city was not easy for him. Each team he played for he left something behind. Each of these clubs produced a piece of the puzzle to move on to the next piece.
>
> If it were not for Pro Vercelli, there would be no Lazio version of Silvio Piola. He achieved his dream during his time there – winning the 1938 World Cup finals.'
>
> – Cittaceleste

Following his first full season at Lazio, Piola continued his goalscoring exploits for the club he would call his own.

Scudetti would not come his way but it was in the Eternal City that Silvio finally become Capocannoniere. No, he didn't win back-to-back awards and no, he didn't score the most amount of goals in a solitary season. He didn't win a Scudetto, but surely he won a ton of Capocannonieri with that many goals, right?

It seems many expect too much from Piola, not understanding that what he brought to the clubs he played for was by far greater than any accolade. He ended up as top scorer for three of the four professional clubs he turned out for while also bringing vast support to these teams and ended up with two stadiums named after him. For what does it matter if Pro Vercelli's success came before Piola played for them, or Lazio earned their first Scudetto long after he had left? What needs to be known about Silvio is the man behind the 274 figure, the one who battled on through the war period and played until he was 41 while others his age were already nice and cosy in their retirement.

Let's not jump ahead too far though, as Piola was arriving at his pomp, and he was earning money all of us would dream of – £1.83 a week. His goalscoring had seen him enter the Italy squad for the first time and he scored twice on his debut against Austria.

Another 21 goals for 1936/37 meant he not only guided Lazio to a second-place finish in the table, but also became Capocannoniere for the first time. It may have taken eight years for the title to arrive but then again he didn't have to wait as long as Alessandro Del Piero. At least Ale had his Scudetti to keep him company. That should have been the season that Piola held the trophy aloft, with his side scoring more and winning more than eventual champions Bologna, but their eight losses to the Rossoblu's three meant they missed out by three points. They failed to beat Bologna on both occasions.

It meant that his finest moment came not in Serie A, but in France when he won the 1938 World Cup, the last before the Second World War. With three goals already under his belt, including a brace to knock out the hosts, Italy would play Hungary in the final. Silvio was pivotal to their success on the day, regaining his side's lead after Pál Titkos had cancelled out Gino Colaussi's early opener. It was a goal of real beauty too, with a mixture of superb passing and a classy finish to cap it off. Colaussi started the move, feeding Piola who played the ball into Giovanni Ferrari. In any modern game, Ferrari would have been yelled at for not shooting, seeing as he had the goal at his mercy from six yards.

He opted to flick the ball out on to the right of the area for Meazza, the man Piola was finally partnering, who would then find Silvio unmarked in the box. With little to no backlift, Silvio dug the ball out from under his feet before powering it into the roof of the net. It was everything that epitomised Piola and Italy at the time. He wrapped the game up late in the second half with a first-time finish that nestled neatly in the bottom corner. The damage was done – the win secured – Piola was a World Cup winner.

With the Second World War starting in September 1939, Piola soldiered on in terms of his footballing presence, finding the net 19 times until 1941. Lazio hadn't been performing to an expected level and Silvio nearly arrived in Serie B earlier than expected, surviving by just four goals over Novara. Two valuable points were secured in the Derby della Capitale halfway through the campaign, with *Piola-gol* scoring both. A typical occurrence surely? Maybe so, but the opening goal came with Silvio four stitches better off and a bandage wrapped around his head. A quite apt parallel to draw on in comparison with his first-ever goal in top-flight football – the bandage of brilliance.

Piola's time at Lazio was nearly up at this point with just two years remaining at the Biancocelesti. He ended it in style, securing 21 goals to earn his second Capocannoniere, equalling the same tally that saw him lift the accolade back in 1937. But that was that for Silvio's Lazio adventure with

143 goals in 227 appearances all done and dusted and after competing in the 1943/44 Campionato Alta Italia with Torino FIAT, he signed for Juventus in 1945.

He spent two years at the Old Lady following the war, where he ended up tutoring Giampiero Boniperti, a then 18-year-old who officially made his debut in 1947, just before Piola moved to Novara. Boniperti spoke of Piola in his foreword to Gianfranco Capra's book *Hai mai visto giocare, Silvio Piola?* – 'Have you ever seen him play, Silvio Piola?' – mentioning how Silvio helped him progress as well as what he thought of the legendary Italian:

> 'He was the centre-forward we all looked up to. To think of my astonishment when I moved to Juventus in 1946 and the most famous Italian football player was there. He was one of the first players who I met and who spoke to me, offering me tips. He helped me on my movement inside the penalty area and other useful pointers. While he was finishing his adventure at Juventus mine was just beginning. Two destinies crossing paths. He is a man I will never forget. The true teacher of football and life.'

It was here at Juve that *Piola-gol* came the closest to winning the Scudetto, finishing second in both seasons he was at the Turin-based club. What is more remarkable was the fact the ageing striker managed 26 goals over those two years, despite the fact it was right after the war, in a time where travelling was near impossible and food was at a premium.

What is odd is that 16 of those 26 goals are not rated as official, as it was part of the war tournament won by Torino in 1946 that included Serie B teams. Torino's Scudetto is still ranked as official, so it seems a little unfair that Silvio lost out on 16 strikes that would have see him on a total of 290 instead. Secretly, Francesco Totti is probably over the moon about this as it's already unlikely he'll beat the 274 record left by Silvio, let alone 290.

With another runners-up finish in 1946/47 and at 34 years old, an age when many players would be contemplating retirement, Silvio would give Italian football one last hurrah at Novara. He dropped down to Serie B, and it appeared as if his career would play out in Italy's lower leagues. Yet 30 games and 16 goals later, the Biancoazzurri topped Group A, and all of a sudden the serial goal-getter was back in his righteous home – Serie A. He spent seven years with his new side, continuing his goalscoring, and even managed 37 goals in 68 appearances between 1950 and 1952 – when approaching the age of 40. To see a man of his age scoring freely must have been a sight to behold.

He bowed out on 7 March 1954 in a 4-0 drubbing handed down by Atalanta, but the real ending came a month earlier against AC Milan. With Novara trailing 1-0, Piola connected with a cross with what had become his trademark *rovesciate a bicicletta* – a bicycle kick. At 40, he became the oldest goalscorer in Serie A. You'd expect most men of such an age to not attempt such a feat, but with Silvio it came naturally.

Rather unfairly, that record as the oldest scorer was beaten in 2007 when Alessandro Costacurta, a man who had previously only scored two goals in his career, netted a penalty in his final game. Despite the fact it was done as a farewell for one of Milan's longest-serving players and arguably the last thing Alessandro was thinking about at that time was this record, he also won seven Scudetti in his career. A little unjust one would think. Piola had to take what he could get, even if many people would see it as a minor record. Silvio later revealed he 'never played for great teams', much to the amusement of Romanisti, which was his reasoning behind why he didn't win a Scudetto.

Roma fans continue to focus on Piola, not for his Lazio links but for the supposed battle with their golden boy Francesco Totti. Now all references to Piola are followed with 'can Totti better his tally of goals' or 'if Totti was playing then he would have scored more'. It's the age-old problem people make when comparing the two forwards. Why can't both be applauded for their own achievements, rather than bringing up ifs and buts about what football was like 80 years ago?

All readers will hopefully now understand the man behind the three-figure statistic. As Gianni Brera mentioned in his open letter to Piola, 'The history of Piola could be told with just numbers, but what sort of story would that be?' You'll know him as the gentleman he was, both on and off the pitch. While we all revel in his goals, if he was still with us now he wouldn't want the fuss – he wasn't that type of person. He achieved his dream of winning the World Cup however, and always wanted to better others with his goalscoring. With a goal record that looks like it will never be beaten, Silvio will always top one chart regardless, and that is something no one will take away from him.

GIGI RIVA

'Football was an outlet for me. My uncle told me to find a real job, but football was the one for me.'

– *Corriere della Sera*

AT the end of the 1969/70 season, Cagliari's captain Pierluigi Cera held the Scudetto aloft. It signified the club's greatest achievement in their entire history – their one and only title. One man was pivotal to the success – a 26-year-old from Leggiuno who had the task of leading his team from the front. That man was *Rombo di Tuono*. That man was Gigi Riva.

Gigi grew up scoring goals. It was in his blood. In a single season at the age of 17 he scored 30 goals for Laveno Mombello, a small club based in Varese just along the tail end of Lake Maggiore. He loved scoring goals and it was no wonder Serie C side Legnano beckoned, where he made his debut aged 18. Football was the escape for the talented young man – avoiding the harsh reality of life in a poor family. Gigi's parents had passed away in his early years and it left his sister, Fausta, to attend to his parenting needs in the suffering household that surrounded Gigi. His father, a working man, had sadly lost his life when hit with a loose piece of machinery in the factory he was employed at. Riva himself worked long hours as a mechanic repairing cars prior to his own factory job while simultaneously playing for Legnano. The beautiful game was his constant break from his troubled life. Riva was enjoying his football and opted to try out at Inter where he was swiftly, but expectedly, rejected. It seemed every time a door was being opened by the Italian, it would close abruptly in his face, although another would be left slightly ajar a few steps ahead.

Beppe Galluzzi, coach of the National Juniors for the Azzurri, elected to pick Riva for their qualifier with Spain and the Legnano boy helped his country to a tournament held in England. Gigi netted in the 2-1 semi-final defeat to Bulgaria while abroad – a major learning curve for the young man whose name was slowly appearing upon the lips of supporters in Italy. Riva was of course still a Serie C player and many thought he was still far from the standard needed to play at the very top.

He remained at Legnano for the remainder of the season, finishing 15th in Group A before making the move to the club that would become his beloved home – Cagliari. His new team had just finished top of Group B in Serie C and secured promotion to Serie B. The Rossoblu faithful will be forever thankful to director Andrea Arrica who made the decision to bring Riva in.

Gigi was considered a stranger when Cagliari made the move for the 19-year-old – he was thin, lacking major upper-body strength and failed to show any blistering pace at the time, a gamble for Arrica to make. Enrica Rocca, president of Cagliari, remained unmoved but Arrica saw potential.

He saw the powerful left foot Gigi possessed, along with his ability to pull away from defenders with quick turns and darting runs. Rocca's right-hand man had persuaded him to part with 37m lire and Riva would be welcomed ahead of the 1963/64 season.

Coach Arturo Silvestri opted to throw Riva in instantly, making his debut against Prato at the start of the campaign. Gigi was of great importance to the Sardinian side – scoring the equaliser in the penultimate game against Udinese to mathematically secure promotion. They finished second at the close of the season and secured back-to-back promotions as they entered Serie A. It was only now he believed his future lay in football – this was his profession for life and yet he still longed to share it all with his parents:

> 'My only real regret was not being able to share my life and success with my parents. If anyone could help me with this problem I would say to him: bring them back to life. I had suffered from depression for a year and a half at the time but this is now just a memory for me.'
>
> – *Corriere della Sera*

The 1964/65 campaign saw Cagliari back in Serie A and a disappointing start ensued – the Rossoblu sat bottom alongside Mantova with only nine points at the midway point. Riva had only scored twice beforehand, his first coming three games in against Sampdoria and his second versus Genoa. Cue the turnaround for the Sardinian side and wins were soon coming. Gigi was right at the forefront of the complete change in fortunes, scoring against Juventus, Atalanta and Lazio in quick succession. Varese, Foggia, Genoa and Milan would feel his force – Riva and Cagliari had found their feet in Serie A. It was quite unexpected seeing as they had been languishing at the bottom for so long. They finished seventh in the end, gaining 25 points in the second half of the season. Their nine-point neighbours at the midway point, Mantova, managed only another 11 points and were relegated. The contrast between the two teams was astounding and Riva knew he had found his home. Nine goals was his total, not bad for his first season, considering Cagliari's poor start to life in the top flight. Gigi was beginning to develop as a footballer. He was no longer the scrawny young man he had been at Legnano. His apparent lack of upper-body strength seems a mere urban myth. Riva was built to withstand any battles on the pitch, standing tall above the rest.

The seasons that followed were not the true fairytale story someone would create for Riva and Cagliari. The following seasons saw them finishing 11th, sixth and ninth. The team were slowly building themselves. Riva was still the main man – he was scoring goals and becoming a club and national icon. The fans were loving him and he was loving his football. He was able to score 11 in 1965/66 and became Capocannoniere in 1966/67 when he notched up 18 goals. At this stage Cagliari were attracting some talent and some very able players were being added to their ranks. Roberto Boninsegna – another of our *Calcio's Greatest Forwards* – partnered Gigi at the start of this season and they both found the net on the opening day against Lecco. Riva then helped himself to a hat-trick in the third week of the Serie A season, cementing himself alongside Roberto for the up-and-coming games.

In 1967/68 Riva added another 13 to his growing tally. Milan felt his force twice when he was able to bag a super brace. Pierino Prati also found himself on the scoresheet for the visitors as he went on to become Serie A's top scorer for the season with 18. His side were still just biding their time. They finished ninth in the end but were only six points – or three wins – away from runners-up Napoli.

Cagliari and Riva could sense something big on the horizon. Manlio Scopigno gave the Rossoblu their first sniff at a historic Scudetto success in 1968/69. Gigi bagged 21 in a remarkable season that saw his team finish second, four points behind champions Fiorentina. Runners-up seemed to be the story of this year for the Rossoblu as they also had to make do with being second best to Roma in the Coppa Italia – losing out by three points in the Group Final that also contained Foggia and Torino. It was quite the season filled with various thrills and spills expected at the highest level.

Riva's Cagliari were dominating the league during most of the season and were top of the table going into March 1969. It was then they began to falter – they were winless in four until a 3-1 home victory over Milan but by then Fiorentina were above them in the standings. They would fail to claw back the four points they needed to draw level with la Viola and a 0-0 draw against Pisa confirmed they would have to make do with being second best.

Following the season Scopigno was ready to make some changes. Riva was constantly attracting interest from many clubs, mainly Juventus, who he had rejected in 1967. Riva believed the Bianconeri were actually offering too much money for him and even mentioned to his team-mate Pierluigi Cera that he could not play under such a burden. However, Scopigno had instead opted to sell Boninsegna, the only other major player the club had to offer, and he was sold to Inter, the team Roberto stated was his 'beloved'. The Rossoblu had acquired a nice sum of money as well as three new players – Cesare Poli, Angelo Domenghini and Sergio Gori. It added much needed depth to a squad that had only 17 players previously.

It was time for the 1969/70 Serie A campaign, the greatest and most iconic in Cagliari's history. Scopigno had his team ready to go. The incredible season began with a scoreless draw against Sampdoria but they registered their first win the following week by turning over Lanerossi Vicenza 2-1. Riva and new man Domenghini were both on the scoresheet and the two also struck against Brescia a week later. It was

GIGI
CAGLIA
Paine

all beginning to come together for Cagliari. Riva's men had found a rhythm for the season that consisted of winning a couple then drawing a couple.

Losses rarely occurred – just twice they walked away from a game with their tails between their legs in a 30-game season. It was remarkable to watch for those who were lucky enough to witness the 'Sardinian slayers' in full force. Even defensively the Rossoblu could not be thwarted, as they only conceded 11 goals all season.

The hopes of the fans were beginning to rise throughout and Riva kept helping himself to more goals. He scored possibly every type of goal imaginable as well. He found the net from the spot in week five against Fiorentina, rolled the ball in from two yards in week seven against Napoli and spanked a free kick into the top corner against Milan in week 14. Gigi was performing brilliantly for Cagliari. Week 17 saw them visit Vicenza and Riva scored a superb overhead effort in an important 2-1 win.

A header back across goal saw the forward leap elegantly into the air, hooking back his left foot as he rose to meet the ball and plant the acrobatic effort into the roof of the net at a colossal speed. Pietro Pianta can count himself lucky he did not lose his head when attempting to save such an effort. Riva threw back his head and held his arms aloft – it was his 11th of the season and kept his side three points above the chasing Juventus and Inter.

The two sides met a month later and Riva was leading the line as he had done in the previous 23 matches. He scored to level the game on two occasions, securing a valuable point. Neither goal was particularly memorable – a scrappy header and a penalty – but it showed that Riva was the striker everyone wanted because he knew how to score goals whatever the circumstance. It was a match full of controversy – Juventus were awarded a penalty to have the chance to go ahead despite protests from the Cagliari defence. Enrico Albertosi got down well to save but was deemed over his line when it was struck and the spot-kick would be taken again. Even though Albertosi was unable to save the second one, it seemed the referee was always trying to make amends for his error in awarding the penalty in the first place and when Riva was being slightly tugged by Sandro Salvadore he pointed to the spot. The result saw them stay at the top of the table.

The games ticked down and they weren't to be stopped. Along came 12 April 1970 – the day Riva and Cagliari won the Scudetto. The ground was full four hours before kick-off, anticipating the possibility of witnessing such a historic day in Sardinia. The Stadio Amsicora welcomed Bari, who themselves needed the points to defy the odds and remain in Serie A. Riva made sure it would be his team that went home celebrating as he launched himself on to a set piece, connecting beautifully with a diving header to break the deadlock a few moments before half-time. The second half hadn't produced much but Lazio were doing them a huge favour as they led 2-0 against Juventus. In the 88th minute, Gori doubled Cagliari's lead and that was that, the Scudetto was theirs.

Sheer euphoria broke out in the stadium as a pitch invasion occurred. Everyone in attendance was celebrating what they had just seen. Apparently two escaped prisoners had attended the game and were caught – yet they were allowed to watch in handcuffs for the remainder of the game before 'attempting to' applaud Scopigno's team. There were to be mass celebrations for days upon days. According to John Foot's *Calcio: A History of Italian Football,* the publication *L'Unione Sarda* had sold 125,000 copies the day after the game and the city was full of fans still stunned by what their club had just achieved. Riva and his team-mates were of course in ecstasy and the success of the Scudetto had all but secured Gigi's future with the Rossoblu forever. Riva's best memory of this success was the fact he had achieved it with Cagliari despite all the interest Juventus had shown in him previously:

> 'The Scudetto triumph had secured my decision to stay at Cagliari even though Sardinia had already won me over. I saw people leaving Sassari at 8am and they were in the ground by 11! I understood that football was everything to Sardinians. Cagliari was everything for every single one of those supporters and I could not possibly have left them. Leaving for Juventus would have been cowardly. I would have earned triple but Sardinia had made me a man. It was my land. They called us the shepherds and bandits around Italy. I wanted the Scudetto for my land. We did it, the bandits and shepherds.'
>
> – *La Gazzetta dello Sport*

As the parties began to die down and the realisation the Scudetto was theirs had sunk in, preparations began for the defence of their title. Riva had gained his third Capocannoniere success during the incredible previous year but unfortunately Cagliari would not experience such a high again. Riva had spent the summer with the national team at the 1970 World Cup finals but was coming under heavy criticism from the media as he was putting in below-par performances. He did score three times across the tournament as Italy made it to the final, only to lose 4-1 to Brazil. He was joined by his Rossoblu team-mates Albertosi, Cera and Domenghini for the game but despite the result it seemed it had not affected the Sardinian boys as they went into the 1970/71 season ready and raring to go. They started as they meant to go on, winning 2-1 with Riva scoring from the spot to defeat Sampdoria. Things seemed to be going well and despite a couple of blips they were only three points behind leaders Napoli in October.

European football had also become part of their season and Cagliari eased past Saint-Etienne 3-1 on aggregate in the first round. *Rombo di Tuono* grabbed himself two during the first leg in a 3-0 win to secure them a place in the second round against Atlético Madrid. Even though they were knocked out by the Spaniards, they won the opening encounter 2-1 with Riva scoring. The striker had one of his best performances in his career and Italian sports journalist Gianni Brera gave him a 9+ rating on the report cards but even then it was deemed not high enough by some of Brera's comrades.

Following the first leg success Riva and Cagliari's fortunes took a turn. Gigi had broken his leg in a tackle by Austrian Ronald Hof. It was not the first time the Italian had badly injured himself on international duty – he had been out for a number of months in 1967 following an injury sustained against Portugal. The injury meant Riva missed much of the Rossoblu's season and did not return until April. By that time Cagliari were seventh and 15 points adrift of Inter at the summit. They finished in the same position with Riva concluding the Serie A campaign with eight goals.

The next season saw Gigi back to his best, smashing shot after shot past helpless goalkeepers as his goalscoring tally grew considerably. It took him just 44 minutes in the first game to grab a goal in a 3-1 victory against Hellas Verona and he scored again the following week against Atalanta. He continued to score at a consistent rate and closed with 21 goals across the 30 games. Former team-mate Boninsegna had the last laugh this time around, pipping Gigi to Capocannoniere by a single goal. Juventus knocked on the door once again following the exit of Scopigno as coach seeing it as an opportunity arising, but Gigi was firmly glued to Sardinia and would never budge.

As the seasons wore on it was clear Riva was beginning to decline. He had never been one to let his injuries stop him showcasing his incredible talent but such setbacks were beginning to take hold of him. Despite the fourth-place finish they had secured prior to the 1972/73 campaign, the Rossoblu began to decline once more and followed that up by finishing eighth – Riva scoring 11 of their 26 goals. The continuous slip was fully visible to calcio fans as Cagliari then ended up tenth two seasons running before coming rock bottom in 1975/76. Riva had got just 12 during those two and the relegation campaign was to be his last in football.

His final Rossoblu goal was at home against Como in a 1-0 win on 12 January 1976, one of only five victories they achieved that season. When Cagliari welcomed Milan to Sardinia on 1 February, it would prove to be Riva's final match. Milan came out 3-1 victors and the Italian went down in a heap by the corner flag without any contact. It was clear something serious had occurred and a later examination revealed that Riva had ruptured a tendon in his right thigh – the Italian's career was over. The sheer drive of such a specimen meant he did not officially draw the curtain on his career until two years later, constantly disregarding any advice given to him by doctors or physios.

That was the end of Gigi Riva's footballing career. His goals were his payment to all those who had carried faith in him and it brought about some rather clever negotiations:

> 'When I first joined Cagliari I was able to get my first car – a co-owned Fiat 600. I was able to drive in secret on the track around the stadium to learn. The instructor told me that he would give me my drivers' certification if I scored on Sunday. I managed to get two in Verona. I got my licence!'
>
> – *La Gazzetta dello Sport*

In among such an incredible career he shared spectacular highs and lows. He was a man who lived and breathed football, and no Sardinian will ever forget *Rombo di Tuono*.

ANDRIY SHEVCHENKO

'I visited the San Siro at 14 and remember thinking how unbelievable it was. I vowed that one day I would play there.'

– CNN Sport

VICE-PRESIDENT Adriano Galliani knew from the start he had to bring Andriy Shevchenko back to AC Milan. The second most prolific striker in their history was to return to the San Siro after leaving the Rossoneri for Chelsea back in 2006. The transfer to the Blues was arguably the wrong move for the Ukrainian. He spent two disappointing years in England and he never fully recovered from his transfer to Chelsea, having left behind a superb Serie A goalscoring record.

His performances in Italy saw him become one of the finest recent strikers to have graced Serie A. He won everything there was to win at Milan, scoring freely in the process. Every team felt the pain of Shevchenko one after the other. He could strike them with his left, curling them so elegantly into the top corner. His right wasn't bad either – volleyed efforts were driven home at will when he was thwarted from cutting inside and unleashing a left-footed thunderbolt. That didn't happen often though – defenders couldn't stop this man when he was in full force. Shevchenko made his own career, his own lifestyle and his own free-scoring ability. Dynamo Kyiv gave him a chance to lay out his plans of turning into one of Europe's finest attackers back in 1994, beginning the topsy-turvy ride of Andriy Shevchenko.

However, you never see a rollercoaster start off with a massive drop, and yet this is what happened to Andriy when he was just nine years old. The Chernobyl nuclear disaster had recently occurred, with Shevchenko's family forced to leave their home – located all but 80 miles from the nuclear plant. Fortunately for Andriy, none of his close family members lost their lives and the turmoil caused by the catastrophe hadn't hampered his spirits as he continued to focus upon his love for football. The young man grew up playing the sport on a regular basis and was scouted by Dynamo Kyiv's Alexander Shpakov. Leading on from some impressive displays as a youth player, he moved up the ranks to play for Dynamo-2, and then finally for the first team in October 1994 against Shakhtar Donetsk. Andriy would go on to spend five glorious seasons there, winning the Ukrainian Premier League five times and the Ukrainian Cup three times.

His incredible performances and ability in front of goal meant a move beckoned for Sheva. At 22 years old one of the wealthiest and biggest clubs in the world were ready to see if the forward could fulfil his potential at the highest level – AC Milan. The deal had been in the pipeline for a number of months and the proposed fee of £16.3m to be paid across the course of five years was finalised. The deal sparked a new change in Shevchenko's life. The Ukrainian believed he was ready for the move, but even he was stunned by the club he became a part of:

> 'The first time I came here and looked at all these cups, I said to myself, "My God, what a team I've joined!"'
>
> – *Corriere dello Sport*

Shevchenko was back at the San Siro after visiting eight years prior to his move from Ukraine. He had begun to understand the formalities of football in Italy, engaging in a tough training session a day after moving to the country. Milan had won the Scudetto in 1998 so the new forward on the block needed to hit the ground running in order to keep up with the standards expected by coach Alberto Zaccheroni.

He played in the Supercoppa Italiana versus Parma and realised the differences in what occurred on the field in Italy, as opposed to his homeland. They lost 2-1 on the day, but it was a chance to learn about the style of the Italian game. Much like Gabriel Batistuta and Hernán Crespo, Sheva just needed to find his feet in Serie A.

The opening game of the 1999/2000 season followed a week later and Andriy travelled to Lecce for his league debut. With the match at 1-1 and nearing the final 15 minutes, Sheva announced himself to the Milanese faithful. A lofted ball from George Weah on the left found Oliver Bierhoff, who would head back across the face of goal in the direction of the new boy. Andriy nipped ahead of the lunging defender to side-foot the ball through the goalkeeper's legs. Shevchenko sprinted off to the advertising hoardings, lifting his shirt over his head with his arms aloft before directing a fist pump full of ecstasy toward the away support.

The match would finish 2-2 but Andriy wasn't to mind too much – he was in possession of his first Serie A goal. It spurred him on unquestionably and he was craving goals – lots of them. The next game gave the San Siro crowd a peek at the ability the forward held as he netted again when taking on Perugia in early September. It was a straightforward finish – heading home into an empty goalmouth thanks to an intricate cross from Weah.

A fine display came on matchday five when Milan went to the Stadio Olimpico to face Sven-Göran Eriksson's Lazio. The Biancocelesti led Shevchenko's team 3-1 after 40 minutes but Andriy had other ideas. Two minutes before the interval he broke away from the Lazio defence and rounded goalkeeper Luca Marchegiani before smashing the ball into the roof of the net. With the match finely poised at 3-2 Lazio were wary of Shevchenko's threat and attempted to subdue him in the second half.

But a poor mistake from Marchegiani saw Weah fouled and Shevchenko was given the chance to add his second as the game entered the final 30 minutes. The long run-up was put into place, putting off the Italian between the sticks, as Andriy rolled the ball into the opposite corner to level the game at 3-3. Galliani could be seen attempting to stay in his seat following the equaliser but the emotion was clear on the vice-president's face – he'd found a gem.

Five minutes later and the hat-trick was complete. Weah again was the provider, stroking a pass into the path of Andriy who shifted the ball so swiftly on to his left foot before drilling it back across goal to give Milan a remarkable 4-3 lead. He was finding his home at the Rossoneri. But much like his debut, his team-mates were unable to secure the win and Sven's men grabbed a valuable point in the grand scheme of things as they went on to lift the Scudetto ahead of Juventus.

Andriy was scoring all types of goals as the Serie A season motored along at a constant pace. Free kicks were dispatched, penalties stroked home and even a shinned effort in the Derby della Madonnina saw off Inter. Everything he touched was flying past unfortunate goalkeepers and adding to his ever-growing tally. He ended with a flourish, finishing off a penalty on the last day to defeat Udinese 4-0 in front of 75,000 spectators.

The spot-kick signified his first individual accomplishment for Milan and in Italy, securing Capocannoniere with 24 superb strikes, denying Fiorentina's Batistuta by a solitary goal. The Ukrainian capped off the season averaging a goal every 108 minutes. In proportion, it takes one day, 17 hours and 40 minutes taking the train from Kyiv to Milan. If you were to embark on such a journey, Sheva would have scored 20 of his 24 Serie A goals in that time. It proved pivotal in Andriy's continual rise in Italy, gaining the accolade of Serie A's Foreign Footballer of the Year along the way as he slowly developed into one of Milan's greatest forwards.

The 2000/01 Serie A season soon beckoned and Shevchenko secured an opening-day 2-0 success over Vicenza, directing a header into the bottom corner from a Paolo Maldini cross. The Eastern Wind, as he also came to be known, carried on his good fortunes in front of goal – Bologna and Juventus both feeling his wrath in the succeeding weeks. Milan themselves weren't faring too well even though their striker was scoring at a consistent rate. He ended the season with 24 goals to his name yet again, an incredible feat for someone who was playing in Ukraine just two seasons previously. If anything, Sheva's goals distracted fans from the poor campaign as a whole as Milan finished sixth in the standings. The only high point came in mid-May when the Rossoneri crushed rivals Inter 6-0 – Andriy netting twice with a header and a side-footed effort to complete the rout.

The 2001/02 season in Serie A was no better for Milan, and even with his goalscoring tally dropping to 14 in the league it was still Sheva who proved the difference in the

Rossoneri's disappointing campaign. One of his finest goals came in a 1-1 draw when hosting eventual Scudetto winners Juventus. Halfway through the first period, Shevchenko latched on to a flicked header just inside the Bianconeri's half and proceeded to run full pelt at the bewildered defence. His sheer pace took him away from Dutchman Edgar Davids before leaping over a half-hearted tackle from Mark Iuliano. The forward's next touch saw him glide past a stunned Gianluca Pessotto before unleashing a truly spectacular strike from the corner of the box into the opposite side of the goal. It left Gianluigi Buffon with no chance.

The commentator screamed as the ball hit the back of the net, '*Andriy! Incredibile! Impossibile!*' It was moments such as this that made Shevchenko undoubtedly one of the best strikers Serie A has witnessed in the past 20 years. The finish was nothing unexpected. Supporters had come to acknowledge the fact Andriy could conjure up such brilliance out of nothing.

Despite there being nothing to change what Sheva could do in front of goal, there was to be a change of the coaching team at Milan. Silvio Berlusconi had sacked Fatih Terim in November and Carlo Ancelotti was chosen to replace him. Although a finish of only fourth was secured alongside a semi-final exit in the Coppa Italia, Shevchenko was ready to grab his first piece of silverware in the colours of Milan.

Along came 2002/03 with Shevchenko ready to send more ripples through the footballing world with the Rossoneri. Sheva would conclude 2003 with victories in the Coppa Italia and the UEFA Champions League. How was there such a drastic change in Milan's fortunes? Ancelotti's men just seemed to peak at the right time, although it was occurring without their key man. The Ukrainian suffered a knee injury in the third qualifying round of the Champions League and didn't return until a month later. By this stage Milan had finished the job off on the away goals rule against

Slovan Liberec and won their opening four group games. Shevchenko's side were drawn alongside Bayern Munich, Deportivo La Coruña and Lens. With Pippo Inzaghi's brilliance in full swing, Milan had propelled to a maximum 12 points. He had appeared on the bench for the 2-1 win over Bayern, and it didn't take the master long to get going – in the week following there were goals for Sheva in the league away at Chievo and Lens.

Milan were going about their business successfully in Serie A and soon the second Champions League group stage rolled around as well as their entrance into the Coppa Italia. Shevchenko was on hand to give them the winning start in Europe, scoring the only goal against Spanish giants and defending champions Real Madrid. A quite remarkable defence-splitting ball from Rui Costa – well worth looking for online – set Sheva through on goal and he took one touch to set himself before driving the ball low past Iker Casillas. The shirt was pulled over his head as he ran away in jubilation. From scoring his first goal at Lecce four years ago to netting against Europe's finest was a massive accomplishment. He'd learnt the ropes at Dynamo Kyiv and adapted his game to suit the Italian way.

Everything was coming together for the Ukrainian – Milan were top of the league, top of the second group stage and had just knocked out Ancona in the Coppa Italia. By early April, though, the Scudetto was heading towards Juventus but Milan did finish top in their Champions League group and were preparing for a Coppa Italia semi-final second leg against Perugia, having dispatched Chievo in the previous round.

Sheva wasn't scoring much but this was the season where he was proving his mental strength and he contributed the most valuable goals of Milan's successful campaign. He popped up to net in the 3-2 second leg win over Ajax in the Champions League quarter-finals, knocking home a header to give Milan the lead for the second time on the night.

There's a great camera cut seen when Andriy is celebrating that goal. He runs away, arms pumping up and down in a fit of emotion before cutting to Carlo Ancelotti doing the exact same on the touchline. These two knew each other, kicked every ball together, and celebrated every goal together.

After getting past Perugia in the Coppa Italia semi-finals and Ajax in Europe, the biggest game of Shevchenko's career was upon him as Milan had drawn Inter in the semi-finals of the Champions League.

After a 0-0 first leg, the second leg produced two goals with an away goal the difference to separate the two sides. That goal was scored by Andriy Shevchenko. On the stroke of half-time a great ball from Clarence Seedorf fed Sheva deep inside the Nerazzurri box. He side-stepped Iván Córdoba, who then looked more interested in taking the forward's leg out to dinner than trying to win the ball with a swiping tackle after being bamboozled by Andriy's incredible turn of pace. Shevchenko then lashed the ball home over the advancing Francesco Toldo – advantage Milan. Obafemi Martins netted late on for Inter but by then it was too late. Andriy Shevchenko was going to a UEFA Champions League Final to meet another Serie A rival – Juventus.

The week preceding the final in Europe saw Sheva net in the 4-1 first leg win over Roma in the Coppa Italia Final. It proved enough as they then drew the return fixture 2-2 a few days after the UEFA Champions League Final which occurred on 28 May 2003 at Manchester United's Old Trafford.

It was scintillating and quite often breathless for a match that featured no goals in 120 minutes of football. Andriy thought he'd got one after just eight minutes but Rui Costa's offside position cut his celebrations short. To be fair, they weren't exactly short, and it took an eternity for Sheva to realise the linesman's flag was up.

The match went to penalties and with a host of misses happening, it fell on Andriy to take the decisive kick. He looked nervous, glancing over to the referee for the whistle at least four times. Sheva got the signal and it was time for him to either create his finest moment, or his worst. The forward glanced left, directed toward Gianluigi Buffon's right, and began his run-up. As he neared the ball he slowed down – Buffon had already gone the way he believed he had to – it was all a trick. Sheva calmly slotted the ball home into the opposite corner. Nerves? What nerves? Milan's golden boy sprinted straight to team-mate Dida to celebrate, falling to the floor in the process. It's well worth watching the official Milan channel's commentary of the winning penalty to hear the word *'Campioni!'* repeated 101 times. Andriy Shevchenko had won the UEFA Champions League for Milan.

It would be hard to top triumphs in Europe and domestically, but the 2003/04 season brought the Scudetto home for Sheva. It was Milan's first league title in five seasons having won it a few months before Andriy joined. It was quite an incredible 34 games for the Rossoneri as they only lost twice on their way to the Scudetto. Shevchenko got 24 goals along the way and they flowed right from the off. Ancona succumbed to a brace at the Stadio Del Conero before the Ukrainian added to his tally against Bologna, Lecce, Inter and Sampdoria heading into November. Milan wouldn't let up and neither would Andriy and it was he who secured the Scudetto when hosting Roma on 2 May.

The decisive strike came just two minutes in, directing a terrific header into the far corner from 12 yards. Peerless. Sheva's dream season was capped off when he was awarded the FIFA Ballon d'Or for his performances in Serie A, a moment he had wished would be welcomed upon him in his younger years:

> 'I was once a young kid dreaming of winning the FIFA Ballon d'Or for a long while. I came very close on a few occasions but when my time did come I was

> so happy. I felt as if one of my dreams had become a reality.'
>
> – FIFA.com

The Ballon d'Or success of 2004 coupled with all the other accolades and goals of the previous seasons meant interest in Sheva was at an all-time high. Roman Abramovich, owner of Chelsea, spotted the Ukrainian in a Milan hotel when scouting players from Inter as he looked to build up the club he owned. Andriy wasn't interested in the slightest from the outset, and Berlusconi didn't wish to sell his prized asset – the Italian had become Shevchenko's metaphorical godfather as well.

However, another two seasons of goals – 36 across 2004/05 and 2005/06 – meant it would be even harder to keep a hold of the striker. Andriy was still suffering from the pain of the Champions League Final against Liverpool in 2005 which can be read about in more detail in Hernán Crespo's and Inzaghi's sections in *Calcio's Greatest Forwards*. Shevchenko missed the decisive penalty at the end and was also denied in extra time by an astounding save from Polish goalkeeper Jerzy Dudek:

> 'I cannot believe that the ball didn't go in. I have seen Jerzy Dudek several times in the last few years and I have asked him, "How did you manage to save my shot?" It has become a joke between us.'
>
> – *L'Equipe*

Once an offer of £30.8m was laid out on the table of the Milan president, it was an amount he couldn't turn down. The move was complete in the summer of 2006 but Shevchenko wouldn't have a dreamlike playing career in England. He never showed Chelsea what he was capable of after leaving Milan.

When he was finally deemed surplus to requirements at Chelsea following the 2007/08 Premier League, he made what many thought would be a fairytale comeback to his old Italian stomping ground – AC Milan. It wasn't to be, with Sheva participating in 18 league games – nine of those were starts – without scoring.

Shevchenko became one of those players who seemed to just fall off the face of the earth. After the rather subdued return season for Milan he made another switch, this time to former club Dynamo Kyiv after going back to his parent team Chelsea. He rekindled some of his goalscoring form back in Ukraine but never got the desired send-off to his professional career in Milan. He didn't spend an hour after his final home game against Roma blowing kisses to the Curva Sud with tears in his eyes. Instead, he was voted the disappointment of the season in a poll by *MilanNews* online.

This is the man who sits second behind the great Gunnar Nordahl for goals in Serie A for Milan, and yet the ending of such a story was completely underwhelming. It meant he concluded his time in Italy with 127 goals from 226 appearances. In his prime he was unstoppable, powerful and lethal when it came to putting the ball into the net. England will forever see the forward as a failure – someone who never lived up to the expectations. It is a shame, because the Ukrainian really was something special. Andriy Shevchenko epitomised the rise and fall of one of Europe's finest, but the memories will live on, immortalising Sheva into Serie A history.

GIUSEPPE SIGNORI

INTRODUCED BY RICHARD HALL

'He [Zdeněk Zeman] greeted me by saying, "Welcome bomber." I thought he was confused. I only had five goals in Serie B, I was anything but a bomber. He had seen something else, evidently.'

– Sport.it

I HOLD *Beppe* partly responsible. Well, him, James Richardson and Italia 90. At 12 years old and having watched no other football other than all the goals of Italia 90 on repeat for the last two years, Italian football finally came to the UK and I was hooked. *Football Italia* on Channel 4 gave us the first match, Sampdoria 3 Lazio 3. In this game one man was head and shoulders above the rest. He scored twice and that was it, I was in awe.

Giuseppe *'Beppe'* Signori was one of the most complete and ruthless forwards of his era. His name is remembered, but why is he not on a pedestal? When one writes about him the sentence feels like it should start with 'lest we forget'. When he was at Lazio, he was more deadly than the eagle on his shirt; he was immense – so why is he overlooked?

Followers of the Italian game know who *Beppe* is. They know he played for Lazio and they know he scored goals, but there was so much more. He was part of *that* Foggia side, which earned him his move to Lazio in 1992. He blasted on to the centre stage, becoming Capocannoniere in his first season.

It wasn't just me who was stunned by this broadcast in Britain as thanks to Channel 4, many fans in the UK were born that day and won't forget Signori's devastating ability to poach goals and score from set pieces.

His short walk up to the penalty spot had Lazio fans enthralled and opposition goalkeepers baffled but he was also ruthless with a distanced strike. He started to drift away from his marker more in 1994/95 and scored many more goals from open play. He proved much more dynamic and more complete.

The league's top scorer was revisited again the following season. This was his high point, his victory in the amphitheatre. Admittedly, 12 of his goals came from the penalty spot, but his penchant for two-step penalties, ballistic free kicks and tap-ins only fuelled his reputation for being a ruthless finisher.

His career was tainted after he retired with accusations of match-fixing and betting scandals. In 2011 he was banned from all football activity for five years. Perhaps this has muddied the memories.

One thing is for sure, without *Beppe* I wouldn't have been as hooked on the Italian game and many of my life experiences would have been missed. It is for that reason I love Signori and also why I am truly grateful to him.

Richard Hall

What do Giuseppe Meazza, Gigi Riva and Giuseppe Signori all have in common? Although they remain in the shadow of Gunnar Nordahl's haul, each of these players have won Capocannoniere three times during their illustrious careers. Ruthless, clinical and excruciatingly unbearable for defenders, *Beppe* was a thorn in the flesh of all those who attempted to thwart his attacks – he couldn't be stopped.

Signori entered into the enthralling world of football at ten years old, ready to stamp his authority as he became a part of Inter's youth set-up. It would appear Giuseppe was prepared for life in football already, joining up with a side that had lifted the Scudetto 11 times previously. All the signs pointed in the direction of the glitz and glamour of Italy's Serie A, surely?

It wasn't to be that simple for the young Italian, being told his physique, much like that of Riva's, was simply not good enough when it came to professional football. Those who ran the Primavera made it clear to Signori he was too small and lacked the qualities needed to progress. We have to bear in mind that his height is 5ft 7in, the same as Alessandro Del Piero and also two inches taller than Lionel Messi. It is unclear whether the coaches at Inter really were troubled by his height, or if it was down to the fact they saw Signori wearing boots two sizes too small, as he believed it allowed him to improve his touch when in control of the ball.

Whatever the reason, Giuseppe moved on from his days in Milano at 15 years old to Leffe. His first year there began in 1984 with the team gaining promotion to Serie C2. The transition between youth and lower league Italian football seemed to cause no problems for the forward. He worked in a textiles factory run by Leffe's owner where he repaired the machinery alongside wreaking havoc on the pitch – Signori bagged a very respectable five goals in eight appearances during his first season.

The following year was more memorable for the frustration many felt when seeing the clinical finisher on the wing. With his lethal left foot on display for calcio fans to gawp at, Signori was placed on the wing to utilise his talent for crossing the ball instead of putting it in the net. It's a scenario that occurred at a much later date for the Italian national team when coach Arrigo Sacchi kept the prolific striker in midfield for the Azzurri because he liked him to run from deep. Not only did this anger the fans, it also made Signori rather disgruntled, refusing to play against Bulgaria in the 1994 World Cup semi-final unless he was put up front. *Beppe* was later benched for the final against Brazil, revealing to Sport.it that it was a 'choice which practically excluded me from the final'.

For all the dilemmas Giuseppe faced when being popped on the left of the pitch, he still remained a heavy influence. His goal tally did dry up but his mountain of assists meant that even with Leffe succumbing to relegation in Group B of Serie C2, Signori had earned himself a move to Serie C1 side Piacenza. He would be used occasionally across the course of the 1986/87 season, appearing on loan for Trento a year later, before returning to Piacenza, who had worked their way up to Serie B.

The Stadio Leonardo Garilli was the venue in which Signori began to rise up the ranks as a professional footballer and although they finished rock bottom with *Beppe* making 31 appearances during that campaign, he transferred to Foggia who had just been promoted from Serie C1.

Attack-minded coach Zdeněk Zeman would finally get the best out of the Italian forward by playing him as just that – a forward. The previous years on the wing would be a distant memory while at the Satanelli, scoring 14 goals as he led the line in a 4-3-3 formation during his first year at the club and his 11 strikes the following season meant Foggia would star in Serie A for the first time in 13 years.

Signori was 23 and ready to make his debut in Italy's top flight. We may think that his rise to the top had been rather subdued with very little action for a team not many calcio fans believed could survive in Serie A. *Beppe* and his two attacking compatriots, Francesco Baiano and Roberto Rambaudi, set the league alight during the 1991/92 season. On 29 September 1991 Giuseppe got his first of many in a 1-1 draw with Parma. It comes as no surprise that the goal detailed all that is brilliant about Signori – a delicate touch alongside the confidence to go around the goalkeeper meant the striker would get himself off the mark for the season as he rolled the ball into an empty net.

Two weeks later he smashed home a well-worked free kick move from 20 yards at home to Ascoli and all of a sudden the dangerous left foot of *Beppe* was on full show – striking the ball with such venom that all goalkeepers were astounded that they didn't fly into the back of the net with it. An acrobatic effort against Atalanta, a chip versus Napoli and a low drive when Cremonese came to town – all types of goals were being ticked off the imaginary checklist in *Beppe*'s back pocket. Score more than ten goals in your debut Serie A season? Check. Help your newly-promoted side to a top-ten finish? Check. Become one of the greatest goalscorers of the 1990s? Soon enough. Once the Serie A season had concluded, Lazio were soon knocking on the door to enquire about the availability of Signori, despite finishing beneath their target's employer's side. The chance to join a team in the Eternal City was too good to refuse and soon Signori would wear the Biancoceleste shirt.

Without giving away too much, if you are reading on expecting to see a hoard of silverware being dragged around in a massive rucksack by *Beppe* you'll be extremely disappointed. It was Giuseppe who got people captivated by Italian football, creating new calcio lovers all across the globe with every strike of the ball. He would become loved by the Laziali, although sometimes it's not the easiest transition when you can't find your way to your new club:

> 'My first day at Lazio was very traumatic. I missed the meeting. At that time there was no navigation and I got lost with my father on the streets of Rome. I arrived at Lazio to replace an idol, Rubén Sosa. There was curiosity but also scepticism. I had a strong start and this definitely helped me as well as the team to achieve important results. A new Lazio was being born.'
>
> – Lazioland.com

It was a strong start indeed with *Beppe* finding the net seven times in just his first five games. Dino Zoff, coach of Lazio at the time, carried on the idea of playing Signori up front, and his goalscoring began away at Sampdoria with two in three minutes in a thrilling 3-3 draw. The ruthless nature of the Italian shone through with fierce strikes from both feet seeing Gianluca Pagliuca stunned. The classic two-step penalty was displayed the following week when at home to Fiorentina and he then headed home the equaliser against Cagliari. In just three games the striker had scored with both feet, his head and from the spot and really all that was left was a free kick. *Beppe* let us all down – it took him until matchday five, a whole two games later, to secure one in a 5-2 victory over Parma that also saw him bag a hat-trick. Not bad for the new kid on the block.

Signori was pretty much running away with Capocannoniere already due to his stunning displays in the first half of the season. Almost literally in one sense – joining in with a rather odd jogging-on-the-spot celebration with Paul Gascoigne at home to Atalanta which would soon be recognised as *Beppe*'s celebration of choice. He scored a wonder-goal a few weeks later against Inter after running from inside his own half, dribbling around the clueless defenders who looked more like a couple of dogs chasing their tails before firing back across with that lethal left peg of his. Only Juventus and Roma avoided feeling his pain during the 1992/93 Serie A season as he pretty much single-handedly guided his side to a fifth-place finish. How could you stop a man as clinical as Signori? Answer – you couldn't.

The next season brought more joy to *Beppe* despite his side's underwhelming league finish of fourth. He would become just the ninth player in Serie A history to win back-to-back Capocannonieri, something only achieved once since Signori by Antonio Di Natale in 2010 and 2011. Many would think twice about drawing parallels between these two forwards, but they share a lot more in common than meets the eye. They both have an impeccable goalscoring record and neither have any major silverware to show for it. However, when you are loved by a club like Signori was by the Biancocelesti, all the memories moulded by *Beppe* would always remain ingrained on their minds however little the trophy haul was.

The forward fell three short of his previous total, ending with 23, but they came in just 24 matches and he concluded the two seasons with a goal every 0.8 games. Every time you sat down to get your weekly dose of calcio on a Sunday in the 90s, the reality of it was if you didn't see a *Beppe* goal you were downright unlucky. Goal after goal, celebration after celebration, it was almost an endless cycle. Signori shoots – Signori scores. The two-step penalties were crashing into the goal and he threatened to take the net off with a flying effort versus Cremonese on matchday 21. You can imagine all those goalkeepers going to a bar late at night on a Sunday with some form of Campari mix deliberating over which goalscorer they despised the most. Whenever

Signori's name was uttered, a shudder would occur around the table, especially from the man who would have to face him next week.

He finally got his goal against rivals Roma before the season was up in the Derby della Capitale and the passion exuded from his body. There was no simple arm aloft as he ran to the corner flag; this one was all fist pumps as his locks flowed in the wind. With the close of the season seeing his side again finish below expectations, former coach Zeman was instated in replacement of Zoff for 1994/95.

Although no trophies were won during that season, it is still seen as a memorable one by the Laziali and featured a team with names such as Alessandro Nesta, Roberto Di Matteo and Marco Di Vaio as well as Gazza and *Beppe*. One thing many calcio fans love to joke about is Zeman's attacking intent when it comes to football. The Czech-born coach gave us all something to savour when it came to matters on the pitch, making sure his team entertained those in the stands. This is the man who said, 'If you score 90 goals then it shouldn't really matter how many are conceded.'

Signori wouldn't better his previous two tallies but was part of a team that finished runners-up to Juventus in the race for the Scudetto. Lazio managed a truly remarkable 49 goals in 17 home matches that season as they destroyed Fiorentina 8-2, smashed Foggia 7-1 and crushed Inter and Milan 4-1 and 4-0 respectively. In the latter, *Beppe* added a superb goal to his book of strikes when he fired a left-footed volley first time right into the bottom corner. The ever-present comical running celebration was always on show as he sent the Curva Nord into pandemonium after every goal that would reverberate around the entire country and leave the Colosseum shaking.

Although the home form of Signori's side was something to marvel at they struggled to gain enough points away from home and even with five straight league wins to conclude the season – one of which came against rivals Juve – Giuseppe would have to make do with second place. *Beppe*'s brilliance in front of goal still saw them ten points adrift come May and again there was nothing to show for it. Their return to European football after over 15 years wasn't the worst in all honesty, losing out 2-1 on aggregate to Borussia Dortmund in the UEFA Cup quarter-finals.

While Juventus were revelling in Lazio's misfortunes as they celebrated their Scudetto and Signori was coming to terms with life away from the Azzurri following the dispute with Sacchi in 1994, chairman Sergio Cragnotti had other matters to attend to with the Biancocelesti.

Parma's Calisto Tanzi had decided to table an offer of around £8m – a then record fee – for *Beppe*'s services. It seemed inevitable that Cragnotti would accept the offer but a gathering of what was reported to be around 5,000 fans turned up at the Stadio Olimpico to protest the sale of their star striker. The owner opted to make a complete u-turn and kept Signori at the club, becoming the first notable chairman to make such a decision. At first, Giuseppe seemed disappointed with the club taking matters into their own hands, reportedly saying his 'little girl is in Rome and doesn't want to go' in an article published by *La Repubblica* on 13 June 1995. However, he later revealed how he believes it was here that the love between club and player were tied together eternally in the Eternal City:

> 'I was away on tour in Brazil at the time but I knew there was this negotiation with Parma. My will was always to remain at Lazio. For the people, at the time in question, it was clear the most important thing they wanted was to keep a hold of me. They'd rather Cragnotti sold the rest. It is with that reasoning that it showed just what a great love we had.'
>
> – Storie di Calcio

It paid dividends with *Beppe* winning the Capocannoniere crown for the third time in four seasons as he shared the award with Igor Protti of Bari, who also scored 24 goals. The captain was scoring as freely as we all had become accustomed to, but some feel the need to undermine this achievement as 12 of his 24 strikes came from the penalty spot. In reality, as long as your striker is putting the ball in the net it shouldn't matter how they come about. Signori and his team-mates guided Lazio to third that season but things were changing off the field in 1996/97. A dreadful first half to the campaign saw Zoff regain control of the team as coach, implementing his own style of play that was, shall we say, less attacking than what fans were seeing from Zeman. Sven-Göran Eriksson was then put in charge and it was here things would affect *Beppe* directly.

The new man at the helm elected to favour new boy Roberto Mancini up front over Beppe in a 4-4-2 system and he ended up loaning out a rather annoyed Signori to Sampdoria. Giuseppe's last training session, according to *Corriere della Sera*, featured him 'scoring a few goals' then leaving 'without saying goodbye'. Fans also took to kicking Eriksson's car while hurling insults at Mancini, who was unlucky enough to be celebrating his 33rd birthday on the same day.

An injury-plagued time at the Blucerchiati meant Signori scored just three times before moving on to a loan at Bologna at the close of the season. In a situation that can best be described as unfortunate, Lazio went on to win the Coppa Italia that season for the first time in 40 years.

Even with so much being said of Signori thus far, there were still another six seasons to be spent in Serie A with the Rossoblu. His scoring wasn't as impressive when at Lazio but *Beppe* made sure he would score 84 times across 178 games while at the Stadio Renato Dall'Ara. He made himself an instant hero when finally announcing himself on to the European scene in the first season, winning the Intertoto Cup before progressing all the way to the UEFA Cup semi-finals, scoring five in the process against Sporting CP and twice when up against Slavia Prague and Lyon. They would go on to lose on away goals to Marseille.

The ageing *Beppe* wasn't stopping just yet, scoring 15 and then 16 in successive seasons up to the end of 2000/01. He then entered disagreements with coach Francesco Guidolin and saw contract negotiations stall, but the man who had already become a club icon would remain with Guidolin getting the chop. Niggling injuries would prove to be his worst enemy and the loss of his incredible first touch meant his career in Italy would end in 2004 with 188 top-flight goals to his name, the tenth best in the history of the league.

It is a great shame Signori's section must end on such a disappointing note, with the Italian becoming involved in the 2011 *Calcioscommesse*, a match-fixing scandal in Italian football. He was arrested and given a five-year ban from all football activity, tainting a great name that many had fallen in love with over the past 20 years. Signori spoke over the phone in an interview while heading to custody, saying:

> 'Do you not have any mercy in this situation? Have mercy. I cannot say anything.'
>
> – *Corriere dello Sport*

It's a sad way to have to draw the curtains on one of the finest strikers to have played in Serie A as he was truly a force of nature on the pitch. It's impossible to ignore and attempt to glaze over what Signori became involved in but his goalscoring is what should be remembered. Sit back, relax, grab a drink if you will, and go and re-watch all 188 goals Giuseppe Signori provided us with. You'd better make sure you're sitting comfortably as this could take a while.

FRANCESCO TOTTI

'I did not notice the size of the hope, the scale of the dream – to grow up to become a footballer. Now, I'm always sad that I can't say "when I grow up, I want to do this", because I am grown up.'

– Panorama.it

DESPITE being known by many names, carrying an ever-growing gluttony of goals and a cabinet full of trophies, this man has only one team to share it all with. Francesco Totti is Roma's greatest ever player, the epitome of the so-called one-club man, and the Giallorossi wouldn't trade him for all the Scudetti in the world.

Il Gladiatore – the Gladiator – has the second-greatest goalscoring tally in Serie A history, making the net bulge 243 times as of the end of the 2014/15 season. That is a lot of celebrations to adhere to and the inevitable thumb-sucking ensues, or even a selfie because you guessed it – Totti has scored again.

The supporters of Roma can thank Fiorella Totti, mother to their Golden Boy, for not only bringing him into the world, but to the Curva Sud. AC Milan were ready to add a Totti-shaped piece to their ever-growing jigsaw in attempting to monopolise Italian football, yet Fiorella had other ideas for her son's fate.

Totti was 16 when he made his debut on 28 March 1993 against Brescia. The young man was all smiles. He spoke of his emotional attachment to the game exactly 20 years later to Roma's official website:

> 'You never forget your first time in a love story. My Serie A debut in a Giallorossi jersey. That day at the Stadio Rigamonti in March was a dream come true for me!'
>
> – ASRoma.com

Such a love story would continue to evolve into what all football fans can still see to this very day. First of all, it's probably best to decide where Totti actually played, as this is something people deliberate over more than his actual antics on the pitch. For the majority of his career he was deployed in between the strikers and the midfielders, and is referred to in Italian as a *trequartista*. Some will argue he is a *fantasista*, although this is more Roberto Baggio than Totti. The position is used to link up those looking to create from midfield to the person wishing to put the ball into the back of the net, hence the name *trequartista* – three-quarters up the field. It allowed Totti to freely roam around the pitch, supplying his team with goals and assists over the course of his career. Let's not get ahead of ourselves here though. Why jump to a 39-year-old attacking maestro when we have over 20 years of highs and lows to simply scratch the surface of?

With his debut out of the way and the buzz of representing the Giallorossi just beginning to simmer, following a season in which he featured eight times, Totti was soon finding his feet in Serie A and getting regular first team action. In 1994/95 he made 21 appearances despite having to battle out with Daniel Fonseca and Abel Balbo, two players who were eight and ten years older than him respectively. It probably helped the young man that he scored his first Serie A goal on the opening day at the Stadio Olimpico against Foggia. It was a typical Totti goal – connecting with a knock-down beautifully with his left foot to see the ball fly into the bottom corner. He grabbed three more that campaign – a delicate chip at home to Bari, a tap-in versus Brescia and a comfortable side-footed finish past Francesco Toldo of Fiorentina.

It was refreshing to see the confidence of Francesco at such a young age, celebrating his goals as any model professional would – with style. After his Brescia goal he ran straight to the corner flag, placing his hand on the top of the pole and standing with his chest puffed out and back straight like he was reporting for duty. It was as if to say, 'I'm here to serve the Romanisti forever, so you'd better be as proud as I am to be a Romanista.' It was evident that he knew he had the talent to succeed and so did his coach Carlo Mazzone, who said Totti was a 'child prodigy that will change the face of Rome', as reported in *Corriere della Sera*.

His showings that year made him a regular for 1995/96, scoring another two goals and also featuring in the UEFA Cup seven times, scoring twice against Eendracht Aalst and Brøndby IF. Following his antics in Europe and in Italy that year, Totti seemed prepared to continue his improvement when Carlos Bianchi became coach of Roma for 1996/97. He began to form a rather weak relationship with his new coach, and despite picking up a sublime chipped goal against Milan on matchday five, things were not looking good for Totti and Bianchi. The club began to ponder whether it was best to loan out their young star considering the Argentinian man at the helm didn't pick Totti regularly, with Sampdoria and Inter two possible destinations to offload the unused player.

However in February of the same season, Totti did what he has always done – prove people wrong. In the Torneo Città di Roma, a tournament played out this time around with Dutch side Ajax and Germany's Borussia Mönchengladbach, he outplayed the opposition in front of Bianchi's very eyes. Totti bagged a beauty from 20 yards against the latter, which also included a mazy run ending with a delicate chip to finish the job off. As *Corriere della Sera* put it, 'Francesco Totti became Francesco Totti.'

The actions in Rome meant instead of the Italian parting company with the Giallorossi, it would be Bianchi who would return to Argentina. The King of Rome, as he would come to be known, ended the footballing calendar year expressing how he was looking directly to the future:

> 'I am here until at least 2000, which is when my contract expires. If I had my way, I would never move from my town or change this shirt. I want to stay with the Giallorossi for life, but in football you can never take anything for granted.'
>
> – *La Gazzetta dello Sport*

The future held a change that Francesco would benefit from with Zdeněk Zeman becoming the new Roma coach. Zeman came with his attack-minded way of playing the beautiful game, something that was clear with his 4-3-3 formation and the mindset that he simply just enjoyed seeing goals. The Romanisti were a little sceptical about their new tactician, considering he had most recently managed their biggest rivals Lazio – Francesco once said he would rather end his career than sign for them.

The change of coach reinvigorated Totti and he found himself playing on the left wing, a move which worked wonders as he became a provider alongside his consistent exploits in front of goal. It was in this season that Francesco was reaching a new level of maturity, growing stronger and more muscular. He was able to fend off more defenders and opposition players when on the ball but was just as quick and nimble on his feet as before. The confidence of the young man was continuing to grow and he had also been handed the number ten shirt at the start of 1997/98. The shirt wasn't just a number to Totti, it held a significant bond between the player and the club, the idol and the fans.

In that season he scored two brilliant goals at home to Bari – one a low free kick into the bottom corner and the second a stupendous first-time volley that nearly broke the net. The finest was not a thunderbolt of a goal though, but a beautifully controlled lob over the Udinese defence on matchday 31 when he brought the ball under control in one touch before finishing past Luigi Turci with ease.

It was in that campaign that the Golden Boy became *il Capitano* – the Captain. It was an honour that was always forthcoming with Totti, who had continued his rise in Italian football at a phenomenal pace. He marked it by scoring the final goal in a 3-1 win over Lazio in the Derby della Capitale success for the first time over Lazio. Before Zeman moved on and Fabio Capello was getting comfy in the dugout as the new millennium arrived, Totti had scored 25 goals in 61 appearances – for you mathematicians out there, that's about 0.4 per game.

With Capello in place and Roma ready to change their league fortunes, the initial start to the Italian's coaching career at the Giallorossi was fairly underwhelming and they even finished a place below their 1998/99 position of fifth. It was also Totti's lowest-scoring season since 1997, finding the back of the net seven times in 27 games – many of which were penalties – and we got to see his first attempt at the *panenka*, which he executed to perfection on matchday 30 at home to Bologna. It's not to suggest that the forward was not reaching his expected levels on the pitch – the captain was still putting in good performances for a 23-year-old who was leading one of Italy's finest clubs by himself.

At the end of Capello's first year at the club the Golden Boy scooped the Serie A Italian Footballer of the Year award to go alongside his Young Footballer of the Year prize from 1999. He was being recognised for his influence on the pitch as well as on the touchline, and in 2000/01 he was ready to gain the greatest success of his Roma career to date.

The Giallorossi had only previously won the Scudetto twice – 1942 and 1983 being the successful years. Capello had acquired Gabriel Batistuta, the free-scoring Argentinian striker from Fiorentina, ahead of the new campaign. Despite the strong start that saw Roma win all three opening matches against Bologna, Lecce and Vicenza – Totti scoring in each one – fans would protest their disappointment at the team following a loss to Atalanta in the early stages of the Coppa Italia. The angry supporters staged the protest outside the training facilities in Trigoria, only to halt their proceedings when their captain arrived at the gates. Francesco was quick to calm the disgruntled fans, reminding them they were 'right to be angry but need to help us [the team] find tranquillity'. *La Gazzetta dello Sport* also reported that after this incident the attacker went into the press room and stated the players were only 50 per cent to blame, and Capello must take his fair share of the criticism. Totti's relationship with the fans was on full show, and as always, it paid dividends.

Inter defeated them 2-0 on matchday four but following the loss, Totti and co. romped to eight victories in ten, with the other two games being drawn. After a loss to Milan at the San Siro they won seven on the bounce to leap to the summit of Serie A. Totti was loving life, and finally so were the fans on the Curva Sud, as they watched their captain smash a volley in against Udinese of such beauty at the Stadio Olimpico in one of their lengthy unbeaten runs. Capello's men grabbed a vital point away at Juventus with the season drawing to a close and the Scudetto was finally secured on the last day of the season with a 3-1 victory at home to Parma. It had been tense prior to the decider, with Totti believing he'd already handed his side the title against Napoli the previous week, but Fabio Pecchia levelled late on. It was all part of the bigger picture though, as Roma were then able to lift the Scudetto in front of their own adoring fans.

Carlo Zampa, the stadium announcer at Roma, was quick to get the fans buoyant as he claimed it was their 'biggest game in 18 years' and for the fans to put their 'heart, soul, enthusiasm, lungs' and pretty much whatever else they had spare to give their club. It was of course that man Francesco to get the ball rolling, the Italian smashing home inside 20 minutes after a clever pass from Batistuta found him inside the area. Totti ran straight to the Curva Sud – with his shirt off – before being mobbed by his team-mates and even a few ecstatic cameramen. Vincenzo Montella and Batistuta completed the job, albeit with a pitch invasion following a Gialloblu consolation slowing down proceedings, and Roma and Totti were finally presented as Scudetto winners. If that wasn't enough, he was also crowned the Serie A Italian Footballer of the Year for the second consecutive season.

The 2001/02 season began with a bang with Totti securing the Supercoppa Italiana thanks to a 3-0 win against Fiorentina and although he was struggling a little with injuries, he scored eight times including one following a brilliant dribble against Torino and one of his best against rivals Lazio. In a 5-1 win on 10 March 2002 Totti elected to attempt a lob from around 25 yards that left Angelo Peruzzi flabbergasted at the audacity of the goal. He also revealed a shirt saying '*6 unica*' – 'you are unique' – having dedicated the strike to his new girlfriend Ilary Blasi. Totti again donned a similar shirt saying '*6 sempre unica*' – 'you are still unique' – to celebrate nine years together in 2011.

Totti was working wonders off the pitch as well as on it and in the following season he got his first hat-trick in Serie A, against Brescia, a side who were probably sick of the sight of him, while he also gained another set of Serie A and Italian Footballer of the Year awards. The hat-trick was everything expected of him – a well-taken penalty followed by an exquisite free kick, ending with a mazy run and finish from outside the box to seal the three points. The league performances were not what was expected of Capello and the Giallorossi though, finishing eighth.

But there was a spectacular turnaround in 2003/04. Silverware was a distant memory but Totti and his teammates had a superb season goals-wise, finishing off with 68 goals and just 19 conceded. The Italian had a great season individually, scoring 20, and again won the Italian Footballer of the Year award. The pick of his goals include a diving header on matchday 17 at home to Sampdoria which also featured Francesco running half the length of the pitch before lifting the ball into the far corner. It's one of Totti's lesser-known goals and for the quality it holds that must say something about his footballing ability. When you go back to revisit this goal, take a look at all the Blucerchiati players scampering to try and tackle Totti before inevitably just giving up. A little like when you played football with your friends at school, and there was that one kid who was just too fast for your little legs to catch up to – unless you were that kid.

As the Serie A seasons progressed Totti began to meet some milestones, scoring his 100th goal with a fantastic free kick in a 3-3 draw with Inter. The same campaign also saw him net the *Miglior gol* – best goal of the season – when he inflicted more pain on the Nerazzurri. Totti evaded two tackles on his way from the halfway line before clipping probably the greatest *cucchiaio* – directly translating to spoon, therefore meaning chip – over Júlio César that Serie A has ever seen. There's actually a compilation of Totti's brilliant chips – it lasts for four minutes, so keep your jaw from dropping early on.

Luciano Spalletti was instated in 2005/06 after the previous poor season and Totti played a more prominent role compared to his usual *trequartista* position, this time directly up front and it paid off, scoring 15. After a bad injury to his left foot in February 2006 Totti was able to recover quickly and efficiently, meaning he would travel to Germany for the 2006 World Cup finals where Italy went on to win the ultimate prize. It spurred on the Golden Boy for some incredible feats during the next campaign, finally acquiring Capocannoniere honours with 26 goals to his name. One of those included the *Miglior gol* again, for a stunning first-time volley from the most stupendous of angles against Sampdoria on 26 November 2006. It was also the year Roma would secure the Coppa Italia, defeating Inter 6-2 on aggregate.

The Italian kept scoring and Roma were winning trophies here and there, lifting the Supercoppa Italiana for the second time with Francesco by defeating Inter 1-0. For the fifth time in his career he was given the Italian Footballer of the Year award but he then suffered a knee injury that meant he missed most of the end of 2007/08, including the back-to-back success of the Coppa Italia against Inter.

The constant battle with the Nerazzurri was what captivated many supporters, in Italy and abroad, because Juventus were not in the picture due to the *Calciopoli* scandal. Even with Totti and the Romanisti getting one over on Inter every now and then, they would always lose out on the Scudetto, with their rivals lifting the trophy every season from 2006 – if including the awarded trophy after *Calciopoli* – to 2010. In that final season Francesco narrowly missed out on the biggest prize in Italian football despite Roma pushing the Nerazzurri all the way to the very end. The frustration, but also passion, showed during the Coppa Italia Final where they again had to face Inter.

Totti had some scuffles in his time to say the least, and many recall the incident with a young Mario Balotelli as one of the worst, probably due to how recent it was. With the stage set at the Stadio Olimpico when the Giallarossi welcomed Inter, the Nerazzurri had a 1-0 lead going into half-time. The frustration was pretty evident as soon as *il Capitano* entered the field. He clattered goalscorer Diego Milito after being muscled off the ball before giving Thiago Motta a little trim with his studs while the Inter midfielder was on the ground from a previous tackle.

The game was drawing to a close and with Balotelli bearing down on goal from the left with three players around him, Totti elected to kick out at the youngster. Francesco was given his marching orders and received a four-match ban. Totti claimed Mario had provoked him throughout since his arrival on the pitch, calling him 'granddad'. It's clear this wasn't the main reason, and the sheer passion and frustration of Totti had boiled over. It was inevitable the anger and disappointment would show. Some would argue his unconditional love for Roma and the shirt he wears every Sunday makes it justified while others will claim he should know better as an experienced professional.

The thing is, Totti is a player who could easily go from this to playfully kicking Pippo Inzaghi's behind while he was tying his shoelaces, or go around pretending to be pregnant with the ball tucked under his shirt – both incidents are well worth searching for. The Italian had his comical moments alongside the naughty ones, earning himself so much love and hate by many. For every moment that was frowned upon, Totti was always on hand to make fun of himself, or with the help of his Azzurri team-mates. Back in 2003 a book was released by Francesco titled *Tutte le barzellette su Totti* – All the Jokes about Totti – which showcased a number of jokes, all centring around Francesco as the source of amusement. An example is:

Nome? – First Name? Francesco
Cognome? – Last Name? Totti
Professione? – Profession? *Calciatore* – Football player
Sesso? – Sex? *Non tanto ultimamente!* – Not much lately!

It was this aspect of Totti many loved and adored, as well as his heroics on the pitch. He remained more civil in the coming months, revealing that Roma's rivals from the previous season had deserved to win the silverware, and was also quick to dispel rumours he wanted to quit the game. The 34-year-old had mentioned in a press conference that July that it had crossed his mind and that he wanted to 'give up', but he remained due to the support of the fans around him. As for matters on the pitch, he stayed level-headed in the 2010 Supercoppa Italiana where they were again thwarted by Inter ahead of the 2010/11 Serie A season.

In this campaign he scored his 200th goal in Serie A, popping up with the landmark strike from the penalty spot. With Roma failing to gain more silverware in the following seasons, their results were more memorable each time Totti scored a goal to overtake a rival forward in the race for Silvio Piola's Serie A record of 274. He leapfrogged Roberto Baggio with another penalty and in 2011/12 he surpassed Milan legend Gunnar Nordahl. Giuseppe Meazza and José Altafini were both taken out at the same time with a cool finish away at Genoa.

In 2013/14 he marked his 700th appearance in the red and yellow of Roma against Torino – his 553rd league game. As for his successes in 2014/15, Totti found the net away at Manchester City in the UEFA Champions League, becoming the oldest goalscorer in the competition at 38 years and three days. This was also the year many readers will have fresh in their minds when Francesco elected to take a selfie against Lazio on 11 January 2015 – volleying home at the back post before pouting to the camera.

It feels a shame to not only whizz through his past few years, but also to just scratch the surface of the career of Serie A's modern great, with so much left untouched of the incredible Roma forward's days in Italy. The question remains now over whether Totti will beat Piola's goal record. Many would say no and that is the more likely outcome. Aged 38 at the end of the 2014/15 season, he would need to score an extra 32 goals to overtake Piola. The latter had achieved his goal tally of 274 in fewer games but did play until he was nearly 41. With his final two years ending with eight goals each, if he averaged that for another three years, including the 2015/16 season, he would score 24 goals and thus fall short. There are so many factors to take into consideration, and even if he does fail to overtake Silvio, Totti will still be seen as one of the greatest attackers ever to play in Italy regardless.

Grazie il Capitano.

DAVID TREZEGUET

'Being at Juventus for ten years was the best thing that happened to me. I got to know real football, at an ambitious club, with ambitious players.'

– FIFA.com

HE broke Italian hearts in 2000 and mended them in 2006, but David Trezeguet always had the Juventus faithful supporting him – just. David had an intriguing time in Italy, with many fans leading a constant argument on whether the striker was moulded by pure brilliance or simply a liability. The Frenchman experienced every emotion during his time at the Bianconeri – Scudetti were won and lost, some even to circumstances all Juventini wish to forget about. He went down to Serie B with the Bianconeri due to the *Calciopoli* scandal, making crude gestures to the board of directors in the process. It was an intriguing career to follow and away from the scandal, Trezeguet was one of the star forwards in a Juventus side that could not be thwarted by any of their league rivals.

David was clinical when it came to striking the ball anywhere inside the 18-yard box – a natural poacher. The question every goalkeeper would ask themselves was whether their formidable opponent would elect to shoot with his left foot or his right foot. Either way, the end result was the same – gol di Trezeguet. He became known as *Trezegol*, a nickname that needs no lengthy explanation. The Frenchman did what he was paid for and put the ball into the back of the net – simple, if you could call it that. A time in Italy dedicated solely to Juventus, forming a formidable partnership with Alessandro Del Piero in the process, made David one of the best players in recent Serie A history.

Born in Rouen, France, while his father was playing there, David moved to Argentina when he was two years old, ready to truly start his childhood. It was also where he began his journey into football and he was part of Club Atlético Platense. He played only five matches before moving back to his home country to join AS Monaco in 1995. It was here that the 17-year-old would announce himself to the footballing world, winning the Ligue Un title twice during his five years at the club. He was showing everything that was needed to become a true goalscorer during his time in France, leading Didier Deschamps to comment on his amazing qualities and believe he would grow into a great striker.

As he completed the 1999/2000 season with 22 goals, giving him a tally of 52 for the past three years, it meant big-named teams were ready to swoop in to capture the talented 22-year-old. Italy was firmly in the sights of David as he wished to move to the then-greatest league in the world. AC Milan and Lazio were also taking a look but the Old Lady were quick to move in, arranging talks with agent Antonio Caliendo and Trezeguet's father, Jorge. A £14.6m deal was soon sorted in the summer of 2000 – Carlo Ancelotti had his man.

Here stood Trezeguet donning the famous black and white of Juventus just six years after making a handful of appearances in Argentina's Primera División to a 25-time Scudetto-winning side. Trezeguet had simply gone about his business, scoring goals along the way. He made his move to France and Monaco look easy, finding the back of the net countless times yet he didn't even speak a word of French at the time. It was remarkable – astonishing to see a young man adapt to his surroundings so successfully.

Trezeguet made his Serie A arrival for the 2000/01 season with his debut coming against Bari at the Stadio delle Alpi in the second game of the season. He had already got his first goal during a UEFA Champions League match with Panathinaikos but didn't really announce himself immediately on the Serie A scene – picking up a yellow card for simulation before being substituted ten minutes from time.

He would soon banish any memory of that match when he visited Milan in late October. With the Bianconeri trailing 2-0 after quick-fire goals from Massimo Ambrosini and Andriy Shevchenko, David was brought on in the 64th minute, replacing the rather subdued Del Piero. Five minutes later *Trezegol* scored his first for the Old Lady. Some intricate dribbling on the left from international team-mate Zinedine Zidane saw the midfielder whip in a delightful ball that glanced off Alessandro Costacurta. It fell right for Trezeguet, who planted the header well beyond Christian Abbiati. With the goal meaning Juventus still trailed by one there was no wild celebration from Trezeguet. He simply ran into the goal, picked up the ball and jogged back to the centre circle – receiving a number of high fives in the process. He was off the mark.

The rest of the season was one to savour for *Trezegol* in terms of goalscoring, gaining 13 more along the way to cap off a good first year in Italy. He secured braces against Reggina, Bologna and Vicenza while also finding the back of the net in all of the final five games. It may not have been the 20-goal debut season many other players have achieved, but *Trezegol* was adapting to the game – learning what it was like to play for Juventus. Seasons such as these mould a player into what they become, which is why the next one would arguably be David's best for the Bianconeri.

With 2001/02 getting under way, the Juventini were ready to witness Trezeguet's breakthrough season. He scored twice on the opening day in a 4-0 win over Venezia – both goals coming within two minutes of each other. The first was a header back across goal into the far corner, the second a superb volleyed effort at the back post to give his side an early two-goal advantage. The ball was floated in following a mistake in the Venezia defence and Trezeguet was on hand to spank a left-footed volley past Generoso Rossi. He scored away at the Stadio Atleti Azzurri d'Italia when taking on Atalanta the following week, continuing his good start to what would be a Scudetto-winning campaign for Marcello Lippi's men.

The goals flowed throughout and during the penultimate game of the season Trezeguet kept Juventus in the hunt for the Scudetto thanks to a perfect hat-trick of goals with his left foot, right foot and head in a 5-0 victory over Brescia. The final match saw Juventus visit Udinese, with Inter travelling to Lazio and Roma taking on Torino.

With Inter letting a 2-1 lead slip to lose 4-2, it was on the Bianconeri to secure the win that would give them their 26th Scudetto. David Trezeguet was the name on everybody's lips just two minutes in when the number 17 pulled away from his marker at the back post to head home the first of the game. Juventus went on to win 2-0 and, against all the odds, won the league.

The opener during that match in Udine at the Stadio Friuli set *Trezegol* on the way to 24 for the campaign, joint with Piacenza's Dario Hübner, so the two would share Capocannoniere for 2001/02. Out of Trezeguet's 24 goals, ten came from headers, nine with his left foot and five with his right. An all-round goalscorer one would say. Trezeguet also won the Serie A Footballer of the Year and the Serie A Foreign Footballer of the Year awards. Surely any form of criticism would not fly in the direction of the Frenchman? Unfortunately there's always something lurking in the background to bring such an achievement crashing to the ground.

Despite his feats, many fans were starting to see Trezeguet as some sort of thorn in Juventus's passing game. Many goals had been scored by his head and fans were quick to point this out, stating how when Trezeguet plays the team become a crossing side, rather than playing fast-flowing passing football. There was no doubt that the Frenchman was a natural goalscorer – the records speak for themselves – but he was appearing too sluggish and always waiting for something to happen rather than create the chance himself. His link-up play was never the finest and he was sometimes caught flat-footed – never turning and driving at a defence full pelt.

Trying to please everyone is always a tall order and near impossible for a professional footballer but Trezeguet did what he had to do, which was score goals. He vowed to battle on and prove people wrong. However, his 2002/03 Serie A season wasn't one to savour, even though the club secured their 27th Scudetto and triumphed in the Supercoppa Italiana against Parma.

First off, the Frenchman suffered a knee injury during the summer with his national team according to coach Jacques Santini, meaning he wouldn't be able to play in the Supercoppa Italiana or in the season's opener with his side looking to launch their defence of the Scudetto in style. The injuries were plaguing David – he made just one appearance at home to Como – which, in turn, led to him being out for the majority of the first half of the campaign.

Trezeguet's eagerness to get back on the field proved costly, meaning he missed out on around six months of football. Stupid? Possibly, but if anything it proved how much David loved the game – itching to get back as soon as possible – and it proved a good learning curve for him. It was, let's say, a new challenge for the 25-year-old. He had never suffered a truly bad injury that pinned him to the sidelines before and it was an odd feeling for him. *Trezegol* wasn't used to sitting on the bench or in the stands watching his team-mates go about their business on the pitch. He made his comeback on 12 January 2003 by scoring once in a 5-0 thumping of Reggina. Trezeguet managed a hat-trick the following week as well, scoring a tap-in, a low shot and a penalty to get the ball rolling for his goalscoring season. Regardless of the fact the Frenchman had grabbed four goals in two games, some of his performances were not living up to expected standards and speculation surrounding Trezeguet's future at the Bianconeri grew tenfold. David was very clear about where he saw himself in the future:

> 'I can only say that I feel good at Juve and the Italian championship is one which suits me. I'd like to stay here for a long time. I came to Juventus to win important trophies and I think I made a good choice. Serie A is the most difficult and competitive league around. Here every game is a battle. You have to show a lot of will to win and be able to cope with high pressure. I believe I can do that.'
>
> – ESPN

Trezeguet would go on to find the net another five times to finish with nine altogether. His sixth was one to remember, the winner against Udinese. Gianluca Zambrotta put a brilliantly accurate ball into the box and substitute

Trezeguet side-footed a volley home in mid-air. Aside from this wonderful effort, his contribution was limited due to his recurring knee injury. Lippi still successfully guided the team to back-to-back Scudetti with relative ease – Inter being the closest side to Juventus, seven points adrift.

Moving on from Trezeguet's league success and forgetting his restricted playing time, the UEFA Champions League had been a target of Juventus and the club had steadily progressed to the final against Milan on 28 May 2003. David had played his part in the run-up to the game in Manchester, scoring four goals. Two of those were absolutely vital as they came across both legs of the semi-final with Real Madrid. At the Santiago Bernabéu, *Trezegol* latched on to a blocked Del Piero shot to then poke past the despairing Iker Casillas. They went on to lose 2-1, but a 3-1 win back in Italy made sure it would be an all-Italian final.

Unfortunately, as all Juventini know, there is no happy ending to this story, as expressed in Andriy Shevchenko's section of *Calcio's Greatest Forwards*. The game went to penalties after an enthralling yet goalless 120 minutes, with Trezeguet the first to step up and take his spot-kick. He looked a little nervous, but a solitary kick which could decide the fate of your team in Europe's biggest club competition probably does have an impact on your facial expression and stops you doing a song and dance on your way to the penalty spot. Only David knows what was running through his head and how he felt in that moment, yet the part everyone recalls is the miss. It was a poor penalty by any standards, side-footing comfortably into the midriff of Rossoneri shot-stopper Dida. A sporting handshake ensued between the two but by then the damage was done. Shevchenko went on to score the winning penalty, the camera panning to David – down, distraught, and dejected. It put an end to a weird season for the Frenchman, missing the majority through injury and then missing the vital opening penalty in the shoot-out at Old Trafford.

If injuries had been his problem in the previous season, 2003/04 was one for David to focus on his performances on the pitch rather than his absence from it. He himself wasn't satisfied with his performances, saying in an interview following a 2-1 victory over Bologna in October how he had 'rarely played that badly in my career before' and that he 'wasn't pretty to watch'. On the other hand, it also showed how much David strived to give his all each week for the Juventus faithful as he made the promise to be 'back to my best while scoring as many goals as possible' to make amends.

Again it seemed hard to please the supporters – many believing it would have been better for Trezeguet to not speak to the press at all and concentrate on improving rather than talking. The age-old notion of actions speaking louder than words was clearly running through the supporters' heads.

It is rather odd to see such contempt toward a player who brought so much to the Juventus attacking line-up. He may not have been the agile, quick-footed striker the fans wanted, but his rather preposterous goalscoring record says everything about the type of player *Trezegol* was. Thankfully, the unappreciative nature of a select few supporters it wouldn't faze him in attempting to improve. The fact he finished top goalscorer for the club in Serie A and across all competitions while giving what can best be described as 'adequate' performances that season shows just how talented Trezeguet was in his day. His side finished third and the Coppa Italia eluded David once more as they lost 4-2 to Lazio in the two-legged final. It proved enough as the Frenchman was given a new deal to keep him at the club until 2008. He vowed that a target of 100 goals for Juventus would be met, and was delighted with staying on at the club he loved:

> 'I have always wanted Juve and finally we have an agreement. I want to reach a century of goals for

> the club. We both got what we wanted and I proved my worth to earn a new deal. This is a fantastic environment for me.'
>
> – Channel4.com

The next two seasons were extremely successful for Juventus in terms of clinching the Scudetto, as they did so in 2004/05 and 2005/06. Trezeguet found the scoresheet nine times during the former and all seemed rosy. He even scored the goal to seal the Scudetto at the San Siro against Milan. A truly outrageous assist came from Del Piero, applying a bicycle kick cross on to the head of the Frenchman to send the title to Turin.

With the 2005/06 Serie A under way *Trezegol* was doing everything right on the pitch, scoring their first of a total 71 in the 38-game marathon when hosting Chievo. Another two at the Stadio Carlo Castellani, home of Empoli, put Trezeguet in the driving seat to grab his second Capocannoniere. On 21 December 2005 Trezeguet got the second in a 2-0 win over Siena. The goal itself wasn't anything special, lobbing into an empty net after a goalkeeping misjudgement, but it was memorable because the 28-year-old had drawn level with Roberto Baggio on 115 for Juventus across all competitions. Quite an achievement for the man with a love-hate relationship among the fans. He was humble in his feat, thanking his team-mates and also attributing it to keeping himself fit and feeling physically strong.

Such news spurred him on to continue his exploits in front of goal and by the close, David had bagged 23. It was not enough though as he was thwarted by Fiorentina front-man Luca Toni, who scored 31. It was the least of the 28-year-old's worries as the *Calciopoli* scandal had begun to surface. A couple of days after Juventus secured what they thought was their 29th title, tapes were released of Juventus's Luciano Moggi and Antonio Giraudo engaging in conversations with Italian officials to pick which referees they wanted in their 2004/05 games. Trezeguet and co. were subsequently relegated into Serie B and given an initial 30-point deduction. That punishment was later reduced to just nine ahead of the start of the season.

With a mass exodus of players leaving as if a revolving door was in place, David remained at the club. Heroic? Not so much. He did gain a commemorative plate against Vicenza for reaching 125 goals in just 207 matches, but he caused controversy when celebrating his 15th and final goal of the season on the last day. During the 3-2 loss to Spezia, Trezeguet celebrated his goal by making a number 15 with his hands, before initiating an offensive gesture toward the directors' box that meant 'I'm out of here'. The tension had been mounting during the season and David simply wanted to pack up his 140 goals for the club and go, leaving with the mentality he'd given his all for the club for the past seven years.

Incredibly, this wasn't the end of Trezeguet's time at Juventus. The club had come into good fortune on the stock market, increasing funds available to give David the new contract his time at the Bianconeri deserved. He was quick to make his decision, tying himself down to the club for another four years as they prepared for their return to Serie A. In 2007/08 he scored 20 times, falling just behind team-mate Del Piero in the race to become Capocannoniere. It was the same year that David spanked a sweetly hit volley past Júlio César in the 2-1 Derby d'Italia win – well worth looking up. He managed to give one more year to the Old Lady but was hampered by a groin injury that saw his contract ended prematurely in 2010. Before his time was over he did become Juventus's highest foreign goalscorer, and is also fourth in the all-time chart for the club.

After playing for his wife's home-town club Hercules in Spain, he made a brief stop in the United Arab Emirates at Baniyas only to then finally fulfil his lifelong dream to play for River Plate back in Argentina. David may have spent only a season there but his goals helped Los Millonarios back into the Primera División. Spells at Newell's Old Boys and Pune City followed to draw the curtain on a career that included controversy, penalty misses, but mainly goals. Trezeguet still loved Juventus and that would never change:

> 'Ten years in Juve, it was a great love story. I, David Trezeguet, will be a Juve fan forever. Indeed, the day when the Juventus team win the league title I will go to Turin and ask the Agnelli family to invent a jersey with the third star. I'd be the first to wear it. Even my finest moment was the promotion from B to A. It was a fantastic life experience. Fans considered us heroes because we had chosen to stay. I felt loved.'
>
> – BBC Sport

MARCO VAN BASTEN

INTRODUCED BY ANDY BRASSELL

'My first dream was to be a gymnast. I then found out I could play football pretty well. My gymnastic background helped a great deal with my agility when I took up football seriously!'

– *Telegraph*, 11 February 2002

HEATSTROKE isn't fun. The feeling of your forehead being stretched out like a jumbo canvas, and the recurring waves of everything in your throat scurrying to squeeze out of your mouth. You're floored, floating on jelly legs or flat on your back. It was fun once, though. Well, almost. I was 11 and had been burned into deliriousness on a school journey to Derbyshire. As our coach crawled on its interminable journey back through London and I clutched a sick bucket with my knees, the radio brought news from West Germany, and Euro 88. England were playing the Netherlands and Tony Adams, the reporter said, had been turned inside out by a whirling dervish of a Dutch centre-forward. That was my first encounter with Marco van Basten.

The next bucket I saw was more conciliatory. It was full of chilled water, my feet were in it and I was enjoying the rest of the tournament recuperating in front of the television while my friends toiled away at school. From that armchair I got to know van Basten, from the tantalising trundle into the corner of Eike Immel's net of his semi-final winner to sink the hosts to perhaps his most celebrated goal, the rocket of a volley that sealed the trophy in the final against the Soviet Union.

This flight of fancy beyond the boundaries of our estate eventually took me to Serie A. Van Basten's Milan were something special; that much was clear even from snatched glimpses on *Sportsnight*, which eventually led on to that campaign's pinnacle, the 4-0 demolition of Steaua București in the European Cup Final.

That Milan side, and van Basten, were so closely intertwined with the European Cup back then that it's easy to think about their Serie A misses almost as an afterthought, but they weren't to me. Having taken me to Serie A, van Basten kept me glued, along with Maradona, Gullit, Serena and Barros (and Gustavo Dezotti).

It came alive through the *110 Goals Italia Style* video series, bought for me by my mum from Soccerscene in Carnaby Street, a rare window into football exoticism when there were few. It brought van Basten's working environment to life in wonderfully chaotic fashion. The goals weren't in chronological order, with winners sometimes shown before equalisers and so – like the volley against the Soviet Union – they stood on their own, often minus real context.

Interestingly, filling in the blanks later – via hoovering up DVDs of classic matches, supplemented with reading and a bit of YouTube – did pretty much nothing to alter my view of him. Much like another peerless number nine to grace the San Siro, you could waste forever talking about what van Basten could have been if it wasn't for the injuries, but that would just ignore the beauty of what he actually was. Grazie, Marco.

Andy Brassell

There comes a time in every child's life when you have to quickly yell out what footballer you want to be during a kick-about in the park. 'Van Basten!' shout all of your friends in unison. Usually the friend who owned the ball would get his pick of player, so he would be the Dutchman yet again. It was either the former or Roberto Baggio that were picked – they were the epitome of Italian football in the late 1980s through to the 1990s. The question that always arises when mentioning the Dutchman though is simply 'what could have been'. He was the definition of brilliance – the man we all wanted to be. Everyone pretty much knows the gist of the story van Basten created.

After his time at Ajax came to an end, he moved to AC Milan at just 23 years old. Everyone expected years of free-flowing football, his niggling ankle injuries to pass and of course, goals. He was *San Marco*, sometimes *Marco Golo*. Whatever van Basten touched turned to gold, and the Rossoneri loved him dearly.

His brilliance cost him though, receiving his weekly dose of kicks to the shin when in Italy. A mixture of opponents and doctors meant van Basten's time in the beautiful game came to a premature end. We read of Francesco Totti, Luca Toni and Antonio Di Natale still playing on, nearly reaching the tender age of 40. Van Basten however, retired at 31, and hadn't played since he was 28. This shouldn't be a place though to read about the ifs and buts of his career, which has been detailed enough. Let us not look back on his ankle injuries but at his three Scudetti and double triumph in Europe. He was one of the world's finest footballers and should be remembered that way. This is not a tale of tragedy but a tale of beauty.

While all youngsters pretend to be Neymar, Lionel Messi and Cristiano Ronaldo, we'll all be Marco van Basten for the next few pages – showcasing just what the Dutchman brought to world football, and how quickly it was taken away from all of us.

Marco joins a number of our *Calcio's Greatest Forwards* to have hailed from outside of Italy, but is the only man to feature from the land of windmills and wooden shoes. He grew up in Utrecht, located just south of Amsterdam. A mixture of local teams in the surrounding area fed him his regular prescription of football with Marco regarded as having exceptional ability when at school.

In an article written by Joan Makenbach for the *Panorama* magazine in the Netherlands, six former class-mates alongside his teachers reminisced about what it was like at school with Marco. One teacher – Gerard Nilleson – recalled during a football tournament that van Basten had 'great technique' that saw him 'score from the centre circle after juggling the ball like crazy'. It led on to a major tournament that saw them lose in the quarter-final, a day that prompted Marco to 'cry during the whole bus trip back'. He was seen to be brilliant by his class-mates, despite being described as 'puny' with one friend – Bruno Klabbers – telling him he'd 'be the next Johan Cruyff'. To look back on it now, his comrades were more psychic than even they themselves could have predicted.

Ajax came calling for the 17-year-old Marco, offering him a chance to make the step up from Elinkwijk. It was here that van Basten made his name, scoring on his debut against NEC on 3 April 1982. With Ajax 2-0 up at half-time, coach Kurt Linder decided to replace Cruyff with van Basten. It was as if it was signifying a changing of the guard. Johan was just two years away from retirement and was 35 years old. On came a man 18 years younger than him, ready to introduce himself not only to Dutch football but the world game. In front of 21,000 spectators, Marco did what we all remember him doing a lot – he scored. A lofted ball into the box saw the Dutchman rise highest to net a headed goal. His reaction was more of surprise than anything, before he came to terms with what had just happened. A cartwheel of emotions ensued like an unhinged ferris wheel. His arms were held well aloft, followed by a bout of fist pumps ending in an almighty air punch. His morale was up, his first goal secured – not a bad first day at the office.

What followed were scenes of pure football brilliance. Three Eredivisie titles hurtled his way as well as four top goalscorer accolades. He was named Dutch Footballer of the Year in 1985 and waved farewell to Ajax at the end of 1986/87. He scored a stunner that season – an overhead bicycle kick – in early November against FC Den Bosch, well worth watching for those who may not have seen such a brilliant strike.

Marco had also been dealing with a niggling pain in his ankle that had failed to subside and a week prior to his operation to rectify the problem, things went from bad to worse. In a game against Groningen, van Basten was on the end of a collision that led to his right ankle being broken. His desire to fight on and his decision to strive to be the best possible player eventually held him back. In Zeger van Herwaarden's book *Marco van Basten*, which gives an excellent and insightful look into his injuries in the opening chapter, van Basten is quoted as having said he should have given himself more time and that he should have listened to his body:

> 'Every footballer starts too soon after an injury, but there is a fundamental difference between "to start early" and "starting too early". If you start early, you can still recover – that's sport – there are setbacks, but if you start too early... In retrospect I say that now I have the knowhow and all the misery I experienced with my ankle, I would of course not have continued playing. At the time, someone should have properly examined me and then told me what the sensible decision was, then start to think about football after that.'

It hadn't hindered the interest from Silvio Berlusconi, president of AC Milan. The Rossoneri were building something big – very big. Franco Baresi sat in the heart of the defence while a young Paolo Maldini was emerging from the youth system. Marco was to be joining up with some of the finest players in the world, including Netherlands teammate Ruud Gullit who had signed for a world record fee from PSV Eindhoven. The San Siro was Marco's new arena in which to terrorise defenders, upset goalkeepers and score like never before.

Everything appeared rosy for Marco and he couldn't have dreamt of a better start when he made his debut against Pisa on 13 September 1987. With Arrigo Sacchi's side 2-1 up, a penalty was won with ten minutes to spare. Up stepped the 22-year-old, side-footing the ball with as much power as he could muster. It flew into the far-right corner of the goal – van Basten was off and running.

Or so it would seem. His ever present ankle problems had resurfaced and the dream start had gone up in flames. Again, those who worked to rejuvenate and help Marco claimed this was a problem that had simply not been noticed before, and had probably occurred earlier but had since been aggravated. He didn't help himself prior to his injury either when he criticised Sacchi's tactics. Arrigo Sacchi decided to bench van Basten against Cesena because of this, telling the Dutchman, 'Well Marco, since you are so good tactically, you can sit with me and point out all my mistakes.'

It was clear Marco wanted to be back on the pitch as soon as possible so he kept his mouth shut and looked to fix his ankle woes as Milan were locking horns with Napoli in the race for the Scudetto. He returned during the business end of the season, and on matchday 25 he made sure he would play his part in the battle. The Rossoneri were being held by bottom-of-the-table Empoli and considering they were already four points adrift of the Partenopei, things were not looking good. Up stepped Marco – the man of the moment.

With the second half well under way, the ball found its way to the Dutchman about 30 yards from goal. His first touch was superb, bringing the ball in with a scooped motion to get everything under control. The next was even better, shifting his entire body weight to one side, feigning as if he was going to the left. All of a sudden his direction changed. It completely bamboozled the helpless defender who was left flabbergasted at the skill on show. With the space fully open for Marco to wreak havoc, he unleashed an unstoppable 25-yard piledriver into the net. The Milanisti screamed as he ran to the touchline, arms aloft. As he fell to his knees you could almost feel the emotion Marco was letting out. His ankles were trying to destroy him but he was fighting on, winning matches for a team he would soon call his home. He was *San Marco*.

The result kept Milan firmly in the title race and with three matches left there was just a point to separate the teams. On 1 May 1988 the game was pretty much as big as it gets – Napoli at home to Milan. Sacchi had successfully guided his side to a 2-0 win in the Derby della Madonnina against Inter the previous week, so the morale inside the camp was high. Diego Maradona, the Partenopei's talisman, wanted to see no Milan flags at the San Paolo. Instead, 1,000 red and black supporters showed up and they witnessed history.

Pietro Virdis steered Milan ahead when a free kick fell kindly for him in the box. The stadium fell deathly silent until captain Maradona stepped up to curl home a beauty of a free kick. The noise was almost deafening inside the San Paolo when the ball found its way past Giovanni Galli. With the scores level at the interval, Sacchi made probably the most important substitution in his career. Off came Roberto Donadoni, on came Marco van Basten. The complexion of the game completely changed with Virdis heading home his second to put Milan in the ascendancy. An incredible run by Gullit opened up another chance, one that was gobbled up by Marco. The swift counter attack left the home side stunned as the two Dutchmen combined before van Basten popped the ball into the roof of the goal. Careca's goal a couple of minutes later was a mere consolation as Marco had won the match.

Milan had successfully leapfrogged Napoli with just two matches to go and draws against Juventus and Como brought an end to their Scudetto drought. Van Basten had done it for his new club and he'd never forget it. He played just 11 games that season, scoring only three goals that won his side four points, with one of those strikes coming in the Rossoneri's most important match. His team-mates had built up the crescendo and he had been the climax. If there was a painting to detail Milan's season that year, *San Marco* would have applied the last brushstroke. It details how valuable a player Marco was in calcio right from the start, breaking the hearts of an entire city with just one strike of a football.

Once the festivities had died down, Marco's men had to regroup in a bid to regain their Scudetto. The deadly Dutch duo soon became a trio ahead of the 1988/89 Serie A with former Ajax team-mate Frank Rijkaard joining in on the fun at Milan. Van Basten was a big fan of Rijkaard, naming him in his 'Perfect XI' for *FourFourTwo* magazine, stating, 'He could do everything.' The three players in question had all returned from the 1988 UEFA European Championship as winners, having sunk hosts West Germany then the Soviet Union in the final.

In that match van Basten scored one of the most famous European goals when he volleyed in from an almost impossible angle. He later revealed in an interview with Joe.ie that he 'was a little bit tired so instead of taking it down on my chest it was better to just hit it first time', and was 'thankful it ended up in the back of the net'. He ended up with five goals, the tournament's best, and also the accolade for best player. Typical Marco.

The success that year didn't come in the league however, with Europe the main port of call for Sacchi and co. to quench their trophy thirst. The Rossoneri had already won the inaugural Supercoppa Italiana thanks to a 3-1 triumph over Sampdoria – Marco scoring a penalty in the final minute – which stood them in good stead for the new season. Although the Scudetto didn't return to Milan, the European Cup was there for the taking. Bulgaria's Vitosha, now known as Levski Sofia, were the first on the hit-list, losing out 2-0 in the opener before conceding five at the San Siro. *Marco Golo* provided the brilliance that night when he scored four times. The number nine took to the game like a fish to water after just 120 seconds, rifling a shot past Borislav Mihaylov. The second was a typical thunderbolt into the goal before he completed a first-half hat-trick with a simple finish from a corner. The fourth was a diving header, as if he hadn't shown off enough that day.

The result propelled them on to the challenge of Red Star Belgrade which they won on penalties after the away leg was replayed due to heavy fog cancelling out the original second leg. Marco scooped the Ballon d'Or in December of that year, beating Gullit and Rijkaard to the trophy. It was the first time in the history of the award that the top three had all been from the same club, with 31 Ballon d'Ors having been awarded before then. It signified the brilliance of Marco, the Dutch trio and Milan. They were the heartbeat, the centrepiece even, of world football.

The accolade wouldn't deter *San Marco* or his Dutch entourage one bit with a solitary penalty by van Basten knocking out Werder Bremen before two goals from our talented striker, along with four others, saw Milan romp to victory against Real Madrid.

Despite acquiring 19 goals in Serie A, the main attraction came at Camp Nou on 24 May 1989 when Milan met Steaua București in the final. It was a match to remember with Gullit and van Basten right at the forefront of their European victory. Ruud tapped home early on before Marco got in on the act, diverting a perfect cross with a precise header to double the lead. Once the former had smashed home a third, *Marco Golo* stroked home his second in Milan's final flourish. Steaua were rightly stunned – the Dutch had destroyed them.

It was arguably the highlight of Marco's finest years in Italy, going on to secure yet another Ballon d'Or at the end of 1989, and also that year he became Capocannoniere, replicating his 19-goal haul from the previous season that had proved good enough to become Italy's top scorer. Winning the European Cup was the standard of the time for him, lifting the silverware yet again in Vienna having defeated Benfica 1-0. Although he didn't deliver the heroics of the previous success, vital goals against KV Mechelen and Bayern Munich got his side to the final.

'Have another Ballon d'Or, and while you're here, take this FIFA World Player of the Year award too,' were probably the words of those who had voted for Marco in 1992. He couldn't stop scoring the previous year when he bagged 25 league goals, and a second Scudetto and Capocannoniere headed in his direction. Marco had also equalled Cruyff's record of three Ballon d'Ors. His class-mate Klabbers had been right all along, he was the next Johan Cruyff. If anyone wishes to pay kudos to Bruno, he works as a senior office manager in the Netherlands – good luck finding him. With three Ballon d'Ors, two Scudetti, two Capocannonieri and a host of other souvenirs he'd pick up along the way nicely positioned in his cabinet, things wouldn't be the same again.

It should have just been any other match on 13 December 1992 when Ancona hosted Milan, yet a dark cloud had emerged from the sunny intervals of goals, trophies and accolades. Marco's right ankle was again the unwanted antagonist, leaving him with pain that he just couldn't deal with.

It was the beginning of the end for van Basten. Surgery after surgery, yet nothing was making the problem go away. He managed 13 goals that season in just 15 matches, an incredible statistic of a goal every 0.87 games that helped Milan to back-to-back Scudetti. After the 1993 UEFA Champions League Final, in which van Basten managed 86 minutes and the Rossoneri succumbed to a 1-0 defeat against Marseille, *San Marco* would not play again.

Paolo Maldini spoke about how unfortunate the injury and surgery was, reminiscing about the best player he ever played with:

> 'Oh yes. He was easily the best player I ever played with. Right foot. Left foot. Heading, so strong, fast. He could score, he could pass the ball. He was the best. The way he played was timeless. Stupid surgery to the ankle. It was such a pity.'
>
> – *Daily Mail*, 23 May 2015

Along came the day every Milan fan, player, and lover of football wished would never arrive. On 17 August 1995 during a friendly with Juventus and two years after his game against Marseille, dressed in his suave jacket and jeans, Marco van Basten said goodbye to the sport that had both loved and destroyed him. Those at the San Siro stood to applaud the man who just never wanted to say no. Although many will never share his pain, we all can connect with Marco for what he brought to football.

As he waved to those that loved him it's a miracle he kept back the tears. He was a fighter after all. One man who let the waterworks flow was his coach, Fabio Capello, who simply couldn't keep it in. He knew him as well as Sacchi and Cruyff, growing into his managerial work with Marco the entire time.

Tears were shed for not just a professional, but for a colleague and a friend. Capello later revealed he showed videos of van Basten to Zlatan Ibrahimović when at Juventus, telling him 'to play just like that' as reported by *La Gazzetta dello Sport*. He knew the talent van Basten crafted was the stuff of dreams.

Sacchi wasn't there to cry with Capello, but did describe Marco as 'the cherry on the cake' and say 'he was the most talented but also the most discontinuous, meaning his class was like crystal', as revealed in his book *Calcio Totale*.

It will forever be asked whether the doctors could have done more for *San Marco*, but it was evident it just wasn't to be. Marco himself opened up about the ongoing surgery, stating he 'didn't know if the doctors always helped as there was no improvement from 1992' and that he also 'had the impression things were getting worse rather than better'. He also said during an interview on a Dutch football talk show that following his retirement he simply wanted nothing to do with football as it hurt too much:

> 'I couldn't watch football. It hurt looking at football players like [Paolo] Maldini and [Alessandro] Costacurta playing for AC Milan because – considering my age – I could have been with them

> on the pitch. That was difficult for me to cope with. It wasn't finished for me. I still had the feeling there had been a lot more to come. For me the bottle was half-empty.'
>
> – RTL 7 show *Voetbal International*

It all ended too soon for Marco, and for football. But we finish off this section as we began it. Let's not trivialise and debate about what could have been. Leave that to the pessimists. The aforementioned moments only just skim the brilliance of one of the beautiful game's finest players. Put this book down, take a break, and go watch some of Marco's magic for Milan. One thing is for sure, you won't be disappointed.

CHRISTIAN VIERI

'To be honest I wasn't very good at football! I loved cricket and I made some big scores for my boys' team. I dreamed of becoming the next Allan Border.'

– *Daily Mail*, 3 June 1998

CRICKET was Christian Vieri's passion. This is probably the most unexpected fact to be true of one of Italy's most lethal strikers and a man who was once the most expensive player in the world. *Bobo*, as he became known thanks to his father Roberto, had a wonderful playing career filled with honours that included the final European Cup Winners' Cup, a Scudetto and Capocannoniere. He'd have traded them all in for a career in cricket though. A decent all-rounder according to the man himself, Christian fell in love with the game thanks to his upbringing in Australia and after receiving a bat signed by Australian captain Allan Border.

Christian still had an avid interest in what we all see as the beautiful game. He played for Marconi Stallions in Sydney at a young age, following in his father's footsteps. With his family heading back to Italy in 1988, cricket was a sport that was hard to come by on his return to Tuscany. His only experience of the joy he once felt as a kid would not occur until 30 years later when he went on holiday to the Maldives in 2003, playing a number of matches with some waiters and chefs from a nearby restaurant. Football would be the path of Christian in his life and career, one that truly ignited in 1991 when at the age of 18 he successfully moved up from the youth team to the seniors for Serie A side Torino. *Bobo*'s career was under way.

The Granata had opted to acquire Christian's services from Serie C side Prato a year earlier. His first season after his time in the youth set-up with his new club would prove to be just a taste of things to come as he made his debut in the Coppa Italia against Lazio, a scoring start. He played in only seven games during the campaign, adding one goal in the process – a well-directed header to help his side to a 4-0 home win over Genoa. Despite the promise shown by Christian, he was sold to Serie B side Pisa. After just two goals in 18 appearances he carried on jumping like a kangaroo around teams – first to Ravenna and then Venezia. But the Italian would be back in the fight for a place in the 1995/96 Serie A when Atalanta came calling to become Vieri's fifth professional club in as many years.

The striker would begin to show fans exactly the type of player he was – a man with a lethal shot, bullet header and no-nonsense attacking approach. It even saw the publication *La Repubblica* compare Christian to Gigi Riva. It didn't take him long to announce himself to his first Nerazzurri side, scoring a 90th-minute equaliser to salvage a point when Parma came to visit the Stadio Atleti Azzurri d'Italia. It was the first time we all got to see his passion for the game, running straight to the Curva Pisani while battling a number of advertising hoardings along the way.

On matchday 22 Vieri scored his fifth goal in Serie A – his previous four goals had come from three headers and a penalty. This one was a little more special, unleashing a powerful strike from 30 yards. Soon Marcello Lippi's Juventus were knocking on president Ivan Ruggeri's door – they wanted Vieri.

A fee of around £2.5m was agreed and soon the Bianconeri had their man, while Christian had his sixth club in as many seasons. He had a decent first year at Juve, scoring eight times in the league, the joint highest with Alessandro Del Piero and Michele Padovano. The Serie A season kicked off with a bang for Vieri, finding the net just seven minutes into his first black and white appearance. Reggina were the poor souls who had to feel such a pain – *Bobo* tapping home from a couple of yards.

However, after his dream start to life back in Turin, things took a turn for the worse between Vieri and Juventus coach Lippi during matchday 16 when they travelled back to Vieri's former club Atalanta.

The Italian had been on the bench but made an early appearance for the injured Alen Bokšić. With the score at 0-0 going into the interval, Lippi and Vieri elected to exchange words in the dressing room and that led to the striker being substituted prior to the second half kicking off. The coach had been in Christian's ear all game, letting him know his disapproval of his performance.

The two went face to face at half-time, neither backing down in their verbal onslaughts at one another, with only the surrounding players separating the two before a fight broke out. Lippi once mentioned he was secretly thankful of the fact nothing became of the situation at the time, stating,

'*Bobo* was big,' doubting that he'd have been able to fend off the bullish forward.

Incredibly the dispute actually led to the two of them forming a close bond in their careers, and it even powered Vieri on to find the back of the net on a more consistent basis at a vital time in Juve's season. In an interview following Vieri's retirement, he opened up about the argument:

> 'It was a boxing match! [laughs] We both took stick off of one another and there was an exchange of views. He said something to me in the dressing room and I retaliated. Luckily my team-mates were there to separate us! Perhaps that was the spark that made us understand one another.'
>
> – Tuttojuve.com

After a couple of weeks on the bench to 'cool down', Vieri was back in the starting line-up to face Roma. In the typical and rather clinical fashion that Vieri was known for, he scored twice in the first half to put his team right in the ascendancy. His celebrations were rather muted and it all just seemed like a job to Vieri. As passionate as he was about football, he knew what his role was in the team.

The brace had clearly got Vieri into what we all know as 'the zone' and he soon added another two in the 6-1 destruction of AC Milan at the San Siro. His third brace of a quite remarkable second half to the season came on 15 May 1997 when Juve entertained Piacenza at the Stadio delle Alpi. The Italian's first in this match is well worth searching for, taking the ball down first time before hitting one on the volley off the tip of his toe right into the top corner. Juventus went on to secure the Scudetto at Atalanta.

Although he had secured his target of winning Italy's top prize, the celebrations were marred a little when supporters ran on to the pitch a few minutes prior to the final whistle. It left an unsavoury taste in the mouth for all but Vieri kept his head about him as many fans had become accustomed to. *La Gazzetta dello Sport* gave the 23-year-old a rating of 6.5, stating that he showed 'great determination' during the whole game. It summed up *Bobo*.

So that was that for Vieri's solitary season at Juventus. He also won the UEFA Super Cup when scoring against Paris Saint-Germain, and earned a runners-up medal in the Champions League after a 3-1 defeat to Borussia Dortmund in the final. All of that would prove to be just a distant memory for *Bobo* as interest had hotted up in the free-scoring forward. A very typical modern-day football scenario occurred during the sale of Vieri in the summer of 1997 – Gianni Agnelli reiterated how he had spoken to Luciano Moggi about Vieri and he then announced to Rai Sport that the Italian was 'going nowhere'. The next day Moggi, alongside Antonio Giraudo and Roberto Bettega announced they'd struck a deal with Spanish side Atlético Madrid for the transfer of him – Vieri was off to Spain.

You won't be surprised to know it wasn't a long stay, as had become the style of Vieri's nomadic career, remaining at Atlético for one season in La Liga. It was here that Christian's goalscoring really kicked off – 24 in 24 being his final total. With the Pichichi trophy – awarded by the newspaper *Marca* for finishing as the top goalscorer for the season firmly in his back pocket – *Bobo* would end up back in Italy yet again. Lazio was to be his next port of call for a reported fee of around £20m.

Before you read on to get ahead to his time at Inter, spare a thought for this year at the Biancocelesti. Vieri made his debut at Piacenza on 13 September 1998 and got his first goal against Bologna with a looping header on matchday 15. From then on it was all goals, unleashing an unstoppable strike a week later to secure an important 2-0 win over Fiorentina. With the season drawing to a close and Vieri scoring freely, Lazio realised they were closing in on only their second Scudetto but they had to deal with the added threat of Milan who were looking to spoil the festivities. Christian knocked in a header against Udinese with three games to go in a game that included a rather comical running celebration in which he fell over like a cartoon character, before again finding the net against Bologna to keep his side above the Rossoneri by a point.

However, despite Vieri's best efforts as he netted an equaliser away to Fiorentina at the Stadio Artemio Franchi and then hit the crossbar late on, Milan defeated Empoli 4-0 and leapfrogged Lazio with just one game to play. Although they defeated Parma 2-1 on the final day, Alberto Zaccheroni's men did their job at Perugia, winning by the same margin. It was heartbreak for Vieri whose individual honours of Serie A and Italian Footballer of the Year seemed worthless to someone who was a real team player.

The real success came in the last European Cup Winners' Cup for Christian, defeating Mallorca 2-1 on 19 May 1999 at Villa Park in Birmingham. *Bobo* scored the opening goal of the game, meeting a cross with a first-time looping header right in front of the Lazio fans. Vieri stood with his arms aloft taking in the rapturous applause from the fans situated behind the goal – this was his moment. Vieri looked back on the success with Lazio Style Radio, reminiscing about the final and how it was probably the 'greatest night of my life'.

In spite of all these accomplishments, it's a shame Vieri took so long to find a club to settle in at for a least a few years and that is possibly why many only recall his career at his next club – Inter. He made so many moves to give himself, in his own words, the 'widest experience'. Arguably he had learnt a lot from his time around various Italian clubs and also abroad in Spain, as can be seen in his latest achievement. Once discussions had opened with Nerazzurri president Massimo Moratti and Christian would be reunited with Lippi, it was evident they wanted Vieri whatever the price. The end result was the world's most expensive transfer at the time, with Inter paying £32m to gain their new prized asset.

Vieri burst on to the scene at Inter instantly, scoring his first professional hat-trick at the San Siro against Verona. He needed just two touches for every goal – one to set himself and one to do the damage. He followed this with one of his best performances in a 5-1 victory over Parma. With the game at 1-1 early in the first half, Vieri took the ball in his stride with his back to goal, swivelled, then hit a left-footed shot right in the top corner with the purest connection you're ever likely to see. There's a great camera shot during Vieri's celebration of the goal as it cuts to the stands where Roberto Baggio is situated, applauding the goal. It symbolised the changing of the guard up front for Inter – out with the old and in with the new. Baggio's time at Inter was nothing to reminisce about, so the acquisition of Christian was vital for the Nerazzurri to progress. Vieri went on to provide a hat-trick of assists for his team-mates as they swept aside the Gialloblu.

Torino felt the force of *Bobo* a few weeks later but he also had to put up with the unruly touch of pain during the same game, and was in and out of the treatment room for the rest of 1999/2000. He ended on 13 in 19 games, the highest tally at the club even though he was affected by injury for some of the season, alongside receiving his first red card against Fiorentina on 9 January 2000. Incredibly, Vieri had found a home at Inter and for the first time in his professional career he remained at a club for more than a year.

The £32m spent on the Italian was paying off as he managed to score 40 goals across 52 matches in the next two Serie A seasons. Those who were able to witness Vieri's antics in front of goal knew just the type of player he was. Game after game and goal after goal ensued alongside his second Italian Footballer of the Year award. It was an odd period for Vieri to deal with at Inter, however.

The first season, 2000/01, may have been a good individual one for *Bobo* but his side slacked considerably in the league and his long-term friend Lippi was sacked as coach. And although he scored on the final day of a superb individual goalscoring season, rumours were soon emerging of Christian's supposed private antics away from the field as well as questions over his future at Inter.

With 2001/02 fully under way and Vieri's side battling it out under new coach Héctor Cúper with Juventus and Roma for the Scudetto that had evaded them since 1989, the Italian responded to what he referred to as 'lies' in an interview while the Nerazzurri entered the business end of the season:

> 'It wasn't an easy summer with people saying I'm overdoing my nightlife, or that I'm changing my women every day. I try not to listen to it but it can teach you a great deal.
>
> If people say lies about me all this can, in fact, make you stronger inside.'
>
> – *WorldSoccer* March 2002 issue

Vieri looked set to be securing his second Scudetto and his first at a club he could finally call home, but poor performances in the lead-up to the final league match meant Juventus and Roma were back in the mix. Inter went into the final game top of the table and they travelled to Lazio where Christian gave his side the lead. It was inevitable given the way that Inter had entered the Stadio Olimpico that day, with Cúper stood in the tunnel patting each and every one of the starting XI on the chest to keep them pumped up. Vieri's concentration was written all over his face as he walked out. It was that mental stability that allowed him to be the first to react to a poorly defended corner. His shirt was off and the celebrations began in the away section – Inter were on their way. But even with Vieri giving his team a one-goal lead it wasn't to be. They went on to lose 4-2, each goal being received with thunderous cheers from the Juventini who were 2-0 up against Udinese – the Scudetto had eluded them, again.

One thing that many calcio fans are disappointed by is the fact that neither Ronaldo nor Vieri, who formed a formidable partnership at the time, ever won the Scudetto with Inter. The Brazilian moved on at the end of 2002. As much as the tears may have fallen from all the Inter faithful, it's much more painful to hear from Vieri that he rarely talks to his old colleague anymore because he 'rarely picks up his phone'. They were the terrible two of Inter outside of football according to Christian when interviewed on television after his career at Inter had ended:

> 'We went clubbing. Then, I used to sleep for a couple of hours and train, while he laid down on the bed and ate brioches and drank cappuccinos. The big problem was that the following day at midnight, he used to show up at my house and honked until I came down so we'd go out again.'
>
> – Italia 1 show *Chiambretti Night*

Losing his partner in crime didn't faze *Bobo*, and he became Capocannoniere for the first time in 2003 thanks to 24 goals in 23 games, an astounding record that led his team to second in the table. On matchday 12 Vieri made the headlines with what *La Gazzetta dello Sport* called a 'quadruple dream' as he grabbed all four goals in a win against Brescia. They may not have been the greatest to watch – his goals included a scrappy header and mis-hit volley – but it was a brilliant achievement nonetheless. He also scored the winner in the UEFA Champions League quarter-final against Valencia at home and seized an important away goal back in Spain but was forced off due to a recurring knee problem.

The next two years would be his final flourish at Inter, and he scored his 100th goal for the club with a composed finish into an empty net after evading a lunging tackle from the Lecce goalkeeper on 6 January 2004. After the goal his team-mates mobbed him in jubilation, presenting Vieri with a crown originally bought by Marco Materazzi two months prior – he was *King Bobo*. After scoring three times in the run-up to winning the 2005 Coppa Italia, Vieri's Inter adventure was over by mutual consent.

Once *Bobo* had ended his six-year stay at Inter, there wasn't much else to do than go back to his nomadic roots and play for various clubs across Italy and abroad. He moved to rivals Milan but spent only six months there. It became all too obvious the move to the Rossoneri had been a mistake, shown all too well in a poor performance in the Derby della Madonnina. Once the January transfer window was open, Vieri sailed off to Monaco.

Unfortunately only bad news would follow with *Bobo* picking up a serious injury to his left knee in a game against PSG. It even left the prolific international goalscorer out of Italy's 2006 World Cup finals squad. He did sign a contract that summer with Sampdoria, but the 33-year-old left after just a month following a rather heated discussion with chief executive Giuseppe Marotta. He moved on to his former club Atalanta, scoring twice. This did however include what many believe to be Vieri's greatest goal.

In a home game against Siena, a ball came into the path of *Bobo* close to the centre circle. With one touch he had the ball in the air at what can best be described as a 'good height for a striker' to then swivel and unleash a left-footed volley from 40 yards.

It was so unexpected that the commentator in question was in complete silence during the build-up. As the ball hit the back of the net our supposedly timid commentator screamed out, '*Vierrrrrrrrrrrrrrrrrrri!*' Christian was still producing brilliance.

A year on from this incredible strike and after six goals in 2007/08 at Fiorentina, he returned for the third time to Atalanta. He played nine times there, scoring another two goals in the process – his final Serie A goal coming from a header against Juventus. On 20 October 2009 Vieri finally brought an end to his intriguing career. He stated:

> 'It had already been quite a while that I didn't feel the same desire to train or to go to team meetings. I didn't have the same motivation. When that happens, it's time to stop.'
>
> – FIFA.com

He ended with 142 goals to his name in a remarkable 264 games – a goal every 1.8 matches. That was our *Bobo*.

FACT FILES

The fact files detail each player's appearances and goals. They only reflect time spent in Italy's Serie A, so European competitions are not included and some years may appear disjointed if they played in a lower domestic league, were relegated, or played abroad in their career.

JOSÉ ALTAFINI

Club	*Years*	*Appearances*	*Goals*
AC Milan	1958–65	205	120
Napoli	1965–72	180	71
Juventus	1972–76	74	25
TOTAL		459	216

ROBERTO BAGGIO

Club	*Years*	*Appearances*	*Goals*
Fiorentina	1985–90	94	39
Juventus	1990–95	141	78
AC Milan	1995–97	51	12
Bologna	1997–98	30	22
Inter	1998–2000	41	9
Brescia	2000–04	95	45
TOTAL		452	205

GABRIEL BATISTUTA

Club	*Years*	*Appearances*	*Goals*
Fiorentina	1991–2000	243	152
Roma	2000–03	63	30
Inter	2003	12	2
TOTAL		318	184

ROBERTO BONINSEGNA

Club	*Years*	*Appearances*	*Goals*
Varese	1965–66	28	5
Cagliari	1966–69	83	23
Inter	1969–76	197	113
Juventus	1976–79	58	22
TOTAL		366	163

GIAMPIERO BONIPERTI

Club	*Years*	*Appearances*	*Goals*
Juventus	1948–61	444	178
TOTAL		444	178

HERNÁN CRESPO

Club	*Years*	*Appearances*	*Goals*
Parma	1996–2000	116	62
Lazio	2000–02	54	39
Inter	2002–03	18	7
AC Milan	2004–06	28	10
Inter	2006–09	62	20
Genoa	2009–10	16	5
Parma	2010–12	46	10
TOTAL		340	153

ALESSANDRO DEL PIERO

Club	*Years*	*Appearances*	*Goals*
Juventus	1993–2012	478	188
TOTAL		478	188

ANTONIO DI NATALE

Club	*Years*	*Appearances*	*Goals*
Empoli	2002–04	60	18
Udinese	2004–	362	189
TOTAL		422	207

KURT HAMRIN

Club	*Years*	*Appearances*	*Goals*
Juventus	1956–57	23	8
Padova	1957–58	30	20
Fiorentina	1958–67	289	150
AC Milan	1967–70	41	10
Napoli	1970–71	17	2
TOTAL		400	190

PIPPO INZAGHI

Club	*Years*	*Appearances*	*Goals*
Parma	1995–96	15	2
Atalanta	1996–97	33	24
Juventus	1997–2001	120	56
AC Milan	2001–12	202	73
TOTAL		370	155

ROBERTO MANCINI

Club	*Years*	*Appearances*	*Goals*
Bologna	1981–82	30	9
Sampdoria	1982–97	352	118
Lazio	1997–2000	87	15
TOTAL		469	142

GIUSEPPE MEAZZA

Club	*Years*	*Appearances*	*Goals*
Ambrosiana	1929–40	286	195
AC Milan	1940–42	37	9
Juventus	1942–43	27	10
Inter	1946–47	17	2
TOTAL		367	216

GUNNAR NORDAHL

Club	*Years*	*Appearances*	*Goals*
AC Milan	1949–56	257	210
Roma	1956–58	34	15
TOTAL		291	225

SILVIO PIOLA

Club	*Years*	*Appearances*	*Goals*
Pro Vercelli	1929–34	127	51
Lazio	1934–43	227	143
Juventus	1946–47	28	10
Novara	1948–54	155	70
TOTAL		537	274

GIGI RIVA

Club	*Years*	*Appearances*	*Goals*
Cagliari	1964–76	289	156
TOTAL		289	156

ANDRIY SHEVCHENKO

Club	*Years*	*Appearances*	*Goals*
AC Milan	1999–2006	208	127
AC Milan (loan)	2008–09	18	0
TOTAL		226	127

GIUSEPPE SIGNORI

Club	*Years*	*Appearances*	*Goals*
Foggia	1991–92	32	11
Lazio	1992–98	152	107
Sampdoria (loan)	1997–98	17	3
Bologna	1998–2004	143	67
TOTAL		344	188

FRANCESCO TOTTI

Club	*Years*	*Appearances*	*Goals*
Roma	1993–	587	243
TOTAL		587	243

DAVID TREZEGUET

Club	*Years*	*Appearances*	*Goals*
Juventus	2000–10	214	123
TOTAL		214	123

MARCO VAN BASTEN

Club	*Years*	*Appearances*	*Goals*
AC Milan	1987–93	143	90
TOTAL		143	90

CHRISTIAN VIERI

Club	*Years*	*Appearances*	*Goals*
Torino	1991–92	7	1
Atalanta	1995–96	19	7
Juventus	1996–97	23	8
Lazio	1998–99	22	12
Inter	1999–2005	143	103
AC Milan	2005–06	8	1
Atalanta	2006–07	7	2
Fiorentina	2007–08	26	6
Atalanta	2008–09	9	2
TOTAL		264	142

These stats have been compiled to include every Serie A season from the start of 1929/30 to the end of 2014/15. Antonio Di Natale's and Francesco Totti's stats for 2015/16 have not been included.

BIBLIOGRAPHY

Books

Altafini, J. and Pardo, P. (2009). *Incredibile amici!*. Milano: Rizzoli.

Baggio, R., Mattesini, E. and Scanzi, A. (2001). *Una porta nel cielo*. Chiassa Vecchia (AR): Limina.

Caioli, L. (2012). *Roberto Mancini: A Footballing Life*. Thriplow: Corinthian.

Capra, G. (2013). *Hai mai visto giocare Silvio Piola?* Bellesi Francato & Publishing.

Del Piero, A. and Crosetti, M. (2013). *Giochiamo ancora*. Milano: Mondadori.

Foot, J. (2007). *Calcio: A History of Italian Football*. London: Harper Perennial.

Gren, G. (1951). *Med Grenoli i Italien*. Gothenburg: Cirkelförl.

Nordahl, G. (1954). *Guld och gröna planer*. Stockholm: Bonnier.

Sacchi, A. and Conti, G. (n.d.). *Calcio totale*. Reviewed in English by Steve Amoia.

Totti, F. (2003). *Tutte le barzellette su Totti*. Milano: Mondadori.

BIBLIOGRAPHY

Magazines – Italy

Guerin Sportivo

Magazines – UK

FourFourTwo
WorldSoccer
Champions

Newspapers – Italy

Corriere della Sera
Corriere dello Sport
La Gazzetta dello Sport
Lo Sport Illustrato – Supplement
La Nazione
La Repubblica
La Stampa

Newspapers – UK

Daily Mail
The Guardian
The Independent
Telegraph

Newspapers – France

L'Equipe

Newspapers – Germany

Westdeutsche Zeitung
The Rheinische Post

Newspapers – Malaysia

New Straits Times

Television – Italy
Italia 1
Rai 1
Sky Sport Italia

Television – Netherlands
RTL 7

Television – UK
Sky Sports documentary – *Football's Greatest* (5 July 2010)

Television – United States
CNN Sport

Websites
www.fifa.com
www.alessandrodelpiero.com
www.juventus.com
www.acmilan.com
www.asroma.com
www.tuttojuve.com
www.bundesligafanatic.com
www.lazioland.com
www.rsssf.com
www.channel4.com
www.batistuta.com
www.robertomancini.com
www.fiveinmidfield.com
www.forzaitalianfootball.com
www.gunnar-nordahl.com
www.goal.com

www.espnfc.com
www.joanmakenbach.com
www.sportskeeda.com
www.rombodituono.com
www.francescotottiacademy.com
www.milanobsession.com
www.soccertranslator.com (2008–2015)
www.worldfootballcommentaries.com
www.lasamp.com
www.theinsideleft.com
www.joe.ie
it.violachannel.tv
www.acffiorentina.it
www.fiorentina.it
www.udinese.it
www.inter.it
www.interfc.it
www.giuseppemeazza.it
www.liberta.it
www.milannews.it
www.sport.it
www.cittaceleste.it
www.legaseriea.it
www.magliarossonera.it
www.iltempo.it
www.ilsecoloxix.it
www.cinquantamila.corriere.it
www.today.it
www.lalaziosiamonoi.it
www.ricerca.gelocal.it
www2.raisport.rai.it
www.panorama.it

www.panorama.nl
www.nu.nl
www.doria.altervista.org
www.storiedicalcio.altervista.org
www.goaldentimes.org
www.oocities.org
www.beyondthepitch.net
www.football-italia.net
www.bbc.co.uk/sport
www.the100.ru
www.fantasista10.co.uk
www.lrb.co.uk
www.ilpalloneracconta.blogspot.co.uk
www.juveternamore.blogspot.co.uk
www.calciovecchio.blogspot.co.uk

Glossary of Italian Footballing Terms

Bianconeri: Nickname of Juventus. Literally translates as 'white and blacks'.

Biancocelesti: Nickname of Lazio. Literally translates as 'white and sky-blues'.

Blucerchiati: Nickname of Sampdoria. Literally translates as 'blue-ringed'.

Calcio: Although the term does not literally mean 'football' in Italian, when translated into English 'football' is seen to be the best alternative.

Capitano: Name given to the captain of the team. A common nickname for Francesco Totti.

Capocannoniere: Name given to the Serie A top goalscorer award. Plural is Capocannonieri.

Coppa Italia: Domestic cup competition of Italy. Similar to England's FA Cup.

Curva: Name given to a section of a stadium that is a curved shape behind the goal.

Derby d'Italia: Derby match between Inter and Juventus.

Derby della Capitale: Derby match between Lazio and Roma.

Derby della Lanterna: Derby match between Genoa and Sampdoria.

Derby della Madonnina: Derby match between AC Milan and Inter.

Fantasista: A mixture of a trequartista and a creative playmaker. Roberto Baggio and Roberto Mancini exemplified this role.

Gialloblu: Nickname for Parma. Literally translates as 'yellow and blues'.

Giallorossi: Nickname of Roma. Literally translates as 'yellow and reds'.

Gli Azzurri: Name given to Italy's national team. Literally translates as 'the blues'.

La Viola: Nickname for Fiorentina. Literally translates as 'the purple ones'.

Nerazzurri: Nickname of both Atalanta and Inter. Literally translates as 'black and blues'.

Partenopei: Nickname for Napoli. Literally translates to 'people of Queen Partenope' who was the founder of Naples.

Rondinelle: Nickname for Brescia. Literally translate as 'little swallows'.

Rosanero: Nickname for Palermo. Literally translates as 'pink and blacks'.

Rossoblu: Nickname for both Cagliari and Genoa. Literally translates as 'red and blues'.

Rossoneri: Nickname of AC Milan. Literally translates as 'red and blacks'.

Scudetto: Name given in reference to the Serie A trophy. Plural is Scudetti.

Serie A: The highest league possible for all Italian teams to play in.

Supercoppa Italiana: Pre-season competition between the winners of Serie A and the winners of the Coppa Italia. Similar to England's Community Shield.

Trequartista: A player who acts as an anchor between the midfield and attack in a roaming role such as Francesco Totti.